Tim Duffy

MICROSOFT Word 97®

MICROSOFT® CERTIFIED
BLUE RIBBON EDITION

ADDISON-WESLEY

An imprint of Addison Wesley Longman, Inc.

Reading, Massachusetts ▲ Menlo Park, California ▲ New York

Harlow, England ▲ Don Mills, Ontario ▲ Sydney ▲ Mexico City ▲ Madrid ▲ Amsterdam

Acquisitions Editor: *Anita Devine*
Editorial Assistant: *Holly Rioux*
Senior Production Supervisor: *Juliet Silveri*
Copyeditors: *Barbara Conway, Cynthia Benn*
Proofreaders: *Holly McLean-Aldis, Cynthia Benn*
Technical Editors: *Dawn Remmel, Emily Kim*
Indexers: *Mark Kmetzko, Bernice Eisen, Irv Hershman*
Page Checking: *MaryBeth Pitman, Cynthia Benn*
Compositor: *Gillian Hall, The Aardvark Group*
Technical Art Consultant: *Joe Vetere*
Cover Design Supervisor: *Gina Hagen*
Text and cover design: *Linda Wade*
Senior Marketing Manager: *Tom Ziolkowski*
Senior Marketing Coordinator: *Deanna Storey*
Print Buyer: *Sheila Spinney*

ISBN 0-201-44849-1

Addison-Wesley Publishing Company
Jacob Way
Reading, MA   01867
Web: http://hepg.awl.com
Email: is@awl.com

1 2 3 4 5 6 7 8 9 10-DOW-009998

To Wendy and Michael,
The two most important people in my life

PREFACE

Welcome to the *Microsoft Certified Blue Ribbon Edition of Microsoft Word 97®* by Tim Duffy. This text is approved courseware for the Microsoft Office User Specialist program. After completing the projects in this book, students will be prepared to take the Proficient-level exam for Microsoft Word 97®.

Computer literacy is becoming a necessity in a world supercharged with information that is continually evolving and changing. Millions of computers, both individually and in vast networks that span the globe, are constantly processing, analyzing, and organizing information. Advances in hardware and technology that once took decades, then years, now occur with startling frequency.

The challenge is real, it is identifiable, and it is immediate. What does one need to know to achieve and maintain both academic and business success in this technological maelstrom? For more than two decades, Tim Duffy, professor at Illinois State University, and writer, has been answering this question. As a teacher, he has taught introductory computer courses to thousands of his own students; as an author, he has introduced the very same computing concepts and skills to millions of students worldwide through his highly successful series.

In both his classes and his books, Duffy achieves a perfect balance between concept and skill, the why and the how, of computing. The why is the foundation of computing. Learn the concept and why that concept is important, and you can implement any skill. Because he teaches introductory computing throughout the school year, Duffy has intimate knowledge of exactly what conceptual information and what techniques students need and want to learn, and how to present enough of each to interest and challenge these active learners. Duffy knows what works in the classroom and what works in the computer labs. He knows where students can trip up, what assignments will make them think, what examples and exercises will illuminate the concepts, and what techniques will teach.

Duffy teaches what he writes and writes what he teaches. In his books, he brings his classroom teaching experience directly to you with the most innovative, up-to-date material available anywhere. His pedagogy is classroom tried and tested. There are completely new exercises and assignments, an all-new Windows 95-influenced design, and eye-popping graphics for today's visually oriented students. There are Internet and World Wide Web examples and active learning projects. The new Running Case sections are built around everyday problems that require both critical thinking and mastery of specific skills.

BUILDING KNOWLEDGE

For Duffy, learning is like building knowledge. A concept is presented, a feature or task is briefly described, and then students work with it. They complete an exercise or practice a task. Once that task is learned, they add a little more, building on what they are learning. After completing a small group of such tasks, each within its own context, students are presented with projects that unify the concepts and the skills. To achieve this natural balance between concepts and skills, there is constant reinforcement and evaluation throughout the book, including:

- Unifying Features. In the *Microsoft Certified Blue Ribbon Edition of Office 97® Professional* and available as a separate module, *Common Features of Microsoft Office 97®* applications are covered first to give students the big picture of how to use an integrated suite.

- Active Learning. **Exercises** apply software commands and features of each Office 97 application program to a specific problem, reinforcing skills described in the text.

- **Running Case**. Everyday problems are presented with just enough information to challenge the students. The Running Case teaches critical thinking while reinforcing the basic skills that students have learned to that point.

- **Document to Web Presentation**. In-depth coverage shows students how to turn an ordinary document into a professional presentation, enhance its appearance, put it on the Web, and then improve the Web page to produce a professional electronic document.

- Task Steps and Reference. **Reinforcing the Exercise** sections provide students with summary information on how a task is performed to reinforce learning and to provide a reference for the future.

- Self-Learning. **On Your Own** boxes allow students to gain additional mastery of features as they explore Office 97 applications on their own.

- **Timely Tips**. Special notations tell students what potential traps they may encounter with a software tool, what can go wrong, and how to remedy the problem.

- **Toolbar Button Reference**. Tables of toolbar buttons give students a central location to find summaries of buttons found on frequently used toolbars.

- **Keyboard and Toolbar Icons**. Task-specific icons appear frequently in headings and tables to help students identify and remember keystrokes or toolbar buttons.

- Self-Evaluation. **End-of-session exercises** offer reinforcement in multiple formats: true/false, multiple choice, short answer, and project-based questions.

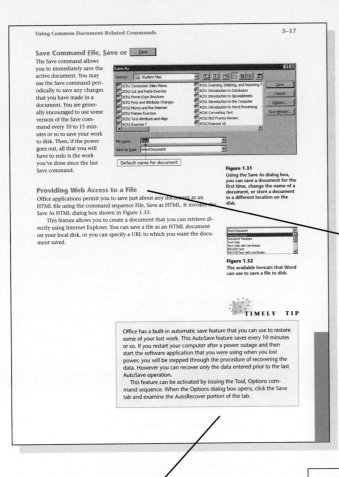

Save Command File, Save or Save

The Save command allows you to immediately save the active document. You may use the Save command periodically to save any changes that you have made in a document. You are generally encouraged to use some version of the Save command every 10 to 15 minutes or so to save your work to disk. Then, if the power goes out, all that you will have to redo is the work you've done since the last Save command.

Providing Web Access to a File

Office applications permit you to save just about any document as an HTML file using the command sequence File, Save as HTML. It invokes the Save As HTML dialog box shown in Figure 1.33.

This feature allows you to create a document that you can retrieve directly using Internet Explorer. You can save a file as an HTML document on your local disk, or you can specify a URL to which you want the document saved.

Default name for document

Figure 1.31
Using the Save As dialog box, you can save a document for the first time, change the name of a document, or store a document in a different location on the disk.

Figure 1.32
The available formats that Word can use to save a file to disk.

TIMELY TIP

Office has a built-in automatic save feature that you can use to restore some of your lost work. This AutoSave feature saves every 10 minutes or so. If you restart your computer after a power outage and then start the software application that you were using when you lost power, you will be stepped through the procedure of recovering the data. However you can recover only the data entered prior to the last AutoSave operation.

This feature can be activated by issuing the Tool, Options command sequence. When the Options dialog box opens, click the Save tab and examine the AutoRecover portion of the tab.

Duffy takes advantage of the **Web-aware tools** provided with Office 97 to help students translate their skills for use with the Internet and the Web.

Timely Tips inform students of helpful shortcuts, potential mistakes, or troubleshooting measures they can use with the text.

---

graphic included in that box varies depending on the type of Office Assistant you choose. Figure 1.4 shows the default Office Assistant called Clippit.

Usually, the Office Assistant feature is activated when you start any Office Application. If it does not appear on your screen, you can activate it by clicking the Office Assistant button on the toolbar. Initially the Office Assistant appears something like Clippit shown in Figure 1.4. The appearance of the box changes, however, as you perform tasks within that application.

If you perform a task that the Office Assistant thinks can be done more efficiently, it offers help without waiting for you to ask. A light bulb appears in the upper-right corner of the Office Assistant box (Figure 1.5). The appearance of the graphic changes, and a bubble displays a brief statement about the task you just performed. When you click an Office Assistant box with this appearance, the Office Assistant provides additional information on how you can make the task easier (Figure 1.6).

If you run into a problem and want the Office Assistant to help you, you can click the Office Assistant box to get its attention. The Office Assistant should look like that shown in Figure 1.7. If, for example, you want information about printing, you type the word *printing* in the box and then click the Search button. A list of topics appears, as shown in Figure 1.8. You can click on any topic to receive further information.

Information about the Print a document option appears in Figure 1.9. As you can see, this option generates a list of printing-related topics. Choosing the Print a range of pages option results in the Help screen shown in Figure 1.10.

You can change the type of Office Assistant from the default of Clippit to one of about eight other versions Office provides. When you right-click on the Office Assistant box, a context menu appears. Click the Options menu item to open the Office Assistant dialog box. Click the Gallery tab, and your screen should appear similar to the one shown in Figure 1.11. Follow the instructions given in the dialog box to examine the various Office Assistants and make your selection.

Figure 1.4
Clippit, the default Office Assistant.

Figure 1.5
The Office Assistant offering to help you with the task of checking spelling.

Figure 1.6
Additional information provided by the Office Assistant on using Word's spelling checker efficiently.

TIMELY TIP

If you have a sound system hooked to your computer, you can hear the Office Assistant making various sounds as you enter an Office document or perform tasks on a document.

Figure 1.7
The Office Assistant ready to help you.

3–4   WINDOWS 95

Shortcut Icons

Check to see if your screen displays shortcut icons like those shown in Figure 1.1. Such shortcut icons may have been placed on your desktop screen by your school computer lab administrator. You can double-click one of these icons to start the application it represents. Notice that shortcut icons have a curved arrow embedded in a square to indicate that they are indeed shortcuts.

Using the Start Button

The menus invoked by clicking the Start button can also be used to start an Office application program. You first click the Start button to activate the Start menu, and then you point to Programs to activate that menu.

The next action you take depends on what appears on the Programs menu. If single application programs are listed, as shown in Figure 1.2, then you can click the desired program and a window will open for that application. If a Microsoft Office option appears on the Programs menu, click that, and then click the desired application when the menu for Office appears.

Figure 1.2
A list of Office-related programs displayed in the Programs menu invoked using the Start, Programs command sequence.

✔ **On Your Own**

Your version of Microsoft Office may include a **shortcut bar** (Figure 1.1), which is a long, narrow bar that appears at the top of the screen. The shortcut bar allows you to quickly access existing documents or create new ones. It also provides direct access to the Schedule+ or Outlook feature (not covered in this text), as well as methods for accessing the Help feature or additional information that might be stored on a CD.

Using an Associated Document

As discussed in Session 2 of the Windows module, you can start an application by double-clicking the icon for an associated document. You can see associated documents when you are viewing the contents of a disk or folder using the My Computer window (Figure 1.3). If the icon for the associated document has an X, Excel starts and the document is loaded. If the icon has a W, Microsoft Word starts and the document is loaded. (Review Session 2 of the Windows module if you have any questions about other associated document icons.)

USING THE OFFICE ASSISTANT

Every Office application provides help through a feature called the **Office Assistant**. There are several types of Office Assistants available. All appear as a box in the lower-right corner of the screen, and the

Figure 1.3
The 97 Student Files folder window with files shown for the Internet Explorer, Word, Excel, and the Binder.

On Your Own boxes encourage students to explore the full range of features available in Office 97 applications.

Hands-On Exercises, based on the Running Case, give step-by-step instructions for learning each application. Numerous screen captures and button icons show students exactly what they need to know.

3–18   COMMON FEATURES OF OFFICE 97 APPLICATIONS

Figure 1.33
The Save As HTML dialog box allows you to create a file that can be accessed using a Web Browser like Internet Explorer.

Hands-On Exercise: Using File Commands

Isabel wants to examine several of the file-oriented commands that are found in various Office applications.

1. **Start Word.**

   Start Click to open the Start menu.

   Programs Click to open the Programs menu. If your computer has an Office 97 option, click that option.

   Microsoft Word Click to start Word. You should see a screen like that shown in Figure 1.34.

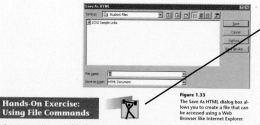

2. **Open two documents using the Open button on the toolbar.**

   Click to open the Open dialog box. Make the necessary changes to access the disk or folder containing the student files used with this textbook.

Figure 1.34
The Word application window.

Using Common Document-Related Commands   3–19

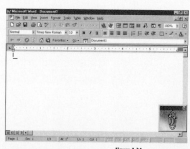

Figure 1.34
The Word application window.

4. **Verify the number of documents that you have opened.**

   Window Click to display the Window menu (Figure 1.38). You should see the names of the two files you have just loaded as well as the name of the blank document (Document2).

   4Ch1 Introduction to Databases Click this document name. You should now see this document displayed in the Word window.

Figure 1.35
The Word window with the 4Ch1 Introduction to Databases document loaded.

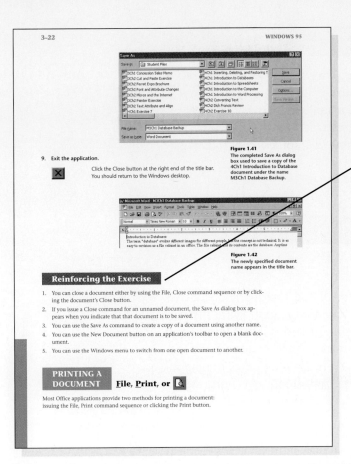

Reinforcing the Exercise sections help students recall and refer to the work they have completed.

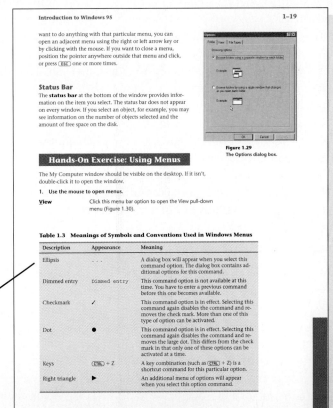

Tables of keyboard or **toolbar icons and symbols** provide students with a quick reference to the conventions and uses of Office 97 applications.

WEB INTEGRATION

The Web site created for this text is **http://hepg.awl.com/office97**. Web-based exercises appear at the end of each session in the Internet Exercises section. The Web site provides an interactive experience for students as they complete exercises in the text that send them to the site for information or files. In the Web exercises, Duffy teaches students how to view and save graphics, how to navigate on the Web, and how to download files; he even offers a guide to buying a personal computer and help on creating personal home pages.

ANCILLARIES

Instructor's Printed Supplements

The printed Instructor's Manual includes a Test Bank and Transparency Masters for each project in the student text. The Test Bank contains tests with answers, and consists of multiple choice, true/false, and fill-in questions that refer to pages in the student text. Transparency Masters illustrate key concepts and screen captures from the text. The Instructor's Manual also offers teaching notes to help integrate current technology (such as the text Web site) into a modern course on Office 97, along with objectives and an outline for each session, and grading tips.

Instructor's Web Site

Instructors get extra support for this text from supplemental materials from our Instructor's password-protected Web site, including screen shots, diagrams, and tables from the text, and files that correspond to key figures in the book that can be used as electronic slides. Screen-by-screen steps in a project can be displayed in class or reviewed by students in the computer lab. The Instructor's Web Site also includes the entire Instructor's Manual with Test Bank in Microsoft® Word format, PowerPoint presentation slides to support classroom lectures for each session (the slides can be printed six per page and distributed to students to facilitate note taking), and a Computerized Test Bank to create printed tests, network tests, and self-assessment quizzes for the Internet. Student data files and completed data files are available. All electronic files can be downloaded from the Instructor's Web site at http://hepg.awl.com/office97. Contact your Addison Wesley Longman Sales Representative for your ID and password.

Student Supplements

QWIZ Assessment Software is a network-based skills assessment-testing program that measures student proficiency with Windows 95, Word 97, Excel 97, Access 97, and PowerPoint 97. Professors select the tasks to be tested and get student results immediately. The test is taken in a simulated software environment. On-screen instructions require students to perform tasks just as though they were using the actual application. The program automatically records responses, assesses student accuracy, and reports the resulting score in a printout or disk file as well as to the instructor's gradebook. The students receive immediate feedback from the program, including learning why a particular task was scored as incorrect and what part of the lab manual to review.

TECHSUITE PROGRAM

The Duffy Office 97 applications texts are available separately or in a single *Microsoft Certified Blue Ribbon Edition of Office 97® Professional* volume. The Office 97 Professional suite includes Common Features of Office 97, Windows 95 with Active Desktop and Windows 98, Internet Explorer 4, Word 97, Excel 97, Access 97, and PowerPoint 97.

In addition to the Duffy *Microsoft Certified Blue Ribbon Edition of Office 97® Professional* lab series, Addison Wesley also offers dozens of proven and class-tested lab manuals within the *SELECT Lab Series*; from the latest operating systems and browsers to the most popular application software for word processing, spreadsheets, databases, presentation graphics, and integrated packages to HTML and programming. Knowing that you have specific needs for your lab course, we offer the quick and affordable custom TechSuite program. Lab Manuals from the *SELECT Lab Series* can be packaged with any of the Duffy Office 97 Professional lab books. Many of the *SELECT Lab Series* are available in *Brief*, *Standard*, or *PLUS* Editions that best suit your classroom needs. Your choice of lab manuals will be sent to the bookstore in a TechSuite box, allowing students to purchase all books in one convenient package at a significant discount.

In addition, your school may qualify for Office 97 upgrades or licenses. Your Addison Wesley Longman representative will be happy to work with you and your bookstore manager to provide the most current menu of application software. Your representative will also outline the ordering process, and provide pricing, ISBNs, and delivery information. Call 1-800-447-2226 or visit our Web site at http://hepg.awl.com and click on ordering information.

ACKNOWLEDGMENTS

I am amazed that fifteen years have passed since I started the first edition of Four Software Tools. At that time, I was totally unaware of the time-consuming efforts needed to produce a college-level textbook. Since then, however, I have developed a sincere appreciation of what is required to make a successful text. The success formula includes family, friends, colleagues, and many individuals in the publishing business. I remain deeply indebted to my wife, Wendy, who encouraged me to write the original version of Four Software Tools. Without her encouragement, the original text would never have been finished, and without her continued support, these projects would be impossible to accomplish.

I also want to express my sincere appreciation to the reviewers of this manuscript:

Jill Betts, Tyler Junior College
Bill Daley, University of Oregon
Kathryn A. Drexel, Drexel Associates
Peter Drexel, Plymouth State College
Seth Hock, Columbus State Community College
Marie McCooey, Bryant College
Vincent J. Motto, Asnuntuck Community-Technical College
Stephen C. Solosky, Nassau Community College
Melinda C. White, Santa Fe Community College

Individuals at the publishing company also play an important role. Addison Wesley Longman's editorial staff is superb. With warm feelings, I would like to acknowledge Anita Devine and Ed Moura. Maureen Allaire initially signed this book and over the years has had much to do with many of my books. I am pleased to be working with Anita Devine, who brings a wealth of editorial experience in microcomputer texts. Ed Moura, Editor-in-Chief, brought a number of excellent ideas to this project. Holly Rioux, editorial assistant, made certain that everything was going on an even keel. Juliet Silveri, Jennifer Pelland, Bess Deck, Sue Purdy Pelosi and Barbara Conway made the publishing process smooth and professional. Emily Kim's and Cynthia Benn's technical edits and copyedits helped to assure internal consistency of the textbooks.

An often-overlooked ingredient in the success of textbooks is the publisher's marketing and sales staff. Tom Ziolkowski's experienced efforts in developing a marketing plan are greatly appreciated. I am convinced that the Addison Wesley Longman sales staff is one of the best in the business.

A dedication is not complete without including my son, Michael. Michael continues to make any writing project a challenge. His requests to go biking, swimming, or pursue a new interest are much appreciated. Michael especially likes to surf the Web to complete home-work assignments and has become a ten-year-old master at ferreting out information from the Web.

CONTENTS

WORD 97

PREFACE v

SESSION 1: Introduction to Microsoft Word 97 for Windows 4-1
Introduction to Word Processing and Word 97 4-2
Introduction to the Word Window 4-2
Application Window 4-2
Document Window 4-4
Operating Word 4-9
Entering Text in a Document 4-9
Hands-On Exercise: Entering Text 4-10
Moving Around a Document 4-12
Working with Page Breaks 4-14
Hands-On Exercise: Using Keyboard Cursor Movement Commands 4-14
Selecting Text 4-17
Hands-On Exercise: Selecting Text in a Document 4-18
Deleting and Restoring Text 4-22
Hands-On Exercise: Inserting, Deleting, and Restoring Text 4-22
Performing Elementary Document Control 4-25
Controlling Line Spacing 4-25
Hands-On Exercise: Changing Line Spacing 4-25
Controlling Page Appearance 4-29
Hands-On Exercise: Controlling Page Layout 4-30
Converting Word Documents to HTML for Placement on the Web 4-33
Hands-On Exercise: Saving a Word Document in HTML Format 4-33
Session Review 4-37
Key Terms and Concepts 4-37
Session Quiz 4-37
Session Review Exercises 4-38
Computer Exercises 4-39
Internet Exercises 4-44

SESSION 2: More Elementary Features of Word 4-45
Using Hotspots 4-46
Hands-On Exercise: Using Word Hotspots 4-47
Using Word Views 4-48
Normal View 4-48
Online Layout View 4-48
Page Layout View 4-49
Outline View 4-50
Hands-On Exercise: Using the Various Views of Word 4-51

Using Margin and Indent Commands 4-56
Margins 4-57
Indents 4-57
Hands-On Exercise: Setting Margins and Indents 4-58
Setting Tabs 4-68
Changing Tabs Using the Ruler 4-68
Tabs Dialog Box 4-69
Hands-On Exercise: Creating Tabs 4-70
Hands-On Exercise: Creating Tabs with Leaders 4-72
Using Find and Replace Commands 4-75
Find Command 4-75
Replace Command 4-77
Hands-On Exercise: Using the Find and Replace Commands 4-77
Additional Commands 4-81
Change Case Command 4-81
Hands-On Exercise: Using Case Conversion 4-81
Date Command 4-82
Hands-On Exercise: Entering Dates 4-83
Saving and Backing Up Files 4-84
Timed Backup Feature of Word 4-84
Session Review 4-85
Key Terms and Concepts 4-85
Session Quiz 4-86
Session Review Exercises 4-87
Computer Exercises 4-88
Internet Exercises 4-93

SESSION 3: Word's Document Accent Features 4-95
Using Document Enhancement Commands 4-96
Adding Page Numbering 4-96
Hands-On Exercise: Using Page Numbering 4-97
Using the Style Gallery 4-100
Using AutoFormatting 4-100
Adding Bullets and Numbering 4-101
Hands-On Exercise: Using Styles, AutoFormat, and Lists 4-102
Inserting a Picture 4-108
Creating Borders and Shading Paragraphs 4-110
Hands-On Exercise: Inserting Borders and Pictures 4-111
Adding Headers and Footers 4-120
Hands-On Exercise: Inserting a Header and Footer 4-121
Adding Footnotes and Endnotes 4-124
Hands-On Exercise: Inserting Footnotes 4-125
Inserting Symbols 4-128
Embedding and Linking to Other Application Files 4-129
Embedding a Worksheet in a Document 4-129

Hands-On Exercise: Embedding a
   Worksheet as a Table   4-130
     Linking a Worksheet with a Document   4-132
Hands-On Exercise: Linking to a Worksheet   4-132
Session Review   4-137
Key Terms and Concepts   4-137
Session Quiz   4-137
Session Review Exercises   4-138
Computer Exercises   4-139
Internet Exercises   4-144

**SESSION 4: Advanced Document
Features of Word**   4-145
Using the Columns Command   4-146
     Editing Columnar Text   4-146
Hands-On Exercise: Creating a Newsletter   4-146
     Adding Clip Art   4-153
Hands-On Exercise: Accessing and
   Manipulating Clip Art   4-153
Using the Table Feature   4-159
     Creating Tables   4-160
     Entering Data in a Table   4-160
     *Enhancing and Editing the Appearance
     of a Table*   4-160
Hands-On Exercise: Using the Table Feature   4-161
Sorting Text   4-166
     Entering and Sorting Text   4-167
Hands-On Exercise: Sorting Names
   and Addresses   4-168
Using the Macro Feature   4-172
     Creating a Macro   4-172
Hands-On Exercise: Creating a Macro to
   Put Your Name in Boldface   4-172
Hands-On Exercise: Building a Letterhead   4-174
     Editing a Macro   4-181
Session Review   4-182
Key Terms and Concepts   4-182
Session Quiz   4-182
Session Review Exercises   4-183
Computer Exercises   4-184
Internet Exercises   4-191

SESSION 5: Word's Productivity Tools   4-193
Finding Words with the Thesaurus Feature   4-194
     Starting the Thesaurus   4-194
     Using the Thesaurus   4-194
Hands-On Exercise: Using the Thesaurus
   to Replace Text   4-194
Counting Words with the Word Count
   Feature   4-196
Hands-On Exercise: Using Word Count   4-197
Merging Documents with the Mail Merge
   Feature   4-197
Hands-On Exercise: Creating the Data
   Source File   4-199
     *Attaching the Data Source File to the
     Main Document*   4-203
Hands-On Exercise: Creating the Main
   Document   4-204
     Executing the Merge Operation   4-209
Hands-On Exercise: Performing the Merge
   Operation   4-210
     Entering Merge Data from the Keyboard   4-210
     Using an Excel Workbook as Merge Input   4-211
Hands-On Exercise: Using an Excel
   Workbook as Input in a Merge Operation   4-211
     Generating Mailing Labels   4-213
Hands-On Exercise: Creating a Label
   Definition   4-213
Session Review   4-217
Key Terms and Concepts   4-218
Session Quiz   4-218
Session Review Exercises   4-219
Computer Exercises   4-220
Internet Exercises   4-221

OPERATIONS REFERENCE   EM-1

GLOSSARY   EM-7

INDEX   EM-11

Microsoft Word 97
for Windows

SESSION 1

Introduction to Microsoft Word 97 for Windows

After completing this session, you should be able to:

- Explain the basic concepts of word processing
- List the major features of Word
- Identify parts of the Word window
- Interpret the parts of the status bar
- Use several insertion point movement commands
- Use elementary Word commands
- Enter a Word document
- Perform elementary formatting of a document
- Convert a Word document to an HTML document for placement on the Web

Isabel is putting together a Word training program for her employees as well as deciding what she wants to cover in the class she will be teaching at the local community college. She knows that her employees and students will need to be introduced to the elementary features of Word so they will be able to move around a document, change the line spacing and margins, and enter simple documents. The exercises in this session will follow her progress.

This session introduces word processing concepts and Word 97 for Windows. It assumes that you have been introduced to various Windows operations, such as how to use the mouse, start Windows applications, and issue Windows commands. It also assumes that you have read the sessions that discuss the common features of Office 97.

INTRODUCTION TO WORD PROCESSING AND WORD 97

People who write often want to clarify and refine what they have already committed to paper. **Word processing** can be defined as the computer manipulation of text data—creating, revising, storing, retrieving, and printing text.

Composing at the keyboard may require some practice, but you can soon get used to it. One great advantage of word processing is that once you have created a rough draft, you can print it, revise it, and print it again with minimal effort. This means that you do not have to carefully plan the original document; a rough outline is all you need to start writing. Because you can think and record your ideas more freely as you write with a word processor, you will be less likely to forget or fail to record points that may slip your mind when you are using pen and paper.

Microsoft Word 97 for Windows is judged by many software reviewers and users to be one of the best, most powerful word processing packages on the market. As well as being powerful and flexible, Word is also among the easiest word processing packages to use. The Word for Windows software package comprises word processing, a merge program, a spelling checker, a thesaurus, a grammar checker, and other advanced features.

Word 97 for Windows also includes desktop publishing capabilities. Its "what you see is what you get" (WYSIWYG) preview environment lets you see more or less how your printed document will appear. Any changes in type size, margins, or embedded graphics automatically appear on the screen exactly as they will on the printed page. Some enhanced text, graphics, footnotes, headers, and other advanced features can be made to appear in a different display mode.

INTRODUCTION TO THE WORD WINDOW

To load the Word for Windows program, click the Start button, drag the mouse pointer to Programs, and then click once on Microsoft Word.

Unless Word has been reconfigured for your computer, when Word is loaded, the window shown in Figure 1.1 appears.

The Word window contains two basic parts: the Word application window and the document window. The vertical line in the upper-left corner of the empty screen is the insertion point, or **cursor.** Its position shows where you will enter text or where a command will take effect.

Application Window

The **application window** shown in Figure 1.1 contains the title bar, application control buttons, menu bar, document control buttons, Standard toolbar, Formatting toolbar, ruler, Office Assistant, split bar, status bar, scroll bars, view icons, and a blank document window with an **end-of-document marker.** In the application window you can have multiple document windows open at the same time (Figure 1.2).

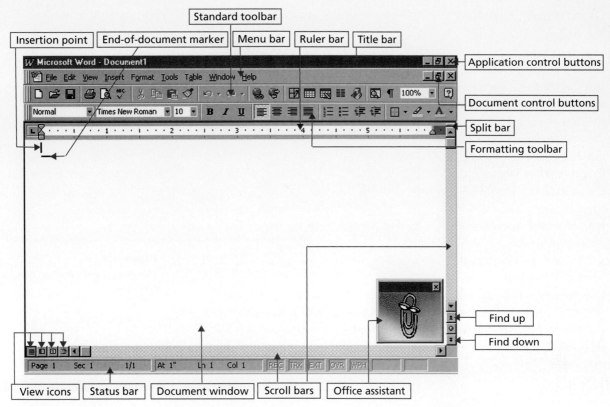

Standard toolbar

Insertion point | End-of-document marker | Menu bar | Ruler bar | Title bar

Application control buttons

Document control buttons

Split bar

Formatting toolbar

Find up

Find down

View icons | Status bar | Document window | Scroll bars | Office assistant

Figure 1.1
The various parts of the Word window.

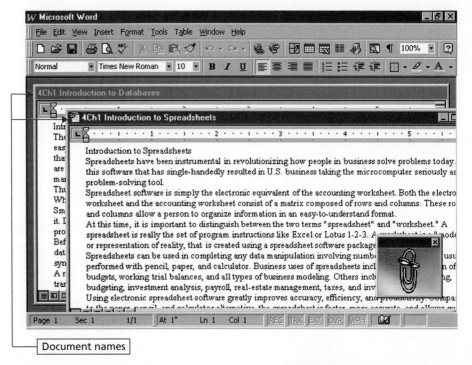

Document names

Figure 1.2
The Word application window with two document windows open and displayed at one time.

Document Window

The document window, shown in Figure 1.3, is where you create, view, and edit a document. Each document window has its own title bar (see Figure 1.2) that shows the name of the document being edited (such as Document1 or Document2, if you have not yet saved the document). You can have multiple documents open at one time.

If only one document is open or displayed at one time in an application window, the name of the document becomes part-of the title bar of the application window (Figure 1.4). Otherwise, the document name appears in the title bar of the document window (Figure 1.2).

Figure 1.3
The document window portion of Word.

Title Bar

The title bar (Figure 1.5) is located at the top of an application or document window. It contains the application name (Microsoft Word) along with the name of the document being edited. It also contains the Minimize, Maximize or Restore, and Close buttons.

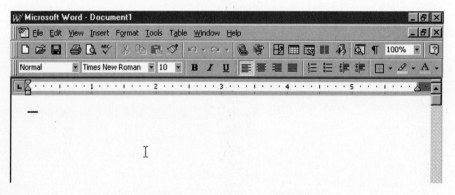

Figure 1.4
The Word application window with one document window open and the document name in the application window title bar.

Figure 1.5
The title bar containing the application name and the Minimize, Maximize or Restore, and Close buttons.

Menu Bar

The menu bar (Figure 1.6) contains menu options that activate pull-down menus. The menu options and menus displayed follow standard Windows conventions. The Minimize, Maximize or Restore, and Close buttons that appear here affect only the document in the document window, not the entire application.

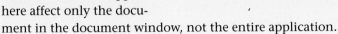

Figure 1.6
The Word menu bar.

Standard Toolbar

The **Standard toolbar** (Figure 1.7), located beneath the menu bar, contains buttons that enable you to execute commands more quickly than you can by going through various menus. Table 1.1 shows and describes each button.

Figure 1.7
The Standard toolbar for Word.

Formatting Toolbar

The **Formatting toolbar** (Figure 1.8) enables you to format characters and paragraphs. Using this toolbar, you can select formatting styles, such as the typeface and point size, or apply predefined styles to text. Table 1.2 shows and describes each button.

Figure 1.8
The Word Formatting toolbar.

Ruler

The **ruler** (Figure 1.9) displays the tab, paragraph, and margin settings for the current line. You can use the ruler **handles** to drag margins to control the indentation of the first line of a paragraph or the amount of space on the left and right to indent the rest of a paragraph.

Tabs appear as black marks on the ruler. Tabs work the same as typewriter tabs, positioning the insertion point at the next tab stop when you press (TAB).

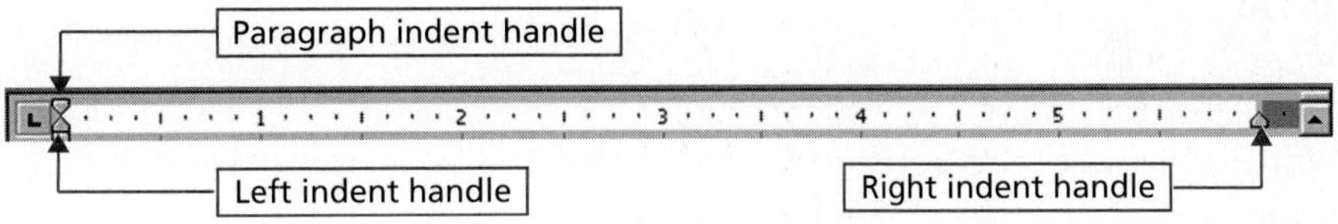

Paragraph indent handle

Left indent handle

Right indent handle

Figure 1.9
The ruler and the handles used to control the first indent and margins.

Office Assistant

The Office Assistant provides information on more efficient ways to perform a task. This feature was discussed in Session 1 of Module 3: Common Features of Office 97 Applications.

Split Bar

When you click the **split bar** (Figure 1.10) the screen divides into two sections, allowing you to have two different views of the same document. You can move the split bar by placing the mouse pointer on the bar (the pointer takes the shape of a double arrow) and then dragging the bar to the desired location. You then have two rulers visible on the screen.

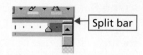

Figure 1.10
The split bar allows you to display two different views of your document.

Status Bar

The status bar (Figure 1.11) is at the bottom of the application window. The left side shows the current page number, section number, and total number of pages. Near the center of the status bar, the cursor's vertical depth from the top of the page is displayed in inches, along with the line and column numbers of the cursor location.

The status bar also shows when some of Word's special features are open. On the right side of the status bar, Word lists the toggle keys and current mode. When you access a menu, the status bar changes, and a description of the currently highlighted command is displayed.

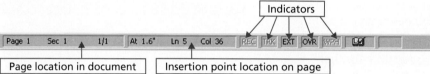

Figure 1.11
The status bar showing the location of the cursor in the document as well as other information.

Scroll Bars

For most documents, only a small portion of the text can be displayed on the screen at a time. The scroll bars provide a way to move through the document in the document window. A horizontal scroll bar is located just above the status bar, and a vertical scroll bar is located along the right side of the document window.

View Icons

At the left end of the horizontal scroll bar are four view icons (Figure 1.12), which control how the document is displayed on the screen. Table 1.3 shows and describes each button.

Figure 1.12
The view icons, which control how your document is displayed.

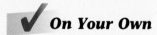

On Your Own

Word has a number of templates (already formatted blank documents) available for your use. To access these document templates, use the File, New... command sequence. The New dialog box appears. Click one of the tabs other than the General tab to see one of these document templates. Use the Elegant Resume from the Other Documents tab to prepare a resume. Use the Mailing Label Wizard from the Letters & Faxes tab to create a sheet of labels containing your name and address that you can use as return address labels on envelopes.

Table 1.1 Standard Toolbar Buttons

Button	Name	Function
	New	Creates a new document based on the Normal template
	Open	Opens an existing document or template
	Save	Saves the active document or template
	Print	Prints the active document using the current default settings
	Print Preview	Displays full pages as they will be printed
	Spelling and Grammar	Checks the spelling and grammar in the active document
	Cut	Cuts the selection and puts it on the clipboard
	Copy	Copies the selection and puts it on the clipboard
	Paste	Inserts the clipboard contents at the insertion point
	Format Painter	Copies the formatting of the selection to a specified location
	Undo	Reverses the last action
	Redo	Redoes the last action that was undone
	Insert Hyperlink	Creates a link that can jump to a location in the current document, a different document, or a Web page; also allows you to include a multimedia file to be executed
	Web Toolbar	Displays the Web toolbar
	Tables and Borders	Inserts a table or border within a document
	Insert Table	Inserts a table
	Insert Excel Worksheet	Inserts a Microsoft Excel worksheet object
	Columns	Changes the column format of the selected sections
	Drawing	Shows or hides the Drawing toolbar
	Document Map	Invokes the Document Map, a separate pane that shows an outline of a document's headings; allows for quicker navigation through a document
	Show/Hide ¶	Shows or hides all nonprinting characters
100%	Zoom	Scales the editing view
	Office Assistant	Displays or hides the Office Assistant, which provides additional information on how to perform a task you are working on

Table 1.2 Formatting Toolbar Buttons

Button	Name	Function
Normal	Style	Applies an existing style or records a style by example
Times New Roman	Font	Changes the font of the selection
10	Font Size	Changes the font size of the selection
B	Bold	Makes the selection bold
I	Italic	Makes the selection italic
U	Underline	Formats the selection with a continuous underline
	Align Left	Aligns the paragraph at the left margin
	Center	Centers the paragraph between the margins
	Align Right	Aligns the paragraph at the right margin
	Justify	Aligns the paragraph at both the left and right margins
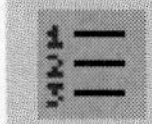	Numbering	Creates a numbered list based on the current default settings
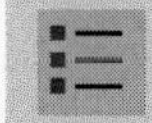	Bullets	Creates a bulleted list based on the current default settings
	Decrease Indent	Decreases the indent or promotes the selection one level
	Increase Indent	Increases the indent or demotes the selection one level
	Outside Border	Shows or hides the Border submenu
	Highlight	Marks text so that it stands out from surrounding text; the down arrow displays the colors
 A	Font Color	Changes text color; the down arrow displays the colors

Table 1.3   View Icons

Button	Name	Function
☰	Normal View	Changes the editing view to Normal view. This is the default view that shows data as it appears on the screen but not how it will appear on the printed page.
▤	Online Layout View	Splits the screen into two panes. The headings are in the left pane. Clicking a heading takes you to that part of the document. This makes it easier to view, move through, or rearrange the document.
▣	Page Layout View	Displays the page as it will be printed and allows editing. This WYSIWYG view takes up a lot of computer resources. If you don't have a really powerful computer, it is best to use the Normal view.
▦	Outline View	Displays the document's outline. This view allows you to see the entire document, with chapter headings, section headings, and so forth. It allows you to expand and contract whole parts of the document.

OPERATING WORD

You are now ready to practice creating, saving, and retrieving documents.

Entering Text in a Document

Entering text in Word is almost the same as typing at a typewriter, except you have more control over the look of the text and can freely edit the text and perform many other operations without having to retype your work.

A useful feature of Word, and of all word processors, is word wrap. When you are typing and reach the end of a line of characters, Word automatically moves the word that doesn't fit on the line down to the next line; this feature is called **word wrap.** The only time you have to press (ENTER) is to start a new paragraph.

Hands-On Exercise: Entering Text

The first Word task that Isabel will teach is the most basic: how to enter text.

1. **If necessary, start your computer and then start Word.**

2. **Turn off the Office Assistant by clicking its Close button.**

3. **Type the following letter.** Press (ENTER) at the end of each short line or paragraph. Don't be concerned if the text on your screen looks different from that shown here. Remember, Word underlines in red any word that doesn't match its default dictionary. Make any necessary corrections and proceed.

   Sports Center Civic Arena
   3015 S. Main
   Bloomington, IL 61701

   March 2, 1998

   Michael Dowd
   1216 W. Brentwood
   Danvers, IL 71763

   Dear Mr. Dowd:

   The purpose of this letter is to confirm your reservation of the Civic Arena for the weekend of April 19 for your organization's Ferret Frolic.

   Enclosed are separate receipts for the Civic Arena rental and security deposit. Any unused portion of the security deposit will be refunded to you by April 30.

   Thank you for selecting the Civic Arena.

   Sincerely,

   Isabel Ortiz, Business Manager

4. **Make the embedded Word codes visible.**

       Click the Show/Hide ¶ button on the Standard toolbar. Now you can see the nonprinting symbols that Word embeds in your document (Figure 1.13). These codes will not print; they allow you to see where you have entered specific commands in the document. Word saves a lot of information about how text in a paragraph is formatted as hidden instructions in the paragraph symbols.
   You can also see any words marked in red that Word thinks might be misspelled.

5. **Display the additional information that is not displayed about a document paragraph.**

   (SHIFT) + (F1)   Press to turn on the Help feature. A question mark now appears next to the mouse pointer.

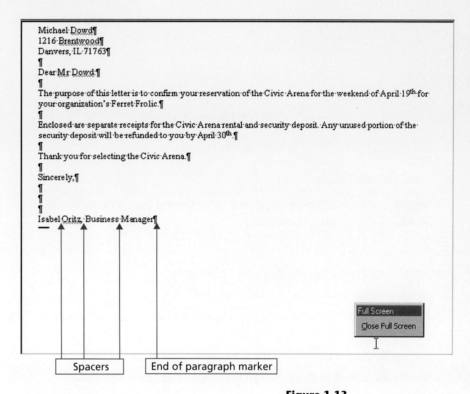

Spacers   End of paragraph marker

Figure 1.13
The Word document with embedded control codes.

Click   Click anywhere in the word *Sincerely*. A bubble with for-
                         matting information appears as shown in Figure 1.14.

SHIFT + F1   Press to turn off the Help feature.

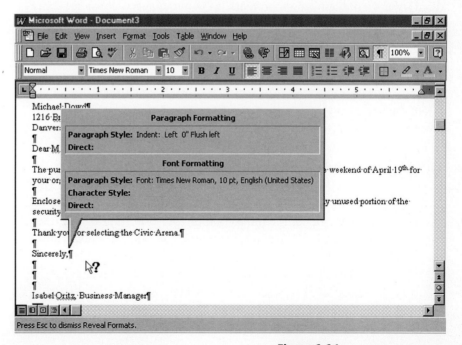

Figure 1.14
Formatting information stored
in the paragraph symbol.

6. **Save the document.**

File   Click to open the File menu.

S̲ave A̲s . . .   Click to open the Save As dialog box. By default, the first
                             line in the document is used as the document name.

Type the name of the document: **M4Ch1 Sample Letter 1**

| S̲ave | Save the file.

7. **Close the document.**

| ✕ | Click the document Close button on the menu bar to
                       clear the screen.

Reinforcing the Exercise

1. When you enter text, Word automatically moves text to the next line—a feature called word wrap.

2. Press (ENTER) only at the end of a paragraph or to insert a blank line.

3. The Show/Hide ¶ button allows you to see embedded Word codes.

4. The (SHIFT) + (F1) key combination activates the point method for obtaining Help. If you click anywhere in the sentence, formatting information appears.

Word's Hidden Paragraph Codes

When you type text and eventually press (ENTER) to end that paragraph, Word inserts a hidden paragraph mark (¶). A paragraph is considered any amount of text that ends when you press (ENTER). The paragraph mark contains all of that paragraph's formatting features, such as line spacing, indents, tabs, boldfacing, underlining, and other features. Word's default mode hides the paragraph marks. However, you can display paragraph marks by clicking the Show/Hide ¶ button on the Standard toolbar. If you delete the paragraph mark, you also delete all of that paragraph's special text features. To get those features back, you can click the Undo button.

Moving Around a Document

As you saw in Session 1 of Module 3: Common Features of Office 97 Applications, you can use the mouse or the keyboard to move the insertion point around a document. To use the mouse, simply position the **I-beam** (the cursor that looks like a capital I) where you want to make a change, and click the left mouse button. If you want to go to a location that is not on the screen, use the scroll box on the scroll bar.

To issue the keyboard **cursor movement commands,** you use the ten-key numeric keypad (Figure 1.15) or other keys with arrow symbols, depending on your keyboard. Session 2 of Module 3: Common Features of Office 97 Applications introduced keyboard cursor movement commands common to all Office applications. Table 1.4 shows additional cursor movement commands for Word, including one that displays the convenient Go To function shown in Figure 1.16.

Figure 1.15
Functions of the numeric keypad and other cursor movement keys supported by the standard 101-key extended keyboard.

Table 1.4   Word Keyboard Cursor Movement Commands

Keys	Action
Horizontal Movement	
→	Moves one position to the right
←	Moves one position to the left
CTRL + →	Moves one word to the right
CTRL + ←	Moves one word to the left
END	Moves to the end of the line
HOME	Moves to the beginning of the line
Vertical Movement	
↑	Moves up one line
↓	Moves down one line
CTRL + ↑	Moves up one paragraph
CTRL + ↓	Moves down one paragraph
PGUP	Moves up one screen of text
PGDN	Moves down one screen of text
CTRL + PGUP	Moves to the top of window
CTRL + PGDN	Moves to the bottom of window
CTRL + HOME	Moves to the beginning of the file
CTRL + END	Moves to the end of the file.
CTRL + G (or Go To from the Edit menu or F5)	Displays the Go To tab of the Find and Replace dialog box (Figure 1.16), where you can enter the page number you want to go to. Two additional tabs, Replace and Find, are also part of this dialog box. To move the cursor to the top of page 10, press CTRL + G (or F5), type **10** in the dialog box and then press ENTER or click OK. The dialog box remains on the screen until you click the Close button.

Working with Page Breaks

Word lets you see where a page break will appear when the document is printed. A **soft page break,** which in Normal view appears as a line of dots across the page, shows where one page ends and another begins (Figure 1.17). Word automatically places a soft page break in a file according to the margin settings and the amount of text. A **hard page break** occurs whenever you create a new page by pressing (CTRL) + (ENTER). In Normal view, a hard page break appears as a dotted line with the words *Page Break* centered on it. Page breaks appear on the screen, but the dots do not appear in your printed document. Making changes to a document before a soft page break can change the location of the soft page break (it moves forward or backward as text is added or deleted), but a hard page break always stays in the same location.

Depending on how your page breaks occur, you may see widow or orphan lines in your document. If the first line of a paragraph appears alone at the bottom of a page, that line is called a **widow**. If the last line of a paragraph appears alone at the top of a page, the line is an **orphan**.

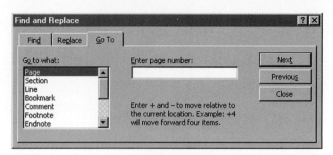

Figure 1.16
The Go To tab in the Find and Replace dialog box for moving to an exact page or other location in the document.

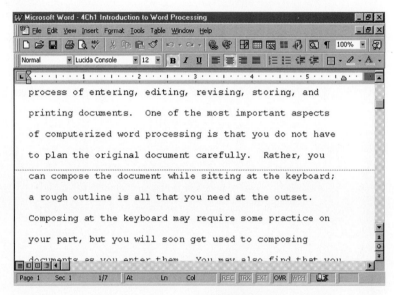

Figure 1.17
A soft page break appears as a row of dots or dashes.

Hands-On Exercise: Using Keyboard Cursor Movement Commands

The next task that Isabel wants to teach is how to navigate swiftly through a document.

1. **Open a file.**

   Click to open the file called *4Purchasing a Computer* from your Student Data Disk using the Open button.

2. **Move around the document.**

Click   Click in the first line of the second paragraph.

(END)   Click to move the insertion point to the end of the line.

(HOME)   Click to move the insertion point to the beginning of the line. Note your location indicated in the status bar.

(CTRL) + (→)   Press to move the insertion point to the word *you*.
three times

TIMELY   TIP

Use the View menu to turn on/off toolbars to make your screen look like Figure 1.14. Use Normal view.

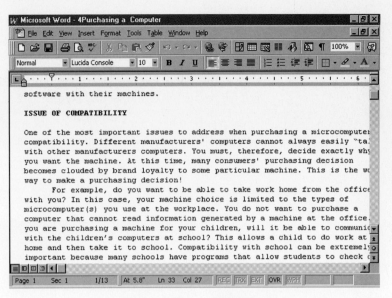

Figure 1.18
The 4Purchasing a Computer document as it appears after moving forward by pressing (PGDN) twice.

(CTRL) + (←)	Press to move the insertion point to the beginning of the word *functions*.
(CTRL) + (END)	Press to move to the end of the document.
(CTRL) + (HOME)	Press to move to the beginning of the document.
(PGDN)	Press twice to move down the document two screens (Figure 1.18). Note your location indicated in the status bar.
(PGUP)	Press to move up the document one screen. Note your location indicated in the status bar.

3. **Practice moving around the document using other commands shown in Table 1.4.**

4. **Examine soft page breaks.**

(CTRL) + (HOME)	Press to move to the beginning of the document.

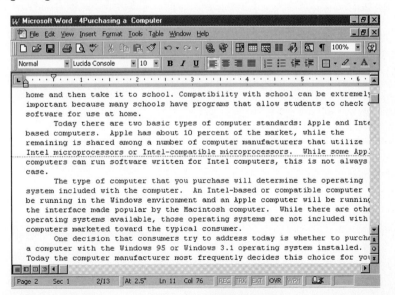

Figure 1.19
The first soft page break in the document.

(PGDN)   Press this key three times. Note the lines of dots em-
                 bedded in the document (Figure 1.19), indicating a soft
                 page break.

Click   Click at the end of the word *consumer* (last word in the
                 first full paragraph of the second page).

(CTRL) + (ENTER) Press to enter a hard page break. Your document should
                 now look like Figure 1.20. Please note that this would re-
                 sult in an unusually short page, so always check your doc-
                 uments page breaks before printing.

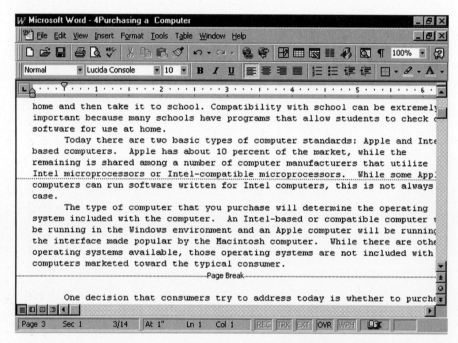

Figure 1.20
The 4Purchasing a Computer
document with soft and hard
page breaks visible.

5. **Click to close the file.**

                 Don't save any changes to the file.

TIMELY TIP

All formatting for a document in Word is based on the Normal template (NORMAL.DOT). You can modify this template to change the
formatting or content of the default document. Word also uses the
Normal template to store the AutoText entries, macros, toolbars, and
custom menu settings and shortcut keys you routinely use. Cus-
tomized items that you store in the Normal template are available for
use with any document.

Reinforcing the Exercise

1. You can use arrow keys as well as other keys on the keyboard to move around a document.

2. You can move both vertically and horizontally through a document.

3. The (CTRL) key, along with a right or left arrow key, moves you a word at a time through a document.

Selecting Text

For many commands to be executed properly, you must first select text by using a click and drag operation. You can also select text by placing the mouse pointer in an area of the document called the **selection bar.** This area is the white space in the left margin of the document (Figure 1.26). The mouse commands in Table 1.5 can also be used to select text using the mouse.

You can extend a selection by using the Select function key, (F8), in combination with any of the cursor movement commands listed in Table 1.4. If you want to select all text from the insertion point to the end of the paragraph, press (F8) + (ENTER).

TIMELY TIP

> When you use the mouse in a drag operation for text that begins at the bottom of the screen and continues, the text scrolls very rapidly, giving you very little mouse control. Use (F8) followed by cursor movement commands. For example, press (F8) + (ENTER) to select all text from the insertion point to the end of the paragraph.

Table 1.5   Using the Mouse to Select Text

Text Selection	Action
Single word	Double-click the mouse anywhere in the word.
Sentence	Press (CTRL) and click anywhere in the sentence.
Paragraph	Double-click in the selection bar.
Any amount of text	Click to position the cursor to the left of the first character you want to select. Press and hold down (SHIFT). Position the cursor to the right of the last character you want to select and click, and then release (SHIFT).
Entire document	Position the cursor in the selection bar, hold down (CTRL), and click. You can also triple-click in the selection bar.
Cancel selection	Click the mouse in any area of the document outside the selection bar.

Hands-On Exercise: Selecting Text in a Document

Many operations in Word require the user to select text. This is the next skill that Isabel wants to teach.

1. **Open the 4Purchasing a Computer document (Figure 1.21).** Click at the beginning of the second paragraph, in front of the *C* of *Consider*.

Click and drag	Using the mouse, create a selection that includes only the second and third paragraphs. Notice that, since all of the paragraphs are not displayed on the screen, it is difficult to create the selection. As you move past the displayed text, it is very difficult to control what text gets included in the selection.

Purchasing a Home Computer[1]

Many consumers are pondering the idea of purchasing a microcomputer for hor
use. Over the past few years microcomputers have become fairly popular
consumer items for adults as well as children. A consumer must consider a
number of important factors when purchasing a microcomputer for the home. *
factors to consider are 1. the use to be made of the computer 2.
compatibility, 3. special requirements, 4. were to purchase the hardware, *
software considerations, 6. hidden costs and 7. components of the typical
computer system,

INTENDED COMPUTER USE

Consider the functions you want your computer to perform. Will you be writ:
letters, a book, or performing any other type of text entry? Will you need
incorporate pictures, drawings, or artwork into your work? Do you have any
need for a computerized address book and/or budget? Do you want to do
financial planning or track your personal finances?

Figure 1.21
The 4Purchasing a Computer document.

2. **Redisplay the same text, and make the text selection using** (F8).

Click	Click anywhere in the document to deactivate the selection.
(CTRL) + (HOME)	Press to move to the beginning of the document.
Click	Position the insertion point at the beginning of the second paragraph, clicking in front of the *C* of *Consider*.
(F8)	Define the beginning of the selection. The EXT indicator in the status bar appears, indicating that you are ready to extend the selection.
(ENTER)	Press to include the second paragraph in the selection.
(ENTER)	Press to include the third paragraph in the selection (Figure 1.22).

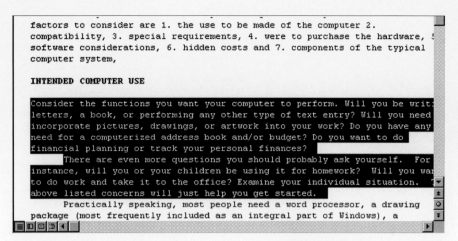

factors to consider are 1. the use to be made of the computer 2.
compatibility, 3. special requirements, 4. were to purchase the hardware, 5
software considerations, 6. hidden costs and 7. components of the typical
computer system,

INTENDED COMPUTER USE

Consider the functions you want your computer to perform. Will you be writ
letters, a book, or performing any other type of text entry? Will you need
incorporate pictures, drawings, or artwork into your work? Do you have any
need for a computerized address book and/or budget? Do you want to do
financial planning or track your personal finances?
　　　　There are even more questions you should probably ask yourself. For
instance, will you or your children be using it for homework? Will you wan
to do work and take it to the office? Examine your individual situation. T
above listed concerns will just help you get started.
　　　　Practically speaking, most people need a word processor, a drawing
package (most frequently included as an integral part of Windows), a

Figure 1.22
The 4Purchasing a Computer document with two paragraphs selected by using F8.

3. **Copy the selected paragraphs to the end of the document.**

Click to copy the selected text to the clipboard.

(CTRL) + (END)　　Press to move to the end of the document.

(ENTER)　　Press to move to a blank line.

Click to insert the copied text in the new location. Your document should now look like Figure 1.23. The EXT indicator in the status bar is turned off. You probably would want to insert a paragraph indent before the word *Consider* because it is the first word of a new paragraph.

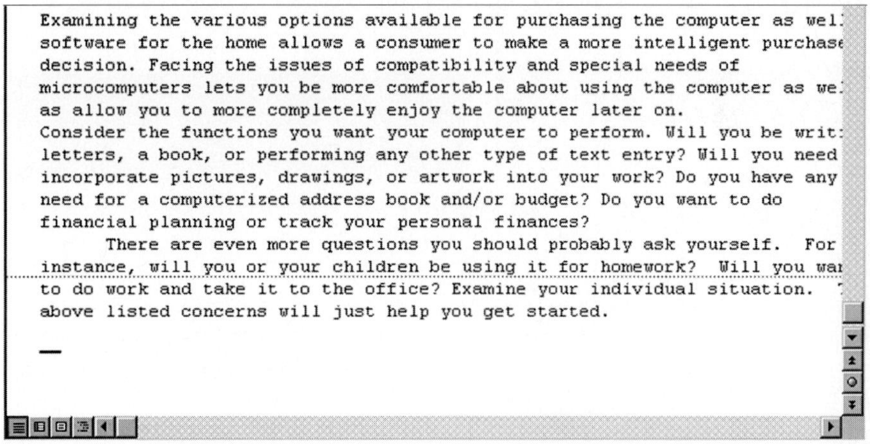

Examining the various options available for purchasing the computer as well
software for the home allows a consumer to make a more intelligent purchase
decision. Facing the issues of compatibility and special needs of
microcomputers lets you be more comfortable about using the computer as wel
as allow you to more completely enjoy the computer later on.
Consider the functions you want your computer to perform. Will you be writ
letters, a book, or performing any other type of text entry? Will you need
incorporate pictures, drawings, or artwork into your work? Do you have any
need for a computerized address book and/or budget? Do you want to do
financial planning or track your personal finances?
　　　　There are even more questions you should probably ask yourself. For
instance, will you or your children be using it for homework? Will you wan
to do work and take it to the office? Examine your individual situation. T
above listed concerns will just help you get started.

Figure 1.23
The manually defined selection copied to the end of the document.

4. **Examine some of the mouse selection commands.**

(CTRL) + (HOME)　　Click to move to the beginning of the document.

Click　　Click the word *computer* in the first line of the second paragraph of the document to move the insertion point.

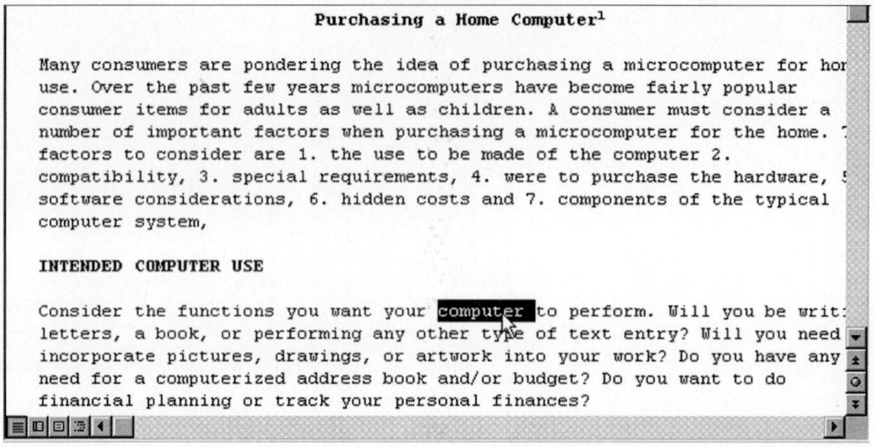

Figure 1.24
A word selected by double-clicking.

Double-click	Double-click to select the word *computer* (Figure 1.24).
Triple-click	Triple-click within that paragraph to select the entire paragraph (Figure 1.25).
Click	Click anywhere in the document to turn off the selection.

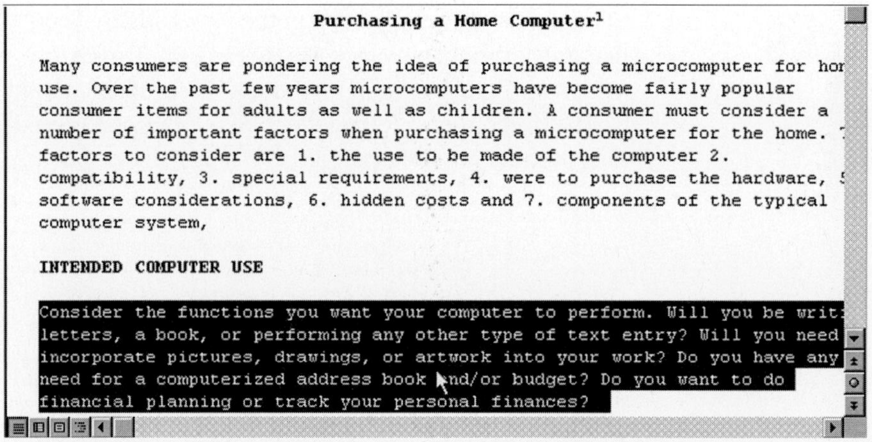

Figure 1.25
A paragraph of text selected by triple-clicking.

5. **Select the entire document.**

Point	Position the mouse pointer in the left margin of the document. The mouse pointer now points up and to the right (Figure 1.26).
(CTRL) + Click	Hold down (CTRL) and click the mouse. The entire document is now selected (Figure 1.27).

6. **Close the document without saving any changes that you have made.**

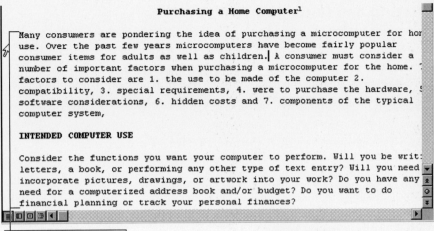

Area of selection bar

Figure 1.26
The mouse pointer pointing up and to the right, indicating that it is in the selection bar of the document.

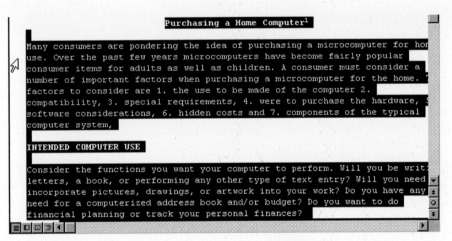

Figure 1.27
The entire document selected by holding down (CTRL) and clicking.

Reinforcing the Exercise

1. The area in the left margin is called the selection bar.
2. You can select text by using the mouse in a click-and-drag operation.
3. You can select the entire document by positioning the pointer in the selection bar, holding down (CTRL), and clicking.
4. You can select text manually using (F8) followed by movement commands.
5. You can use (ESC) to deactivate a manual extension.

Deleting and Restoring Text

Word's keyboard delete commands, listed in Table 1.6, let you delete text in various units. What happens if you delete the wrong text? Fortunately, Word is somewhat forgiving with the delete commands. You can restore deleted text by clicking the undo button. (Refer to Session 2 of Module 3: Common Features of Office 97 Applications for more information.)

Table 1.6 Summary of Keyboard Delete Commands

Keys	Action
(DEL)	Deletes the character at the cursor or any selected block of text.
(BKSP)	Deletes the character to the left of the cursor.
(CTRL) + (DEL)	Deletes from the cursor location to the end of the word. Any trailing spaces are also deleted.
(CTRL) + (BKSP)	Deletes from the cursor location to the beginning of the word.

Hands-On Exercise: Inserting, Deleting, and Restoring Text

Isabel now wants to teach her students and employees how to make changes to their work and correct mistakes.

1. **Open the document called 4Ch1 Inserting, Deleting, and Restoring Text (Figure 1.28).**

> Excel is used to build worksheets.
> Microsoft Word makes creating and editing documents easy.

Figure 1.28
The 4Ch1 Inserting, Deleting, and Restoring Text document.

On Your Own

Where the mouse does not seem to work well for selecting text, use (F8) and any one of the following alternatives:

1. Use some of the cursor movement commands listed in Table 1.4.
2. Use (ENTER).
3. Use various other keys (alphabetic keys, special characters, movement commands, and so forth).
4. Remember to use (ESC) to cancel the extension.

2. Move the insertion point and insert a word.

Click   Click to position the insertion point immediately before the *E* of *Excel.*

Type: **Microsoft**   As you type each character, the existing text moves to the right.

3. Replace a word.

Double-click   Double click the word *build* to select it.

Type: **create**   When you enter the first letter, the text in the selection is deleted (Figure 1.29).

```
Microsoft Excel is used to create| worksheets.
Microsoft Word makes creating and editing documents easy.
—
```

Figure 1.29
The highlighted word replaced by the new text.

4. Move the insertion point.

Click   Click to place the insertion point immediately to the left of the word *Microsoft* in the second line. (Press (HOME) if you have difficulty moving the insertion point to the beginning of the line.)

5. Delete the first two words of the second line.

(CTRL) + (DEL)   Press to delete the first word, *Microsoft.*

(CTRL) + (DEL)   Press to delete the second word, *Word.*

6. Restore the word *Word.*

                         Click the curved arrow of the Undo button to restore *Word.*

                         Click the curved arrow of the Undo button again to restore *Microsoft.*

TIMELY TIP

The Undo command works only for the last command you executed. To undo an operation that you performed some time ago, click the down arrow portion of the Undo button to access a list of tasks that can be undone. Clicking the curved arrow portion of the Undo button automatically reverses the previous operation again.

7. Delete and then restore the phrase *creating and editing.*

Click	Click to position the insertion point in front of the *c* in *creating,* and use a drag operation to highlight *creating and editing.*
DEL	Press to delete *creating and editing.*
Click	Position the insertion point at the end of the line. You will now verify that the position of the insertion point has nothing to do with how the Undo command works.
↰	Click the curved arrow portion of the Undo button to restore the deleted text. Click anywhere to remove the highlighting if necessary. The phrase should now be correctly restored.

8. Use CTRL + BKSP to delete text.

Click	Position the insertion point to the left of the *s* in *Microsoft.*
CTRL + BKSP	Press to delete from the insertion point to the beginning of the word.
↰	Click the curved arrow portion of the Undo button to restore the deleted text.

9. Delete and then restore all of the text in the document.

	Position the mouse pointer in the selection bar of the document, to the left of the first sentence.
CTRL + Click	Issue this command to select the entire document.
DEL	Delete all of the text.
↰	Click the curved arrow portion of the Undo button to restore the deleted text.

10. Close the document without saving your changes.

Reinforcing the Exercise

1. Insert mode moves new text to the right.
2. Entering new text when you have a portion of text selected replaces the selected characters with the newly entered characters.
3. The CTRL + DEL command deletes characters from the insertion point to the end of the word.
4. The CTRL + BKSP command deletes characters from the insertion point to the beginning of the word.
5. Selected text can be deleted pressing either the DEL or BKSP.
6. You can restore deleted text by using the Undo command.

PERFORMING ELEMENTARY DOCUMENT CONTROL

F̲ormat, P̲aragraph

Word provides you with the ability to control how your document appears by allowing you to adjust line spacing, paragraph indents, margins, and vertical positioning of text.

Controlling Line Spacing

Up to this point, you have used only single **line spacing** (or whatever line spacing was set as the default). You can change spacing of any number of lines to single or double line spacing or even to incremental line spacing such as .5 or 1.5. To change line spacing, use the Format, Paragraph command sequence. In the Paragraph dialog box (Figure 1.30), select the Indents and Spacing tab (if necessary). Then, in the Line Spacing or At box, specify a spacing value.

In the Preview box, you will see a sample of how text will appear when the settings you specified in the Paragraph dialog box are applied.

If you want the entire document double-spaced, you must first select the entire document by moving your mouse into the selection bar and clicking the mouse while holding down (CTRL). This operation highlights and selects the entire document.

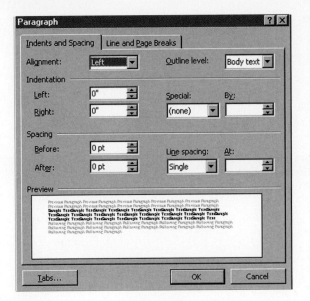

Figure 1.30
The Paragraph dialog box, which controls paragraph indents, line spacing, and spacing between paragraphs.

Hands-On Exercise: Changing Line Spacing

Isabel now wants to introduce ways to change line spacing using keyboard commands and the Paragraph dialog box.

1. **Open the 4Ch1 Introduction to Spreadsheets file (Figure 1.31).**

2. **Select the entire document.**

Point	Move the mouse pointer into the selection bar.
(CTRL) + Click	Issue this command to select the entire document.

3. **Issue the keyboard double-spacing command.**

(CTRL) + 2	Press to double-space the document.
Click	Click the left mouse button once to remove the highlighting. The text should now look like Figure 1.32. Notice that no paragraph is indented, so it is difficult to tell where one paragraph ends and another begins.

4. **Change the spacing back to single-spacing.**

(CTRL) + Click	Move the mouse pointer into the selection bar and issue this command to select the entire document.

TIMELY TIP

If you want to change the spacing of all or only a part of the document, you can use the mouse to select the text and then issue a shortcut command: (CTRL) + **1** for single spacing, or (CTRL) + **2** for double-spacing.

Introduction to Spreadsheets
Spreadsheets have been instrumental in revolutionizing how people in business solve problems today. It is
this software that has single-handedly resulted in U.S. business taking the microcomputer seriously as a
problem-solving tool.
Spreadsheet software is simply the electronic equivalent of the accounting worksheet. Both the electronic
worksheet and the accounting worksheet consist of a matrix composed of rows and columns. These rows
and columns allow a person to organize information in an easy-to-understand format.
At this time, it is important to distinguish between the two terms "spreadsheet" and "worksheet." A
spreadsheet is really the set of program instructions like Excel or Lotus 1-2-3. A worksheet is a "model,"
or representation of reality, that is created using a spreadsheet software package.
Spreadsheets can be used in completing any data manipulation involving numbers and text that is usually
performed with pencil, paper, and calculator. Business uses of spreadsheets include the preparation of
budgets, working trial balances, and all types of business modeling. Others include sales forecasting,
budgeting, investment analysis, payroll, real-estate management, taxes, and investment proposals.
Using electronic spreadsheet software greatly improves accuracy, efficiency, and productivity. Compared
to the paper, pencil, and calculator alternative, the spreadsheet is faster, more accurate, and allows much
more flexibility. Once a worksheet has been prepared, other options can be easily considered simply by
making the appropriate changes. The spreadsheet can then be instructed to recalculate all entries to reflect
the changes. Thus, the process of considering a number of different options ("what if" analysis) can be

| CTRL + 1 | Press to single-space the document. |
| Click | Click anywhere to cancel the selection. The document now appears as it did in Figure 1.31. |

Figure 1.31
The 4Ch1 Introduction to Spreadsheets file.

Introduction to Spreadsheets

Spreadsheets have been instrumental in revolutionizing how people in business solve problems today. It is

this software that has single-handedly resulted in U.S. business taking the microcomputer seriously as a

problem-solving tool.

Spreadsheet software is simply the electronic equivalent of the accounting worksheet. Both the electronic

worksheet and the accounting worksheet consist of a matrix composed of rows and columns. These rows

and columns allow a person to organize information in an easy-to-understand format.

At this time, it is important to distinguish between the two terms "spreadsheet" and "worksheet." A

spreadsheet is really the set of program instructions like Excel or Lotus 1-2-3. A worksheet is a "model,"

or representation of reality, that is created using a spreadsheet software package.

Figure 1.32
The 4Ch1 Introduction to Spreadsheets document double-spaced.

5. **Use the Paragraph dialog box to control paragraph indents, spacing within paragraphs, and spacing between paragraphs.** Do not include the title line in the selection (it will be dealt with later in the exercise).

Click	Position the cursor at the beginning of the first paragraph.
F8	Press to turn on the selection extension feature. The EXT indicator now appears in the status bar.
CTRL + END	Press to select the entire document (Figure 1.33).
Format	Click to open the Format menu.
Paragraph. . .	Click to open the Paragraph dialog box.

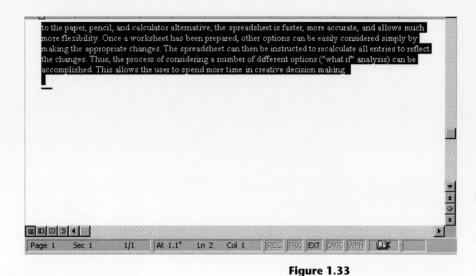

Figure 1.33
The document except for the title line included in the selection.

6. **Change the paragraph indentation to .5 inches.**

Special: Click this list box in the Indentation group to display the list shown in Figure 1.34.

First line   Click to select this entry. Check the entry in the By text box to make certain that it contains the value .5". If it doesn't, change it to .5".

7. **Change the spacing after paragraphs to 6pt.**

          Click the up arrow of the After: spin box in the Spacing group once to display 6pt.

8. **Change the line spacing to double.**

Line spacing: Click the down arrow in the Line spacing list box to display the list shown in Figure 1.35.

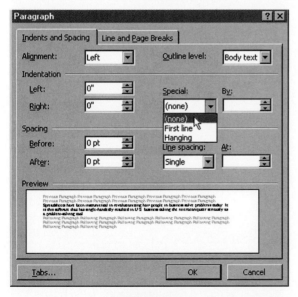

Figure 1.34
The Paragraph dialog box with the entries in the Special list box.

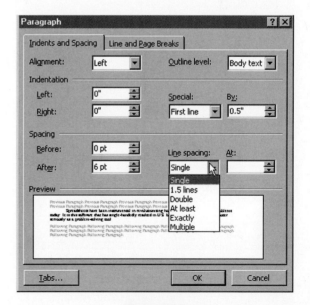

Figure 1.35
The Paragraph dialog box with the options in the Line spacing: list box.

Double   Click to select this entry. Your completed dialog box
                          should now look like Figure 1.36.

9. **Check to make certain that Widow/Orphan control is on.**

Line and <u>P</u>age   Click this tab to display the screen
    Breaks   shown in Figure 1.37. This dialog box controls how text
                          flows from one page to another. Notice that the
                          Widow/Orphan control option is checked, indicating that
                          this feature is on.

          [OK   ]   Click to return to the document.

Click   Turn off text selection.

10. **Center and boldface the document title.** (This line was not included in
    the original selection to avoid indenting the title.)

    (CTRL) + (HOME)   Press to move to the beginning of the document.

    [≡]   Click to center the title.

Click   Place the insertion point in the selection bar immediately
                          to the left of the title line. Click to select the title line.

    [**B**]   Click to boldface the text.

    (CTRL) + 2   Click to double-space the title.

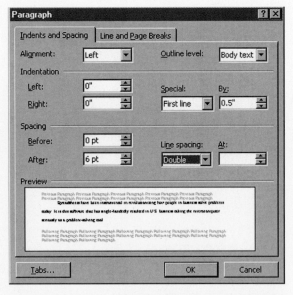

Figure 1.36
The Paragraph dialog box with
the desired changes made.

Figure 1.37
The Line and Page Breaks tab of
the Paragraph dialog box.

Click

Click anywhere to turn off the selection. Your document should now look like Figure 1.38. Notice that the distance between the paragraphs is slightly larger than the distance between the lines inside the paragraph.

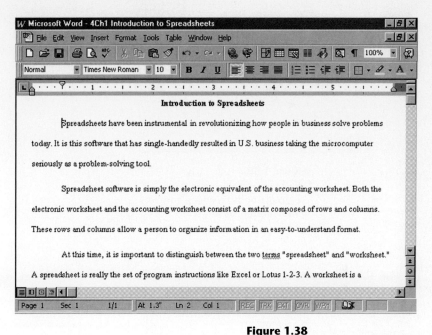

Figure 1.38
The completed document.

11. **Print the document.**

Click the Print button on the Standard toolbar to send the document to the Print Manager for printing.

12. **Save the changed document using the name M4Ch1 Sample Exercise 2, and close the document.**

Reinforcing the Exercise

1. You can use the (CTRL) + click command to select the entire document.

2. You can use the (CTRL) key with a number key (1 or 2) to set the line spacing.

3. You can use the Paragraph dialog box to control a number of formatting features, such as paragraph indentation, line spacing, and spacing before and after a paragraph.

4. You can use the Line and Page Breaks tab of the Paragraph dialog box to avoid widow and orphan lines.

CONTROLLING PAGE APPEARANCE

<u>F</u>ile, Page Set<u>u</u>p

Word allows you to control such aspects of a page as initial margin settings, paper size, and page layout using the Page Setup dialog box. The various tabs found in this dialog box can be seen in Figures 1.39 to 1.42.

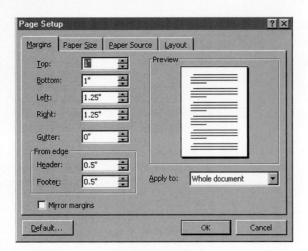

Figure 1.39
The Margins tab of the Page
Setup dialog box, which controls
initial margin settings.

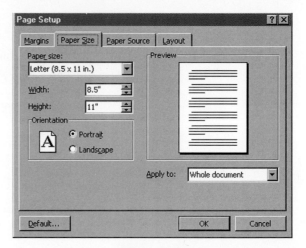

Figure 1.40
The Paper Size tab of the Page
Setup dialog box, which controls
the paper size and orientation of
the paper used in generating a
printed copy of a document.

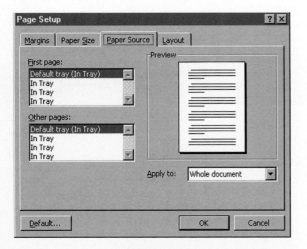

Figure 1.41
The Paper Source tab of the
Page Setup dialog box, which
controls how paper is obtained
for a print operation.

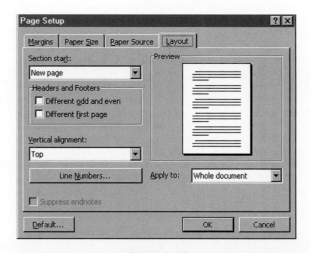

Figure 1.42
The Layout tab of the Page
Setup dialog box, which controls
such items as vertical alignment
of text on a page and the display
of headers and footers.

Hands-On Exercise: Controlling Page Layout

This exercise requires the letter that you created earlier in this session. Isabel wants to teach her students and employees how to center text vertically and change the default margins.

1. **Open the M4Ch1 Sample Letter 1 created earlier in the session.**

2. **Examine how the document is to be printed.**

Click to see how the document will be printed (Figure 1.43). (If necessary, click the One Page button.) Notice that the letter takes up only the top half of the page.

Close   Click to return to the document.

3. **Change the document margins.**

File   Click to open the File menu.

Page Set<u>u</u>p. . .   Click to open the Page Setup dialog box.

<u>M</u>argins   If necessary, click the Margins tab.

     Click the up arrow of the Left spin box until 1.5" appears.

     Click the up arrow of the Right spin box until 1.5" appears. The Margins tab should now look like Figure 1.44.

4. **Change the vertical alignment of the letter.**

<u>L</u>ayout   Display the Layout tab of the Page Setup dialog box.

     Click arrow of Vertical alignment box to display a list of options.

Center   Click this entry. The Layout tab should now look like Figure 1.45.

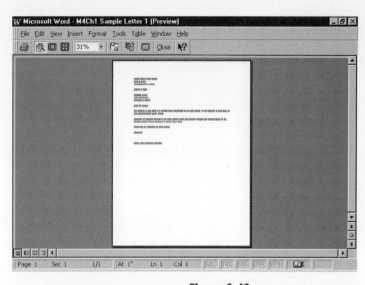

Figure 1.43
The letter in the Preview window.

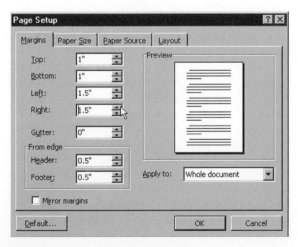

Figure 1.44
The completed Margins tab.

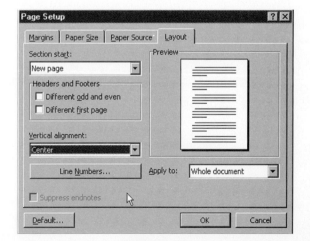

Figure 1.45
The completed Layout tab.

Return to the letter.

5. Examine the impact of the changes.

    Click to see the letter centered on the page, as shown in Figure 1.46.

    Click to return to the document.

6. Print the letter.

   Click to send the document to the Print Manager for printing.

7. Save the changes using the name M4Ch1 Sample Letter 2, and close the file.

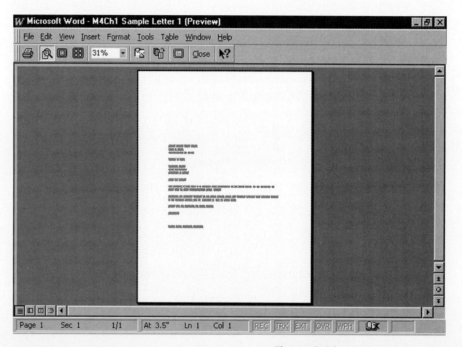

Figure 1.46
The centered letter shown using the Print Preview feature.

Reinforcing the Exercise

1. You can use the Page Setup dialog box to change the margins of a document.

2. You can use an option of the Layout tab of the Page Setup dialog box to control vertical alignment of a page in a document.

CONVERTING WORD DOCUMENTS TO HTML FOR PLACEMENT ON THE WEB

Word, as well as other Office 97 applications, allows you quickly to convert any document to a format (called HTML) that makes that document accessible from the World Wide Web. You use the File, Save As HTML command sequence to make this conversion. The following Hands-On Exercise will illustrate this process.

Hands-On Exercise: Saving a Word Document in HTML Format

For this exercise you will use the ferret brochure you created in Session 2 of Module 3: Common Features of Office 97 Applications.

1. **Open the file M3Ch2 Your Name - Ferret Flyer.**

2. **Save it as an HTML file.**

File	Click to open the File menu.
Save As <u>H</u>TML. . .	Click to open the Save As HTML dialog box (Figure 1.47). This dialog box allows you to save the document as a Web document that can then be accessed by using Internet Explorer or by taking advantage of Word's ability to act as a browser and read an HTML document.
Click	Click in front of the word *Flyer* in the File name text box.
Type: **Web**	Your file name should now be M3Ch2 Your Name Ferret Web Flyer.
Save	Click to save as a Web document. Notice that the text in the title bar has changed. What you now see on the screen is the HTML version of your document (Figure 1.48). The first line of the document was used as the title and now appears in the title bar.

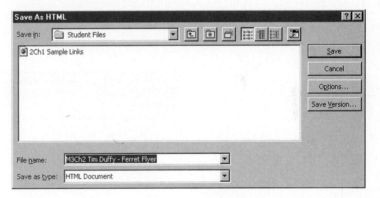

Figure 1.47
The Save As HTML dialog box allows you to save a file as a Web document.

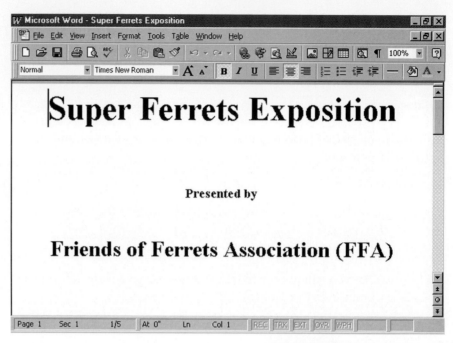

Figure 1.48
The HTML document displayed
by Word.

3. Verify that this is an HTML document.

View   Click to open the View menu.

HTML Source   Click to view the HTML statements used to create the
                          Web document (Figure 1.49).

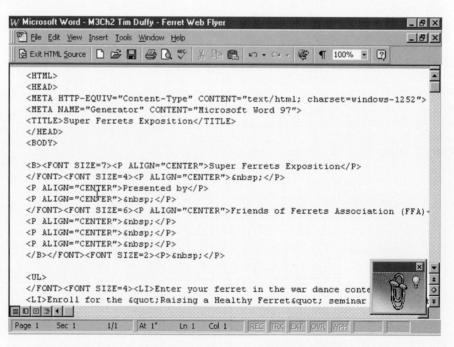

Figure 1.49
The HTML statements for the
Web document.

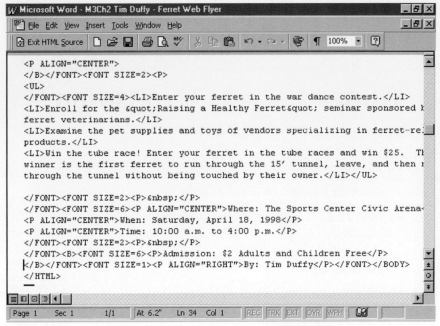

Figure 1.50
The changed HTML code.

4. **Get rid of some of the spacing.** Delete any HTML line that has the character string * </p>* by placing the cursor in the selection bar, clicking to select the line, and pressing DEL. Your document should look like Figure 1.50.

5. **Return to your document.**

   Click to display a box asking if you want to save your changes (Figure 1.51).

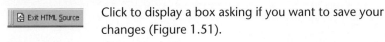   Click to save the changes. The changed Web document now appears as shown in Figure 1.52. Notice that there are no longer large amounts of blank space present.

On Your Own

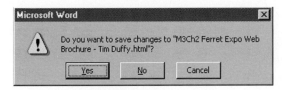

Figure 1.51
Word prompt for saving the HTML changes.

Besides the boldfacing, underlining, and Italics features available via buttons on the formatting toolbar, additional text attributes are available if you use the Format, Font... command sequence. This command sequence invokes the Font dialog box, where such text features as superscript, subscript, strikethrough, small caps, outline, and others are available.

This dialog box also controls various underlining methods that can be controlled by Word. To activate these Underline options, use the Underline pull-down menu.

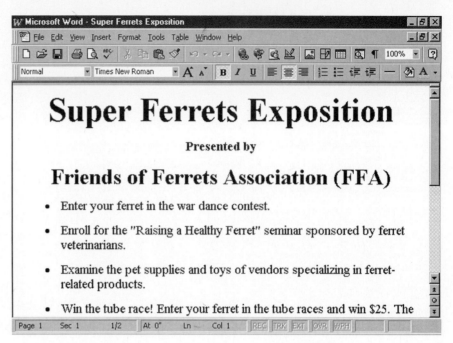

Figure 1.52
The changed Web document.

6. **Close the document.**

    Click the Close button on the menu bar.

7. **Exit Word.**

8. **Access the document using the Internet Explorer (Figure 1.53)**

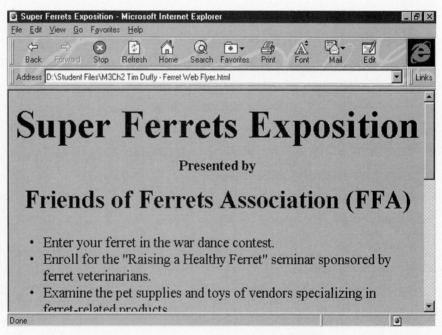

Figure 1.53
The Web document displayed
using Internet Explorer.

SESSION REVIEW

Word processing involves entering, saving, changing, and printing documents and written correspondence. Computerized word processing greatly eases this process.

Numerous word processing packages are on the market. One of the most popular is Microsoft Word, which includes a spelling checker, a thesaurus, merge capabilities, and advanced desktop publishing features. The latest Windows version supports all features found in that operating system.

When you start Word, your screen first displays a blank document window with a status bar that contains information on the location of the insertion point.

The area above the status bar is the document window. The scroll bar, title bar, menu bar, Standard toolbar, Formatting toolbar, and ruler are all part of this window.

Cursor movement commands allow you to move the cursor, or insertion point, around the document. The scroll bars let you move the cursor vertically or horizontally within the document. The mouse lets you move the insertion point within the document window. You can also use keyboard commands to move the insertion point.

Word also allows you to control how the document appears using the Paragraph and Page Setup dialog boxes. The Paragraph dialog box provides control over various types of spacing, and the Page Setup dialog box provides control over document margins.

Word permits you to take a regular document and save it as an HTML file. You can then access that document by using the Word browser or the Internet Explorer.

KEY TERMS AND CONCEPTS

application window 4–2	hard page break 4–14	soft page break 4–14
cursor 4–2	I-beam 4–12	split bar 4–6
cursor movement command 4–13	line spacing 4–25	Standard toolbar 4–5
end-of-document marker 4–2	orphan 4–14	widow 4–14
Formatting toolbar 4–5	ruler 4–5	word processing 4–2
handles 4–5	selection bar 4–17	word wrap 4–9

SESSION QUIZ

Multiple Choice

1. Which of the following commands is used for controlling line spacing?

   a. (CTRL) + L

   b. (CTRL) + A

   c. (CTRL) + 2

   d. none of the above

2. Which of the following statements about Word is/are true?

   a. It allows you to control horizontal and vertical margins.

   b. It allows a document to be viewed before printing to see how the finished document will appear.

   c. It is a tremendously popular word processing package.

   d. All of the above statements are true.

3. Which of the following statements is/are true?
   a. Word is used for entering, editing, and printing documents.
   b. Spacing within as well as between paragraphs can be controlled using the Page Setup dialog box.
   c. The Paragraph dialog box allows you to center a document vertically on a sheet of paper.
   d. All of the above statements are true.

4. Which of the following Word commands affects one word at a time?
   a. CTRL + BACKSPACE
   b. CTRL + DEL
   c. CTRL + →
   d. all of the above

5. Which of the following is not typically contained on the status bar?
   a. column number
   b. vertical position on the page
   c. status of the CAPS LOCK key
   d. line location

True/False

6. WYSIWYG provides the ability to do work that closely approximates desktop publishing quality.

7. Word provides spelling corrections only when the Spelling button on a toolbar is clicked.

8. Word allows you to select text only by using the mouse.

9. You can select text by using either the mouse or F8 in conjunction with cursor movement keys.

10. The terms *hard page break* and *soft page break* are essentially synonymous terms; both types of page break are created in the same fashion.

SESSION REVIEW EXERCISES

1. Define or describe each of the following:
   a. Page Setup dialog box
   b. word wrap
   c. F8 function key
   d. status line
   e. soft page break

2. The term _____ means that data appears on the screen the same as it will appear when printed.

3. Another word sometimes used instead of *insertion point* is _____.

4. The _____ window is used for creating, viewing, and editing a document.

5. The name of the document always appears in a/an _____ bar.

6. A string or line of buttons containing icons that represent tasks that can be performed is called a/an _____.

7. The feature that automatically moves a word that will not fit on the current line down to the next line is called _____.

8. The _____ key is pressed only at the end of a paragraph.

9. The bar at the bottom of the document window is called the _____ bar.

10. The single line of dots that appears in a document is called a/an _____ break.

11. A/an _____ line occurs when the first line of a new paragraph appears by itself at the bottom of a page.

12. The _____ key is used to delete one or more lines of selected text from a document.

13. The shortcut command _____ + _____ is used to change the line spacing in a document to single-spacing.

14. The _____ displays the tab and margin settings for the current line.

15. The I-beam is another form of the _____ _____.

16. Word uses a line with the message _____ _____ in the middle to indicate a hard page break.

17. To go to a specific page, you would use the cursor movement command _____ + _____.

18. Holding down a mouse button and then moving the mouse is done to _____ text before a Word editing command is issued.

19. Use the _____ _____ dialog box to indent the first line of a paragraph automatically.

20. The _____ tab of the Page Setup dialog box is used to control the vertical positioning of text in a document.

COMPUTER EXERCISES

1. Use the Help feature. Use the Help, Microsoft Word Help Topics command sequence. Use the Find tab to search for the following words, and then double-click the phrase indicated. Print the Help screen for the first topic, align.
   a. Align: Adjust the horizontal position of a header or footer
   b. Autocorrect: Automatically correct text
   c. Underlining: Apply a style turns off bold, italic or underlining

   Click the Office Assistant and enter the following queries. Examine the results at your leisure.
   d. page break
   e. line spacing
   f. center vertically

   Click the Options button and select the Print option to print one entry for the page break topic. When you have finished, click the Close button to return to the document window.

2. Experiment with the cursor movement and line spacing commands.
    a. Refer to Table 1.4 for a summary of the cursor movement and scrolling commands covered in this session. Load the file called 4Purchasing a Computer, and practice these commands.
    b. When you have finished experimenting with the cursor movement commands, change the line spacing to double space. Close the file without saving it.

3. Open the file called 4Ch1 Introduction to Databases. The first part of this document is shown in Figure 1.54. Make the following changes to the document:
    a. Double-space the document.
    b. Center and boldface the title.
    c. Change the left and right margins to 1 inch.
    d. Preview the document.
    e. Change the font to whatever form of Lucida you have.
    f. Change the font size to 9 pt.
    g. Print the document.
    h. Save the file using the file name M4Ch1 Exercise 3.
    i. Review the printout and make any necessary corrections. Insert a hard page break after the first paragraph and print the document.
    j. Use the File, Close command sequence, but do not save the file.

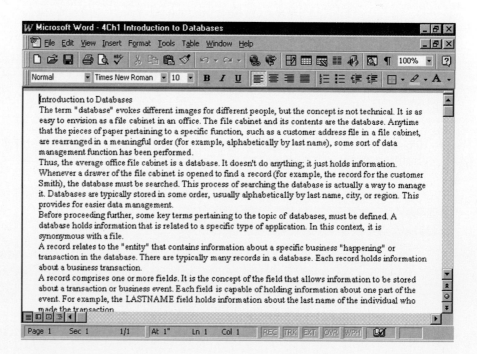

4. Open the document named 4Ch1 Introduction to the Computer. Make the following changes to the document:
    a. Change the font to Times Roman if necessary.
    b. Change the font size to 11 pt.
    c. Single-space each paragraph.
    d. Indent the first line of each paragraph .5 inch.
    e. Put 6 points of space after each paragraph.

Figure 1.54

The first part of the 4Ch1 Introduction to Databases document.

   f. Make any other changes, such as centering or boldfacing, that are indicated in the text shown below.

   g. Print the document.

   h. Save the document using the filename M4Ch1 Exercise 4.

Completed Session 1 Exercise 4:

Introduction to the Computer

The computer has had a greater impact on our society than any other device in the second half of the 20th century. As late as the mid-1970s, relatively few people used computers. For many people today, computers are as much a part of daily life as automobiles, telephones, and electric lights.

In business, computers track and process inventory, accounts receivable, accounts payable, and payroll. They are used in education to schedule classes, train students, and record grades. In the medical profession, computers diagnose and monitor patients. Scientists use computers to analyze the solar system, forecast weather patterns, and conduct experiments.

Of all the computer types, the microcomputer has been most helpful in improving our ability to control information and solve problems. The microcomputer is used by Fortune 500 companies and small businesses alike to file information, produce documents and correspondence, and perform time-consuming financial calculations and projections. It has boosted the productivity of workers at all organizational levels, from the mail room to the board room. Because it has a tireless capacity to perform practice exercises and simulations, the microcomputer is also an excellent teaching tool for primary and secondary school students.

What Is a Computer?

A **computer** is a general-purpose electronic device that performs high-speed arithmetic and logical operations according to internal instructions that are executed without human intervention. The key terms and implications of this definition are examined below.

Electronic. Electricity is the computer's lifeblood. In a high-speed computer, electricity pulses at half the speed of light through the intricate silicon-chip circuits that serve as the machine's brain cells.

Arithmetic Operations. Computers add, subtract, multiply, and divide.

Logical Operations. Computers compare one datum with another. This allows the computer operator to determine if the datum is less than, equal to, or greater than another datum.

Internally Contained Instructions. Computers store the instructions that manipulate data. A complete set of instructions for performing some type of operation is called a program. For example, a payroll program enables a computer to calculate an organization's payroll, taking into account a variety of factors such as salary levels, overtime hours, and part-time employment.

Internal Storage. A program requires some internal storage capability in order to manipulate data. Like its human counterpart, this storage system is called memory. Memory holds the computer's operating system, the program being executed, the data operated on, and any intermediate results that are created by the program.

General Purpose. By retrieving a variety of programs from memory and executing them, computers perform an almost limitless number of tasks—from calculating a business's monthly expenses to drawing architectural blueprints.

5. Enter the following letter and save it in a file called M4Ch1 Exercise 5. Use the default
    font and font size. Single-space the letter. Print, save, and close the document.

Sports Center Civic Arena
3015 S. Main
Bloomington, IL 61701

March 15, 1998

Jeremy Marks, Manager
Twin City Automotive
1022 E. Morissey
Bloomington, IL 61702

Dear Mr. Marks:

As per our telephone discussion yesterday, the purpose of this letter is to request
a bid for three full-size cargo vans to be used for our Civic Arena. Each of the
vans should have a V-8 engine, 1.5-ton capacity, standard five-speed transmission,
and air conditioning.

We would like to take possession of these vans approximately six to eight weeks
from now.

Thank you for your prompt attention in this matter.

Sincerely,

Isabel Ortiz, Business Manager

6. Load the M4Ch1 Exercise 5 letter. Use the Page Setup dialog box to center the letter ver-
    tically. Preview the document. Print the document. Save the document in the file
    M4Ch1 Exercise 6.

7. Load the document 4Ch1 Exercise 7 (Figure 1.55). Delete the underlined text using the
    following commands. You must position the insertion point in the correct location be-
    fore you issue a deletion command.
    a. *evokes different*: CTRL + DEL
    b. *but the concept is not technical*: selection, DEL
    c. *envision as a file*: CTRL + BKSP
    d. *meaningful*: selection, BKSP
    e. *some sort of data management function has been performed*: selection, DEL
    f. *drawer*: CTRL + DEL
    g. *This process of searching the database*: CTRL + BKSP

    Print the file, and save it using the name M4Ch1 Exercise 7.

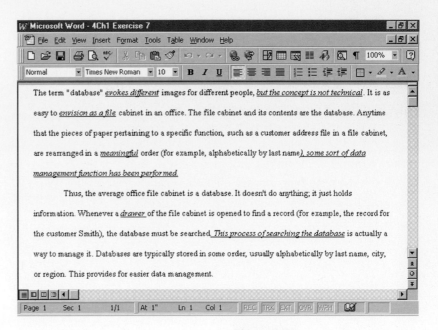

The term "database" _evokes different_ images for different people, _but the concept is not technical_. It is as easy to _envision as a file_ cabinet in an office. The file cabinet and its contents are the database. Anytime that the pieces of paper pertaining to a specific function, such as a customer address file in a file cabinet, are rearranged in a _meaningful_ order (for example, alphabetically by last name_), some sort of data management function has been performed._

Thus, the average office file cabinet is a database. It doesn't do anything; it just holds information. Whenever a _drawer_ of the file cabinet is opened to find a record (for example, the record for the customer Smith), the database must be searched _This process of searching the database_ is actually a way to manage it. Databases are typically stored in some order, usually alphabetically by last name, city, or region. This provides for easier data management.

Figure 1.55
The 4Ch1 Exercise 7 document with underlined text to be deleted.

8. Load the 4Purchasing a Computer document.
    a. Select the first paragraph using a drag operation within the document.
    b. Select the second paragraph using a drag operation in the selection bar of the document.
    c. Select the third paragraph using (F8).
    d. Practice using the mouse commands to select a word or paragraph.
    e. Practice using (F8) along with cursor movement keys to extend ranges. Remember to press (ESC) to turn off the EXT indicator.
    f. Exit the document without making any changes.

9. Return to the M4Ch1 Exercise 7 document, and experiment using the options in the Page Setup dialog box. Print the document first using landscape mode and then using portrait mode. What is the difference between the two modes?

10. Open the 4Ch1 Introduction to Word Processing document.
    a. Use the various methods of selecting text discussed in the chapter to select text. Perform an operation depicted by a button on the Formatting toolbar.
    b. Define five blocks and execute a command against each block.
    c. Use the Undo button to reverse all of your changes.
    d. Use the Delete commands discussed in Table 1.6. against six parts of your document.
    e. Reverse the six deletions using the Undo button.

INTERNET EXERCISES

Get additional information about Word.

   a. Access the Microsoft Web page with your browser (http://www.microsoft.com).

   b. Click the Products button at the top of the Web page, and then choose Word 97 for Windows 95 from the drop-down list in step 1 of the Products page.

   c. On the page that appears, click the <u>Visit the Microsoft® Word 97 for Windows® 95 Website</u> link located in the Contents bar on the left side of the page.

   d. Print the first Web page that is displayed.

SESSION 2

More Elementary Features of Word

After completing this session, you should be able to:

> Use hotspots

> Use Word views for documents

> Work with margins, indents, and tabs

> Use the Find and Replace commands

> Change the case of a text selection

> Insert the date in a document

> Use Word's timed backup feature

Isabel Ortiz wants to continue getting acquainted with Word. She decides to explore the various view modes of Word. She also wants to be able to put together the February schedule for the regional state university's basketball team that uses the Civic Arena's facilities for its games. You will work along with Isabel as you complete the exercises in this session.

USING HOTSPOTS

When you double-click one of the **hotspots** on the Word screen, a dialog box opens, allowing you to perform tasks related to that hotspot. Hotspots give you quick access to frequently used dialog boxes that you normally have to go through menus to open. The Word window has several hotspots. The locations of three of Word's hotspots and the dialog boxes they open are summarized in Table 2.1 and Figure 2.1. The Go To and Page Setup dialog boxes were discussed in the previous session. The Tabs dialog box is discussed later in this session.

TIMELY TIP

You can also activate the Go To dialog box by double-clicking the rectangle on the status bar that gives the location of the insertion point on the page.

Table 2.1   Hotspots

Location	Dialog Box Displayed
Ruler	Tabs dialog box
Margin of ruler (or gray square at right)	Page Setup dialog box
Status bar (location boxes)	The Go To tab of the Find and Replace dialog box

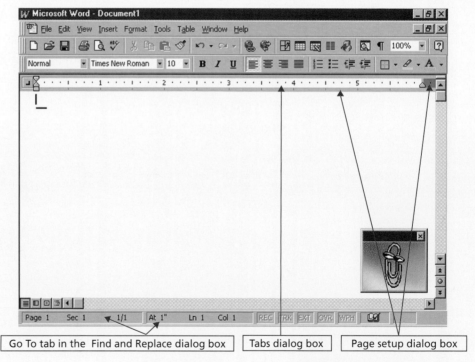

Go To tab in the Find and Replace dialog box   Tabs dialog box   Page setup dialog box

Figure 2.1
Location of hotspots in a typical Word window.

Hands-On Exercise: Using Word Hotspots

Isabel wants to try some of Word's hotspots.

1. **Start Word.** If necessary, open a new document. If the ruler is not present, issue the View, Ruler command sequence.

2. **Activate the Go To dialog box.**

Double-click   Move the insertion point to the rectangle of the status bar that has the word *Page* and double-click. The Find and Replace dialog box shown in Figure 2.2 appears, with the Go To tab open.

          Click to close the dialog box.

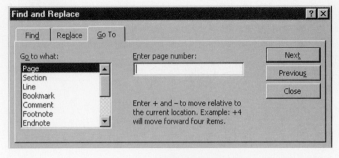

Figure 2.2
The Go To tab of the Find and Replace dialog box activated by double-clicking the hotspot on the status bar.

3. **Activate the Page Setup dialog box.**

Double-click   Move the insertion point to the gray area at the left or right end of the ruler and double-click. If you're careful, you can also double-click on the thin gray area at the top of the ruler. The Page Setup dialog box shown in Figure 2.3 appears.

          Cancel   Click to close the Page Setup dialog box.

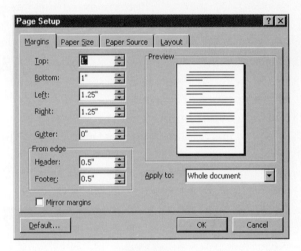

4. **Activate the Tabs dialog box.**

Double-click   Move the insertion point to the numbered rectangle area of the ruler and double-click. (You may have to use the right-hand mouse button.) The Tabs dialog box shown in Figure 2.4 appears. The Tab stop position in the dialog box indicates the location on the ruler that was double-clicked. Any tabs that you set or change take effect beginning at this point in the document. (The Tabs feature is discussed in more detail later in this session.)

          Cancel   Close the Tabs dialog box.

Figure 2.3
The Page Setup dialog box activated by double-clicking the gray ends or top of the ruler.

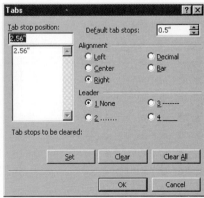

Reinforcing the Exercise

1. You can use hotspots to open dialog boxes that would normally be accessed via the Word menu structure.

2. Double-clicking a hotspot opens a dialog box.

Figure 2.4
The Tabs dialog box for controlling tab settings used in a document.

USING WORD VIEWS

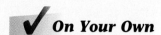

On Your Own

Word allows you to display your document in a number of different ways, or **views.** These different views allow you to see various features that you have applied to your document. You can access a view by clicking one of the view icons displayed above the status bar.

Explore some of the other hotspots that appear in the Word window. See if you can find the following hotspots:

Normal View

Normal view is the view that you have been using so far in this text. Usually you use Normal view for initially building and editing a document. This view does not truly support the WYSIWYG feature that was discussed in Session 1 of this module.

- Record Macro
- Revisions
- Help for Word-
  Perfect Users
- Spelling
- Paragraph

Normal view depicts type sizes, line spacing, indents, and other text appearance features. It does not, however, show more advanced features that affect a document's layout, such as headers, footers, columns, and framed items, as they will appear on the printed page. In addition, as you have seen previously, Normal view displays dotted lines to represent page breaks.

This view also requires the least amount of computer power. If you have an older, slower computer, this is the view that you will use most frequently.

Online Layout View

Online Layout view (Figure 2.5) is especially useful for long documents. This view divides the screen into two panes. The left pane lists elements of

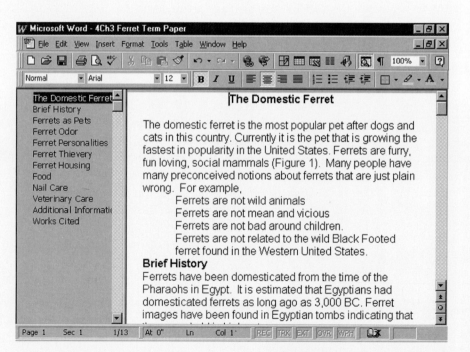

Figure 2.5
The Online Layout view divides the screen into two panes.

the document, such as section headings, table headings, and so forth. The right pane shows the text of the document. The item selected in the left pane is the first item displayed in the right pane.

Figure 2.6 shows the mouse pointer at a heading. If you click a heading, the text in the right pane shows the text at that location in the document. Figure 2.7 shows the displayed Nail Care portion of the document.

To leave Online Layout view and return to Normal view, you issue the View, Normal command sequence or click the Normal view icon.

Page Layout View

Page Layout view (Figure 2.8) shows exactly how the document will appear on the printed page and supports the WYSIWYG feature discussed earlier. Notice that this view contains both horizontal and vertical rulers. A dark border representing the edge of the paper also appears.

Word permits you to edit text in Page Layout view. Text, special features, and graphics are positioned as they will print. Page breaks, rather than being represented as lines, appear as new pages. Using this view, you can quickly verify that you have positioned a special Word feature in the desired location.

Many people use the Normal view of Word to enter most of the document and then switch to Page Layout view to verify that they have used a

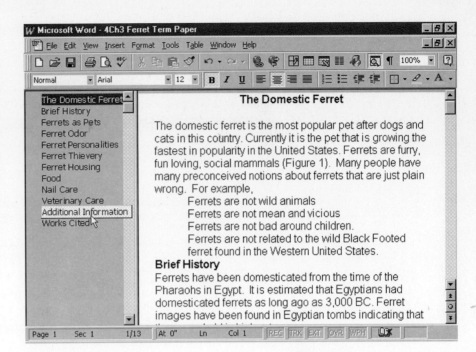

Figure 2.6
A heading in the left side of an Online Layout view screen becomes highlighted when you point to it.

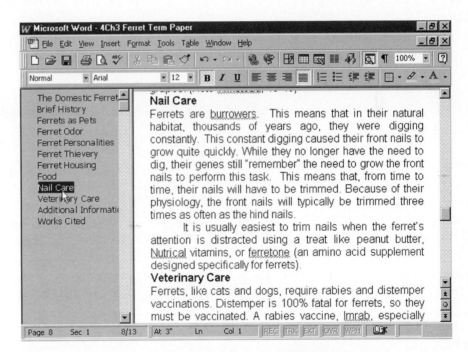

Figure 2.7
When the Nail Care heading is selected, that portion of the document is displayed.

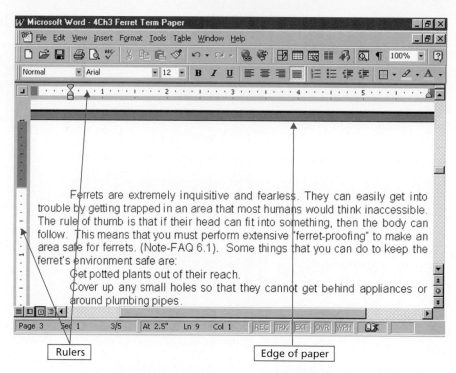

Rulers

Edge of paper

Figure 2.8
The Page Layout view, which shows how the document will appear when it is printed.

feature correctly. Page Layout view works similarly to Print Preview, which was discussed in Module 3: Common Features of Office 97 Applications.

Outline View

Outline view (Figure 2.9) displays the text in outline form. To use this view, you must organize your document properly.

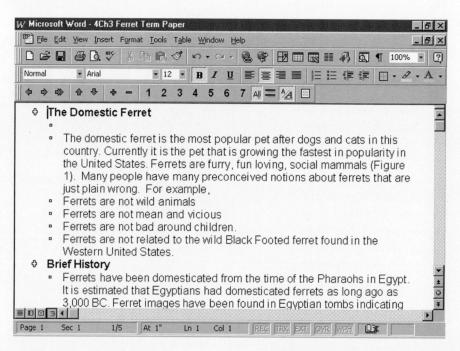

Figure 2.9
Outline view for a document.

Hands-On Exercise: Using the Various Views of Word

Isabel wants to explore the various ways Word views display a document.

1. **Load the 4Purchasing a Computer document, as shown in Figure 2.10.**

2. **Examine the document in Normal view.** Notice that a footnote reference appears after the title.

   (PGDN)   Press three times to move to the page break. Notice that you cannot see the footnote.

3. **Activate Page Layout view and examine the document.**

   (CTRL) + (HOME)   Press to move to the beginning of the document.

   [button]   Click this button at the bottom of the screen to activate this view. Your screen should look like Figure 2.11. Notice that there are now horizontal and vertical rulers present.

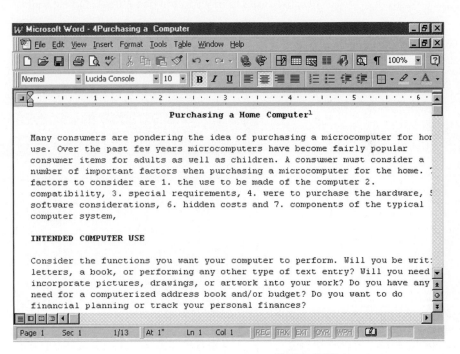

Figure 2.10
The 4Purchasing a Computer document displayed using Normal view.

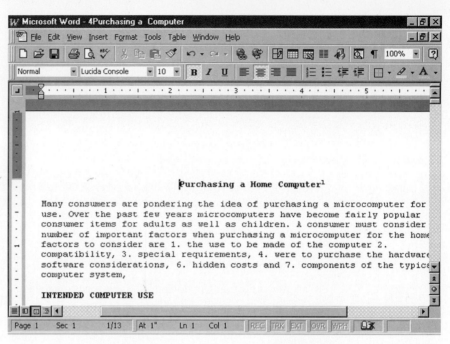

Figure 2.11
The Page Layout view activated for the 4Purchasing a Computer document.

4. **Examine the page break and footnote in the document.**

(PGDN)   Press five times to move to the page break. Notice that you need to press (PGDN) more times to get to the bottom of the page in this mode because the screen displays more of the document. You should now see the footnote on the screen, as shown in Figure 2.12.

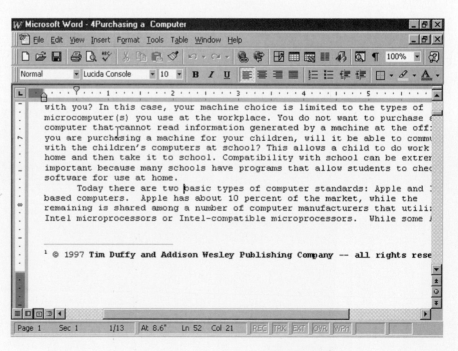

Figure 2.12
The 4Purchasing a Computer document with the footnote visible.

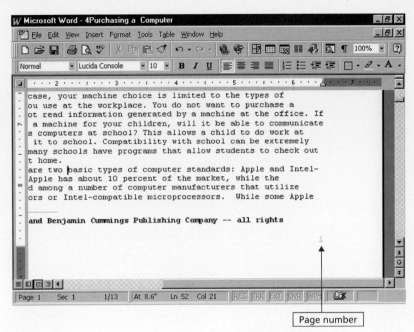

Page number

5. Make the page number visible on the screen.

 Click the right arrow of the horizontal scroll bar. The page number should now be visible (Figure 2.13). If a page code is visible instead, enter the command sequence Tools, Options, View tab, Field Codes to turn off codes.

Figure 2.13
The page number visible in Page Layout view.

6. View the information around the next page break.

Click

Position the mouse pointer in the vertical scroll bar beneath the scroll box, and click four times to move to the next page break (Figure 2.14). Notice that only a page number is present—no dotted line and no page codes.

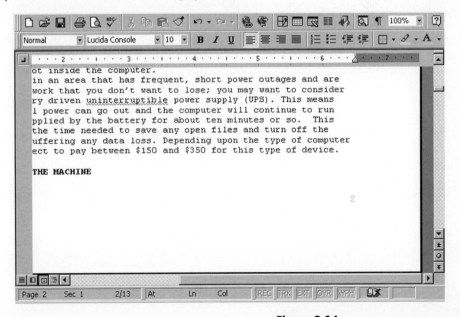

Figure 2.14
The next page break in Page Layout view, which contains only the page number.

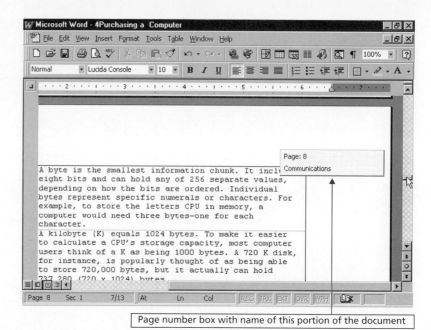

Page number box with name of this portion of the document

7. Display the page number box immediately to the left of the vertical scroll bar.

Click and drag   Click the scroll box in the scroll bar and drag it down. As you move the scroll box, the page number and topic name of the new location should appear as shown in Figure 2.15.

8. Examine the Outline view of the document.

(CTRL) + (HOME)   Press to move to the beginning of the document.

    Click to examine the document in Outline view (Figure 2.16). Notice that a little square indicates the beginning of each paragraph.

Figure 2.15
The scroll box dragged down the screen, showing the page number and topic name of that location.

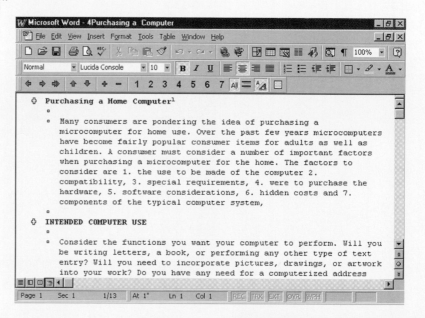

Figure 2.16
The 4Purchasing a Computer document in Outline view.

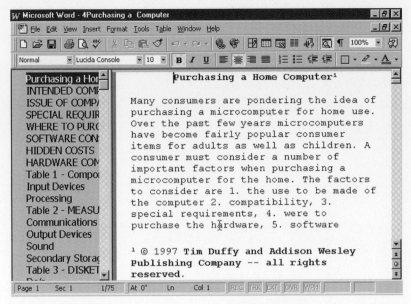

Figure 2.17
The 4Purchasing a Computer
document in Online Layout view.

TIMELY TIP

Once you are in Outline View, you can use the Outline toolbar shown in Figure 2.16 to make changes to the outline. For instance, you can promote, demote, or even enter new text in the document once you have properly defined its level in the outline. Use the (TAB) key to demote text and the (SHIFT)+(TAB) key to promote text. Some further examples of using Outline mode can be found in Session 2 of PowerPoint.

9. **Examine the Online Layout view.**

Click to examine the document in Online Layout view (Figure 2.17). In the left pane, move the mouse pointer from topic to topic. As a heading moves out of view in the pane, the complete heading pops out in a yellow text box, as shown in Figure 2.18.

Click

Click a topic listed in the left pane. The text in the right pane now changes to that area of the document. Figure 2.19 shows the text for the Output Devices topic.

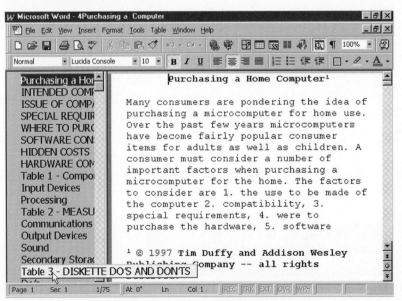

Figure 2.18
The topic text box appears as the mouse pointer is positioned above it.

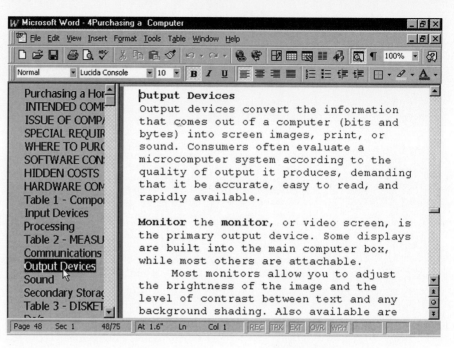

Figure 2.19
The Output Device portion of
the document displayed in Online Layout view.

10. **Leave Online Layout view.**

View   Open the View menu.

Normal   Click the Normal view option. You now return to Normal
                    view.

11. **Close the document without saving any changes that you might have
    made.**

Reinforcing the Exercise

1. You use Normal view for entering and editing a typical document.

2. You use Page Layout view to see special features that you have added to the document.

3. Margins as well as scroll bars with rulers are displayed in Page Layout view.

4. The scroll box, when dragged up or down the vertical scroll bar in any view, shows the page number that you have reached in the document.

5. The online layout view can be used to move quickly to a desired topic in a document.

USING MARGIN AND INDENT COMMANDS

Word lets you change the margins for the entire document or for only selected sections of a document. It also lets you indent individual or selected
paragraphs from the right margin, the left margin, or both.

Margins File, Page Setup or Format, Paragraph

As you saw in Session 1 of this module, the Margins tab of the Page Setup dialog box (Figure 2.20) lets you determine the right, left, top, and bottom margins. The default margin settings are 1 inch for the top and bottom margins and 1.25 inches for the left and right margins. Indicate a new margin width by clicking the up or down arrow in the appropriate spin box until the desired margin value appears in the box, or you can enter the desired margin size directly in the box. For example, if you wish to change the left margin to 1.5 inches, click the up arrow in the spin box to show the value 1.5, or type 1.5 in the Left spin box.

The new margins that you set affect the entire document unless you change the Apply to list box (Figure 2.21). Margin settings remain in effect until you enter new ones.

To change the margins for only a portion of the document in the window, perform the following steps:

1. Select the text for which you want to set new margins.

2. Activate the Page Setup dialog box.

3. From within the Margins tab, make any needed margin changes.

4. In the Apply to box, select the option you want to use to apply the new margins.

5. On the Layout tab in the Section start list box (Figure 2.22), indicate that the new section is to be continuous with the document instead of starting at a new page.

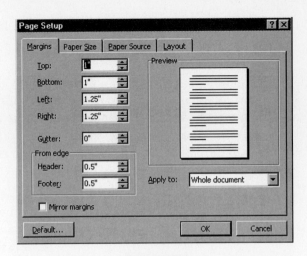

Figure 2.20
The Margins tab of the Page Setup dialog box for controlling margins within a document.

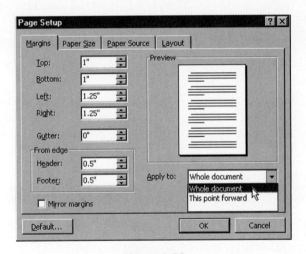

Figure 2.21
The two options of the Apply to list box for determining how the margins will be applied to the document.

Indents

From time to time, you might want to reset the left or right margin for only a single paragraph or selected paragraphs of text. For example, it is a convention to indent a long quotation five spaces from the left margin. Word provides three different types of indents: left, double, and hanging.

Left Indent

The Increase Indent button resets the left margin to the next tab stop. The default tab stops occur every 0.5 inch and operate like those on a

TIMELY TIP

Word uses a standard template for creating new documents. The template in effect for any new document is the Normal template. If you want changes that you make in the Page Setup dialog box to affect all subsequent documents, click the Default button at the bottom of the dialog box. However, when you choose this option, all future documents based on the Normal template will use these same margin settings.

typewriter. You have already used tabs in indenting the first line of a paragraph.

Double Indent

Occasionally, you might want to indent both the left and right margins for a single paragraph. To create this double indent, drag the left and right indent handles in the ruler to the desired locations (Figure 2.23).

Hanging Indent

You use the left indent handle on the ruler to create a **hanging indent,** in which the first line of a paragraph begins at the left margin and the remaining lines are indented.

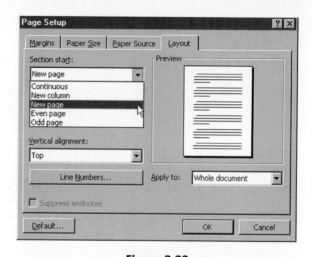

Figure 2.22
The Section start: list box on the Layout tab, which indicates to Word where a new document section is to start.

Hands-On Exercise: Setting Margins and Indents

Isabel wants to help her daughter, Rosa, indent a quotation for a book report. Isabel wants to change the left margin to 2 inches and the right margin to 2.5 inches beginning with the third paragraph.

1. **Open the 4Ch2 Dick Francis Review document.** Your screen should look like Figure 2.23. Position the cursor at the beginning of the third paragraph. If the ruler is not visible, issue the View, Ruler command sequence.

2. **Change the left and right margins.**

Double-click   Double-click the hotspot (the gray square) to the right of the ruler to open the Page Setup dialog box. If necessary, click the Margins tab to make it appear.

Triple-click   Select the 1.25″ value in the Left text box.

Type the left margin value: **2**

(TAB)   Move to the Right text box.

Type the right margin value: **2.5**

Your changed Margins tab of the Page Setup dialog box should look like Figure 2.24.

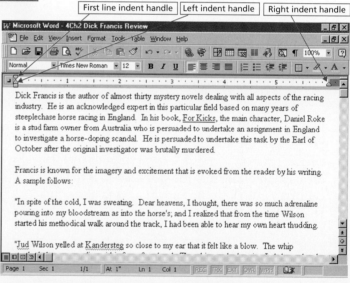

Figure 2.23
The 4Ch2 Dick Francis Review document.

TIMELY   TIP

Word allows you to create a left indent by placing the cursor at the beginning of any line, except the first line, in a paragraph and then pressing (TAB).

3. **Apply these changes from this point forward in the document.**

Apply to: Click the down arrow to the right of the Apply to list box to display the selections.

This point forward Select this entry. Your Margins tab should look like Figure 2.25.

OK Click to close the Page Setup dialog box and apply the margin settings. Your document should look like Figure 2.26.

4. **Examine the document in Page Preview.**

 Click to invoke the Preview window (Figure 2.27). Notice that only a part of the document seems to be present.

(PGUP) Press to see the first page of the document (Figure 2.28). Word has broken the document into two parts at the section break. The page break was created at the Section Break line in the document when the new margins were created using the Page Setup dialog box.

Close Click to return to the Word document.

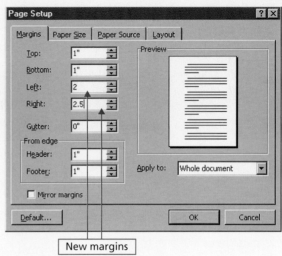

New margins

Figure 2.24
The Margins tab with the required changes.

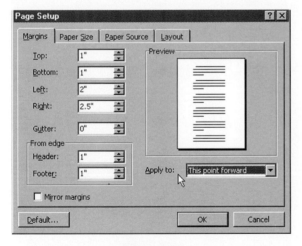

Figure 2.25
The Margins tab with the margin changes and the part of the document to be affected specified.

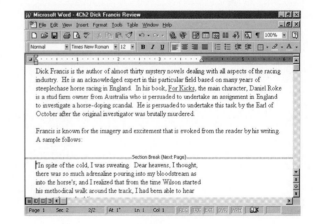

Figure 2.26
The 4Ch2 Dick Francis Review document with the changes made and a document section added.

5. **Delete the Section Break line
   and margin settings.**

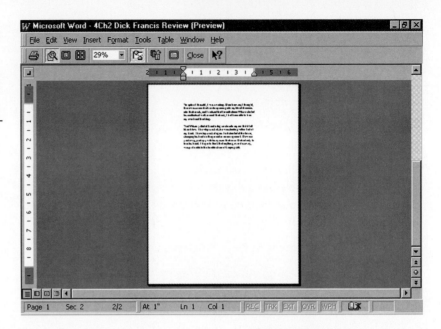

Click the
curved part of
the Undo but-
ton. The docu-
ment appears
as it originally
did in Figure
2.23.

Figure 2.27
The second page of the 4Ch2
Dick Francis Review document.

6. **Make the document text continuous.** Be sure you are at the
   beginning of the third paragraph.

Double-click	Double-click the gray box to the right of the ruler to open the Page Setup dialog box.
Triple-click	Select the 1.25" value in the Left text box.

Type the left margin value: **2**

TAB	Move to the Right text box.

Type the right margin value: **2.5**

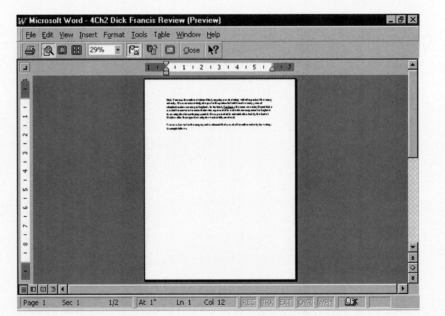

Figure 2.28
The first page of the 4Ch2 Dick
Francis Review document.

Apply to:	Click the down arrow to the right of the Apply to box to display the selections.
This point forward	Click to select this option. Your Margins tab should again look like Figure 2.25.
Layout	Click to activate the Layout tab of the Page Setup dialog box.
Section start:	Click the down arrow to the right of the Section start list box to display choices of where the new section should start (Figure 2.29).
Continuous	Click this entry.
OK	Click to return to the document.

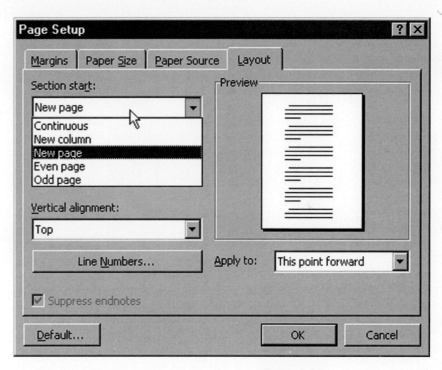

Figure 2.29
The Section start selection box.

7. Examine the document.

Click to activate the Preview window (Figure 2.30). The entire document should now appear on one page.

Click the Printer button of the Preview window toolbar to send the document to the Print Manager for printing.

Click the Close button on the Preview window to return to the Word document. As you can see, resetting margins with the Page Setup dialog box can involve several steps. You will now examine the use of indents to control margin settings.

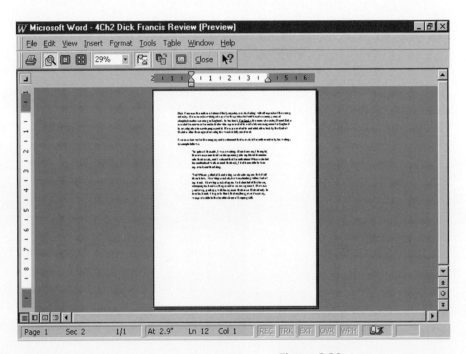

Figure 2.30
The 4Ch2 Dick Francis Review document shown in Print Preview with the changed margins occupying one page.

8. Change the margins back to their original default settings of 1.25 inches. Keep this document on the screen for the next portion of the exercise.

Click the curved part of the Undo button until the document appears as it originally did in Figure 2.23.

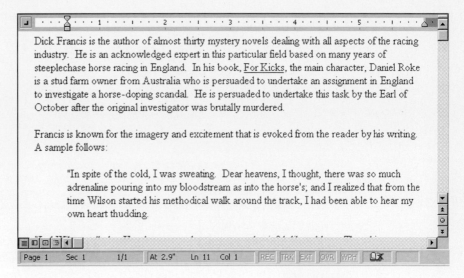

Figure 2.31
The paragraph indented one tab
stop. The ruler handles have also
changed position.

9. **Indent the paragraph in the 4Ch2 Dick Francis Review document that
   starts** *In spite of the cold.* **Position the cursor at the beginning of this
   line of text.**

 Click this button on the Formatting toolbar to indent only
this paragraph (Figure 2.31). Notice that the handles in
the ruler have changed to reflect the new location of the
text.

⊙ Press the down arrow key until your screen looks like Figure 2.32. You should be able to verify that only one paragraph was indented.

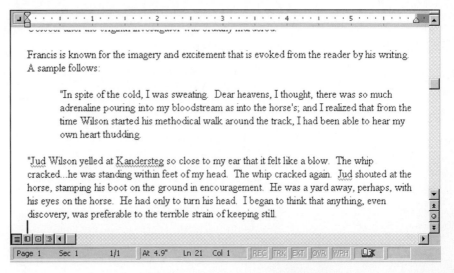

Figure 2.32
The 4Ch2 Dick Francis Review
document with only one paragraph indented.

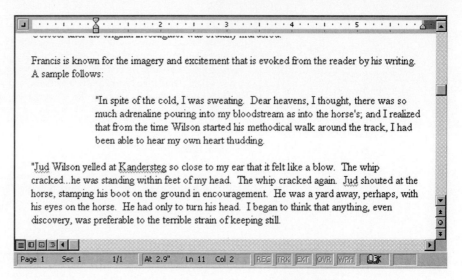

Figure 2.33
Another indent added to the document.

10. **Add another indent.** Position the cursor back at the beginning of the indented paragraph.

   Click to increase the indentation of this paragraph to the location of the next (second) tab stop (Figure 2.33).

   Click to print the document.

11. **Eliminate the indent.**

   Click this Formatting toolbar button twice to return your document to its original formatting.

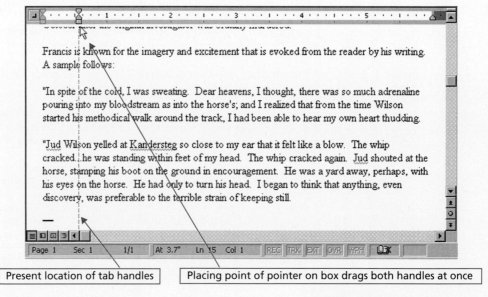

Present location of tab handles   Placing point of pointer on box drags both handles at once

Figure 2.34
Moving the indent handles of the ruler, with a dotted line indicating their effect on the document.

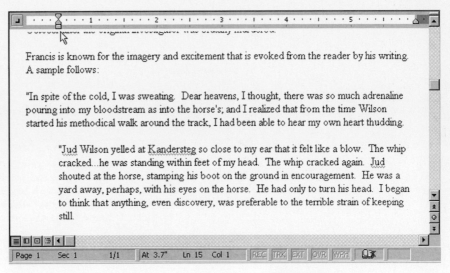

Figure 2.35
The left indent of the document created by dragging the left indent handle to the right.

12. **Create a double-indent to the first default tab stop.** Move to the beginning of the paragraph in the 4Ch2 Dick Francis Review document that starts *Jud Wilson yelled. . . .*

   ■   Click the square portion of the left indent handle of the ruler, and start to drag to the 0.5-inch mark. As shown in Figure 2.34, a vertical dotted line appears in the document, and both of the handles move at once. Once the handles are at the 0.5-inch mark, your document should look like Figure 2.35.

   ▲   Drag the right indent handle of the ruler to the 5.5-inch mark. Your document should now look like Figure 2.36. Notice the new locations of the indent handles on the ruler.

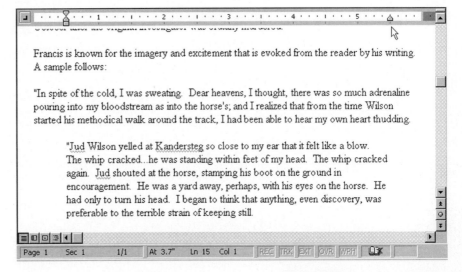

Figure 2.36
The right indent of the document created by dragging the right indent handle to the left.

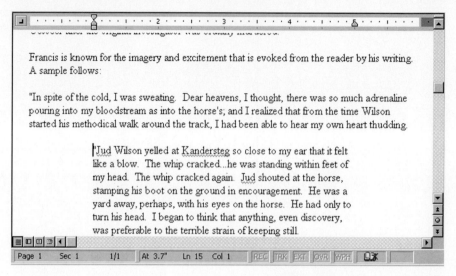

Figure 2.37
The document with both indents increased by an additional 0.5 inch.

13. **Drag both handles in an additional 0.5 inch.** Your document should now look like Figure 2.37. Again notice the locations of the indent handles on the ruler line.

14. **Print the document.**

                    Click to print the document.

15. **Get rid of the indents.**

                    Click the curved portion of the Undo button until the indents disappear (the number of times you need to click will depend on the number of indents you made).

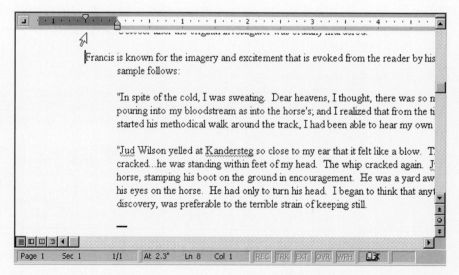

Figure 2.38
The 4Ch2 Dick Francis Review document with a hanging indent.

16. **Create a hanging indent.** Move the cursor to the paragraph that begins
Francis is known. . . .

▼   Click the down arrow portion of the left indent handle of
the ruler, and drag it to the −0.5–inch mark (that is,
down to the left). Your document should now look like
Figure 2.38.

      Click to print the document.

17. **Close the document without saving any changes.**

T I M E L Y   T I P

> You can also use shortcut commands to create indents:
>
>   (CTRL) + M   Creates a left indent
>   (CTRL) + T   Creates a hanging indent
>   (CTRL) + Q   Deletes the formatting (indents as well as any
>   other formatting commands that you have is-
>   sued) for this paragraph

Reinforcing the Exercise

1. You can use the Page Setup dialog box to create new margins for the entire document or from a specific location forward.

2. You can create indents to make temporary adjustments in margins.

3. Unless you have made a selection, an indent change applies only to the paragraph where the cursor is located.

4. You can create indents by dragging the ruler indent handles to the right or left.

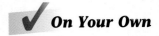
On Your Own

> Besides creating indents with the ruler indent handles, you can also
> use the Paragraph dialog box for this task.
>
> - Enter the Format, Paragraph command sequence, and specify any
>   needed left and right indentation values for the previous Hands-
>   On Exercise.
> - Practice using the shortcut commands listed in the Timely Tip to
>   create and delete indents in a document.

SETTING TABS   F̲ormat, T̲abs

The default tab setting for Word is 0.5 inch, meaning you will encounter a tab every half inch. The **tab stops** in Word work the same as tabs on a typewriter. Pressing (TAB) moves the cursor from one tab stop to the next.

Changing Tabs Using the Ruler

If you want to incorporate only one or two tab stops, the easiest way is to enter the new tab stops directly on the ruler by using the mouse. The icon on the Tab button at the far left of the ruler represents the type of tab stop that you can create (see Table 2.2). To create a different type of tab stop, click the Tab button until the desired tab stop icon is displayed on the button. You can then click the location on the ruler where you want that type of tab stop to appear. The graphical representations of tab stops are shown in Table 2.2.

Table 2.2   Tab Stop Icons

Tab Stop Icon	Type of Tab Stop
⌞	Left-align
⌟	Right-align
⊥	Center-align
⊥.	Decimal-align

Figure 2.39 shows a ruler with right-align, decimal-align, left-align, and center-align tab stops. The default tab stop is left-align, so when you press (TAB) and begin entering text, the left end of the text aligns at that tab stop.

You can delete a tab stop by using the mouse to drag it off the ruler.

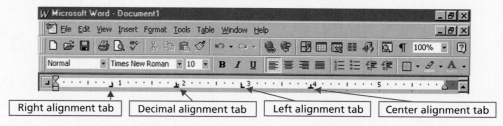

Figure 2.39
A ruler with four different types of tab stops.

Tabs Dialog Box

You can use the Tabs dialog box to create tab stops, change tab stop types, or clear tab stops from the ruler (Figure 2.40). Open the Tabs dialog box by double-clicking the ruler (you may have to double-click the right mouse button to open this dialog box).

TIMELY TIP

When you need tab settings that are different from those currently in effect, you can move to the point in the document where you want the new tab settings to start and create them using the ruler or the Tabs dialog box (see the next section). Tab stops are entered in the document at the insertion point location. You can have any number of different tab settings in one document. Keep in mind that a tab setting affects all subsequent text until a new Tabs command is entered.

As you can see in Figure 2.40, this dialog box allows you to set left-align, center-align, right-align, and decimal-align tab stops, just as the ruler does.

Another type of tab stop you can only create by using the Tabs dialog box is the bar tab stop. A **bar tab stop** places a vertical bar (|) at the tab stop location. This can be used to create a division between units of data that you enter.

To delete all tab stops, click the Clear All button. Usually, you execute this command before entering any new tab stop. (You usually create a tab stop when you open the dialog box.) To create new tabs, enter the location of the new tab in the Tab stop position text box, select the type of tab stop, and click the Set button.

Figure 2.41 shows the Tabs dialog box with a left-align tab at the 2-inch location and a center-align tab at the 4-inch location.

Tab Leader

An additional option of the Tabs dialog box enables you to choose a leader for the tab you are defining. A **tab leader** is a dotted or solid line that fills in a blank area between tab stops (Figure 2.42). For any tab stop, you can create a tab leader by clicking the type of leader desired in the Leader box:

- Click 1 for no leader.
- Click 2 for a dotted leader.
- Click 3 for a dashed leader.
- Click 4 for an underlined leader.

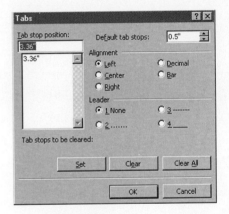

Figure 2.40
The Tabs dialog box, in which you can delete, add, or change existing tab stops.

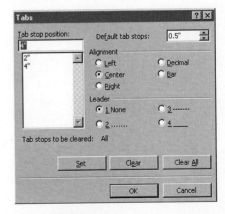

Figure 2.41
The Tab dialog box with locations for left- and center-align tab stops.

Front Office ....CVA 145

Figure 2.42
Example of a tab leader.

Hands-On Exercise: Creating Tabs

Tabs will be useful in creating the February basketball game schedule that
Isabel wants to distribute at the Civic Arena.

1. **Begin with a blank document; close any open documents.** If necessary,
    click the New button to open a blank document. If the ruler is not already
    displayed, enter the command sequence View, Ruler to display it.

2. **There should be no tab stops on the ruler.** If there are tab stops present,
    clear them by using the mouse to drag them off the ruler.

3. **Create tab stops.**

            Click the Tab button on the ruler until the right-align tab
                                icon appears.

    Click   Click the 0.5-inch mark on the ruler. The first right-align
                                tab stop shown in Figure 2.43 should appear.

                                Click the Tab button until the left-align tab icon appears.

    Click   Click the 1-inch mark on the ruler. The left-align tab stop
                                shown in Figure 2.43 should appear.

                                Click the Tab button on the ruler until the right-align tab
                                icon appears.

    Click   Click the 5.5-inch mark on the ruler. The second right-
                                align tab stop shown in Figure 2.43 should appear. Your
                                ruler should now look like Figure 2.43.

4. **Enter the title text.**

Type the name of the school: **Central State Wildcats**

        Click to center the first heading line.

Figure 2.43
The ruler with the desired tab
stops: a right-align, a left-align,
and another right-align.

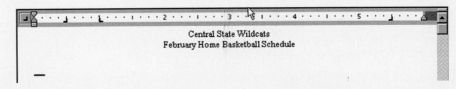

Figure 2.44
The basketball schedule with the first two lines entered.

(ENTER)   Press to move to the next line.

Type the second title line: **February Home Basketball Schedule**

(ENTER)   Press twice to embed a blank line.

            Click to indicate that new text should have left–alignment. Your document should now look like Figure 2.44.

5. **Enter the first basketball game information.**

(TAB)   Press to move to the first tab stop.

Type the date: **8**

(TAB)   Press to move to the next tab stop.

Type the name of the school: **University of Western Wisconsin**

(TAB)   Press to move to the next tab stop.

Type the time: **7:05 p.m.**

(ENTER)   Press to move to the next line. Your document should now look like Figure 2.45.

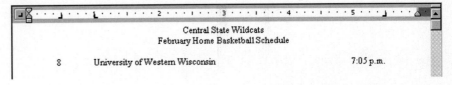

6. **Using Figure 2.46 as a guide, enter the remaining portion of the February basketball schedule.**

Figure 2.45
The February basketball schedule with the first game entered.

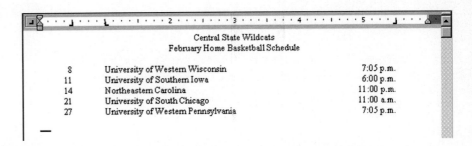

7. **Use the Save command to save the document using the name M4Ch2 Wildcats February Schedule.**

8. **Close the document.**

Figure 2.46
The completed February schedule document.

Hands-On Exercise: Creating Tabs with Leaders

Isabel now wants to create a menu of items available at the Civic Arena concession. She wants to use the Tabs dialog box.

1. **Clear the screen if necessary.**

2. **Clear all tab settings (if any) from the ruler by using the mouse to drag them off the ruler.**

3. **Enter the title.**

 Click the Center button on the Standard toolbar.

Type the title: **CONCESSION MENU**

(ENTER)   Press three times to add two blank lines.

 Click to change back to left–alignment.

4. **Create the tab stops. First, open the Tabs dialog box.**

Double-click   Move the tip of the pointer to the ruler and double-click the right mouse button to open the Tabs dialog box (Figure 2.47). Often a tab stop will be created when you invoke the Tabs dialog box.

 Click to clear any tab stops that you inadvertently created. The boxes in the left portion of the dialog box should now be clear.

Type the position of the first tab stop: **.5**

 Click to place the tab on the ruler.

Type the position of the second tab stop: **5**

 Click to make this a decimal-align tab stop.

 Click to establish a dot leader.

 Click to place the tab on the ruler. Your completed Tabs dialog box should look like Figure 2.48.

OK   Click to accept the tabs and return to the document.

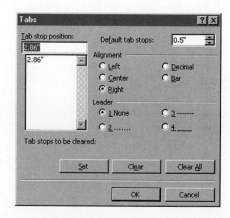

Figure 2.47
The Tabs dialog box invoked by double-clicking the bottom border of the ruler; a tab stop is in effect.

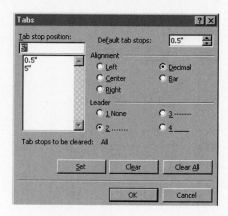

Figure 2.48
The completed Tabs dialog box for the exercise.

5. **Enter the data for the first category and menu item.**

Type the first line: **Sandwiches**

ENTER   Press to move to the next line.

TAB   Press to move to the first tab stop.

Type the sandwich type: **Hamburger**

TAB   Press to go to the second tab stop (notice the tab leaders).

Type the price: **3.50**   Your document should look like Figure 2.49. Notice how the numbers are entered before and after the decimal point.

6. **Enter the second menu item.**

ENTER   Press to move to the next line.

TAB   Press to go to the first tab stop.

Type the next sandwich type: **Cheeseburger**

TAB   Press to go to the next tab stop.

Type the price: **3.75**

ENTER   Press to complete the line.

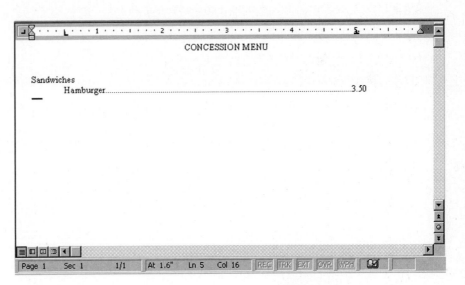

Figure 2.49
The price for the first category and menu item in the concession menu.

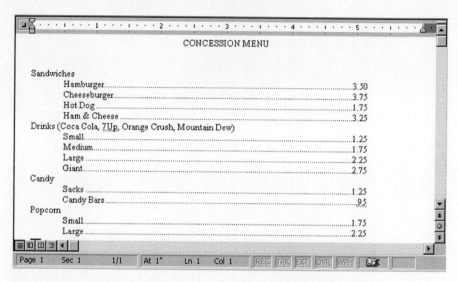

Figure 2.50
The completed menu using tab leaders.

7. Continue entering the remaining lines, using Figure 2.50 as a guide.

8. Print the document.

9. Save the file using the name M4Ch2 Concession Menu.

10. **Close the document.** Notice that the leftmost column is oriented toward alphabetic text; that is, the text aligns at the left side of the column. The numbers in the right column, however, align on the decimal points. With **decimal alignment,** typed text moves to the left until you enter the **alignment character** (a period in this case) or until you press ⟨TAB⟩ or ⟨ENTER⟩. Text typed after the alignment character is inserted normally.

Reinforcing the Exercise

1. You can use the ruler to quickly enter tab stops in a document.

2. You can delete unneeded tab stops from the ruler by using the mouse to drag them off.

3. New tab stops take effect at the location of the insertion point in the document.

4. You can double-click the ruler to open the Tabs dialog box.

5. You can create tab leaders only by using the Tabs dialog box.

TIMELY   TIP

When you add lists in a columnar format to a document, it's best to add them by using tab stops rather than by pressing the spacebar. This approach provides much more flexibility if you wish to change margin settings or the text font. If you have not used tabs and wish to make significant changes to a document, it may be easier simply to retype the portion of the document you wish to alter rather than try to fix it at the keyboard by inserting spaces.

USING FIND AND REPLACE COMMANDS — <u>E</u>dit, <u>F</u>ind/Re<u>p</u>lace

The Find and Replace commands locate, change, or delete a word or phrase wherever it appears in your document.

Find Command

The Find command locates all occurrences of a word or phrase. When you enter the command, Word moves to and highlights the desired text.

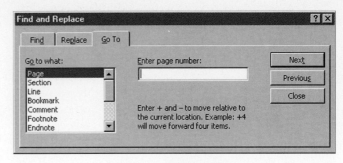

Figure 2.51
The Go To tab of the Find and Replace dialog box.

While the Find command can be invoked using the Edit, Find command sequence, you can also double-click the location boxes of the status bar to display the Find and Replace dialog box shown in Figure 2.51. (You probably remember this dialog box from entering the Go To command earlier in the text.) Click the Find tab to enter the desired text or special characters you want to search for in the Find What text box (Figure 2.52).

If you want to exercise more control over the search, click the More button. The Find tab expands, offering more options (Figure 2.53). Select one or more of the options in the expanded Find dialog box, and then press (ENTER) or click the Find Next button to begin the search. The cursor advances to the first occurrence of the desired text. If you want to edit the selected text or stop the search, choose Cancel or press (ESC). Click the Less button to return the Find tab to its original size.

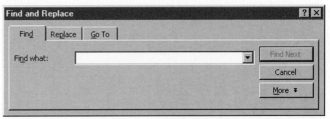

Figure 2.52
The Find tab of the Find and Replace dialog box.

If you want to find only complete words such as *dog* rather than *dogma* or *dogmatic,* you must select the Find whole words only option in the expanded Find tab. Select the Match Case option if you want to match lowercase and uppercase text. Otherwise, entering lowercase characters finds matches with either uppercase or lowercase characters, and entering uppercase characters finds matches with either uppercase or lowercase characters. For example, *dog* will find *Dog,* and *Dog* will find *dog.*

The default Find command searches all text, starting at the beginning of the document and moving toward the end. You can also conduct a reverse search by clicking the down arrow to the right of the Search list box of the Find tab and then selecting Up from the list. Such a search starts at the current cursor location and moves toward the beginning of the file.

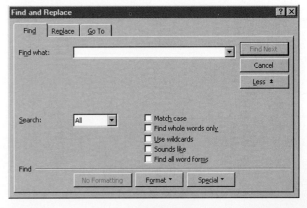

Figure 2.53
The Find tab expands when you click the More button.

By default, Word searches the entire document and includes any special features that have been added, such as footnotes or annotations. If you want to search for text in a specific portion of a document, select that portion and then issue the Edit, Find command sequence. When Word reaches the end of the selected text, the Office Assistant asks if you want to continue searching the remainder of the document and how many, if any, items were found.

T I M E L Y   T I P

If you want to find the next occurrence of the just-found text without reopening the Find dialog box, you can issue the Find Next shortcut command, (SHIFT) + (F4). Word highlights the next occurrence of the desired text without reopening the Find dialog box. You can continue issuing Find Next shortcut commands until the Office Assistant displays a message telling you that you have reached the end of the document and asking if you to want the search to continue at the beginning of the document (Figure 2.54). Click No to return to the place where you began your search.

The Format button in the expanded Find tab allows you to locate the codes of the options shown in Figure 2.55. Clicking the Special button opens a list box that allows you to find special characters and formatting codes (Figure 2.56).

You can also use shortcut commands or toolbar buttons to find special characters or formatting codes. For example, you can find any boldfaced text or a **paragraph mark (¶)**. The following steps enter a code in the Find What text box.

1. Begin the search with the Edit, Find command sequence, and then click the Bold toolbar button. Notice the Format: Bold line that appears below the text box (Figure 2.57).

2. Click the Find Next button. Word finds and highlights the first occurrence of a boldfaced word.

3. To find the next occurrence of a boldfaced word, click the Find Next button again. If there is only one boldfaced word in the document, the Office Assistant will tell you that Word reached the end of the document.

4. Click Cancel to stop the search.

Figure 2.54
The Office Assistant indicating that the end of the document has been reached.

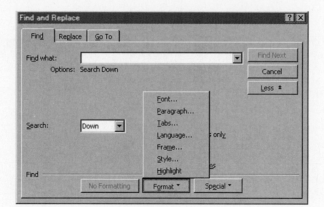

Figure 2.55
The Format option, which allows you to find specific codes affecting the formatting of the document.

Figure 2.56
The Special button displays a menu that enables you to search for the desired special code.

Replace Command

The Replace tab of the Find and Replace dialog box (Figure 2.58) allows you to find and replace a word or phrase with another word or phrase. Click the More button to access an expanded tab (Figure 2.59), which has option buttons like those in the expanded Find dialog box.

Format created using the Bold toolbar button

Figure 2.57
Toolbar button commands entered in the Find what box to locate embedded codes.

You enter the word or phrase you want to change in the Find what text box and the word or phrase you want instead in the Replace with: text box. You can use either the Replace All button to have the change affect the entire document automatically, or use the Find Next button to approve each change before it occurs. If you want to find the string only when it appears as a separate word, choose the Find whole words only check box on the expanded tab. If you want to find the string only when it exactly matches the string in the Find what: text box, choose the Match case check box on the expanded tab.

Click the Replace button if you want Word to replace the string and find the next occurrence. If you want to replace all occurrences of the specified text, click the Replace All button. The Replace All command replaces each occurrence of the Find what text with the Replace with text. Once the Replace All command has been completed, you can close the Replace dialog box by clicking the Cancel button or by pressing (ESC).

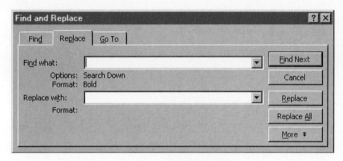

Figure 2.58
The Replace tab of the Find and Replace dialog box.

Hands-On Exercise: Using the Find and Replace Commands

Isabel wants to go through some examples using the Find and Replace commands that she will be presenting to her class.

1. **Open the 4Purchasing a Computer document.**

2. **Issue various search commands.**

Double-click   Double-click one of the location boxes in the status bar. The Find and Replace dialog box appears.

Find   Click the Find tab to open it.

Type the character string you want to search for: **word**

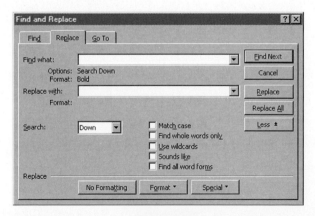

Figure 2.59
The Replace tab expands when you click the More button.

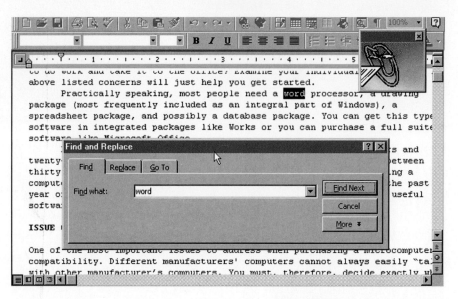

Figure 2.60
The result of finding the text
word.

(ENTER)	Press to start the search. Word highlights the first occurrence of this word (Figure 2.60). The Find dialog box is still on the screen.

3. Find the next occurrence.

Find Next	Click the Find Next button. Because Word's default direction in the Find dialog box is All, the next occurrence of *word* will be farther down in the document. If All is not selected, select All in the expanded tab's Search list box.
Cancel	Click to close the Find dialog box and return to the document.
(SHIFT) + (F4)	Press this shortcut Find Next command. Word highlights the next occurrence of *word* without invoking the Find dialog box.
(SHIFT) + (F4)	Press to issue the Find Next command again. Word highlights the next occurrence of *word.*
(CTRL) + (HOME)	Press to move to the beginning of the document.

4. Issue the Replace command.

Double-click	Double-click one of the location boxes in the status bar. The Find and Replace dialog box appears.
Replace	Click the Replace tab to open it.

5. Tell Word to change every occurrence of *word* to *wurd.*

Replace with:	Click the Replace with text box.

Type the replacement character string: **wurd**   The completed Replace tab should look like Figure 2.61.

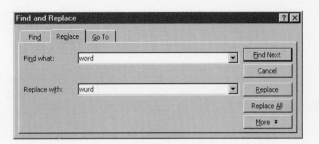

 Click to replace all occurrences. The Office Assistant now displays a dialog box indicating the number of replacements made.

(ENTER)   Press to close the Office Assistant.

 Click to close the Find and Replace dialog box and return to the document.

Figure 2.61
The completed Replace dialog box to change all occurrences of *word* to *wurd*.

(CTRL) + (HOME)   Press to go to the beginning of the document. Confirm that all occurrences of *word* have been changed to *wurd*.

6. **Restore the document to its original condition.**

Click the curved portion of the Undo command to undo the Replace All command you just issued.

7. **Search for paragraph mark codes.**

Double-click   Double-click one of the location boxes in the status bar. The Find and Replace dialog box appears.

Find   Click the Find tab to open it.

More ▼   Click the More button to open the expanded tab.

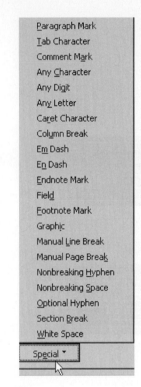

Special ▼   Click to open the menu shown in Figure 2.62.

Paragraph Mark   Select this entry to place a ^p in the Find what: text box (Figure 2.63). The ^p is the Word code for a paragraph mark.

Find Next   Click to begin the Find operation. A highlighted rectangle appears where a paragraph mark is found (Figure 2.64).

Figure 2.62
The Special menu.

8. **Find bold codes.**

Less ▲   Click the Less button to reduce the size of the Find tab and hide the options.

Find what: Triple-click the Find what text box to select the text.

(DEL)   Click to delete the ^p text.

B   Click the Bold toolbar button. A Format: Bold line appears beneath the Find what text box (Figure 2.65).

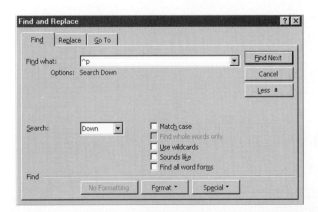

Figure 2.63
The paragraph mark embedded in the Find what text box.

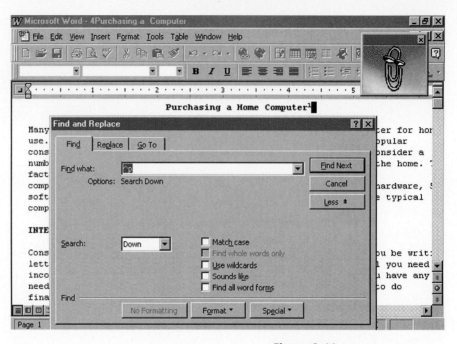

Figure 2.64
A rectangle indicating the location of a paragraph mark.

Find Next   Click to find the first occurrence of a boldface code. *Intended Computer Use* should be selected in the document (Figure 2.66).

Find Next   Click to find the next occurrence of a boldface code. *Issue of Compatibility* should be selected in the document.

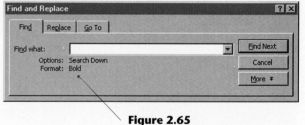

B   Double-click the Bold toolbar button to remove the Format: Bold line.

Cancel   Click to return to the document.

Figure 2.65
The Format: Bold line indicates that a boldface code is being searched for.

9. **Close the document without saving it.**

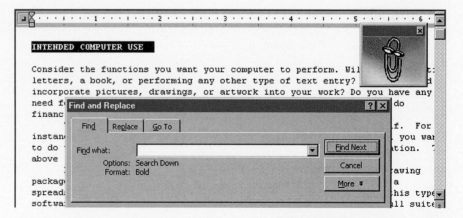

Figure 2.66
The first occurrence of boldfaced text in the document.

Reinforcing the Exercise

1. You can use the Find command to locate text in a document.
2. You can use the (SHIFT) + (F4) shortcut command to locate the next occurrence of search text without invoking the Find and Replace dialog box.
3. You can use the Replace command to find and then replace text.
4. To replace all occurrences of search text, you can click the Replace All button.
5. Word provides a count of the number of times a piece of text is replaced.
6. You use codes as well as text in a Find or Replace command.
7. You can reverse a Replace All command by clicking the Undo button.

ADDITIONAL COMMANDS

Two other Word commands that you will find useful are the Change Case command and the Date command.

Change Case Command (Format, Change Case)

Have you ever entered text only to find later that the characters are unintentionally all in uppercase letters? The Change Case command lets you correct such errors without retyping.

Use the Format, Change Case command sequence to open the Change Case dialog box (Figure 2.67).

You can select the UPPERCASE option in the dialog box to convert selected text to all capital letters. The Sentence case option is used to capitalize only the first character of a sentence.

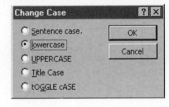

Figure 2.67
The Change Case dialog box.

Hands-On Exercise: Using Case Conversion

Isabel prepares this example for her community college class.

1. **Clear the screen and open the 4Ch2 Converting Text document (Figure 2.68).**

2. **Use the mouse to select the entire document.**

   (CTRL) + click   Position the mouse in the selection bar area. Hold down (CTRL) and click the mouse to select all of the text.

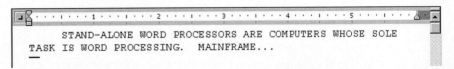

Figure 2.68
The 4Ch2 Converting Text document.

3. **Convert to lowercase.**

Format   Click to open the Format menu.

Change Case. . .   Click to open the Change Case dialog box.

Sentence case   Click this entry.

        [OK]   **Click to close the dialog box and change the case
                        of the text.**

Click   Click anywhere in the document to turn off the selection.
                        Your text should now look like Figure 2.69.

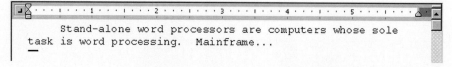

> Stand-alone word processors are computers whose sole
> task is word processing. Mainframe...

Figure 2.69
The converted text.

4. **Close the document without saving it.**

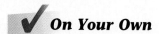

✔ *On Your Own*

You can also use the shortcut command (SHIFT) + (F3) to change the
case of selected text. You may have to issue the (SHIFT) + (F3) shortcut
command several times before the text is converted as you desire. Explore how text is converted using this command sequence.

Reinforcing the Exercise

1. Word allows you to change the case of text you have entered by issuing the Format,
    Change Case command sequence.

2. The Change Case dialog box offers several case conversion options, including UPPER-
    CASE, lowercase, and Sentence case (only the first word is capitalized).

3. Word also allows you to use the shortcut command (SHIFT) + (F3) to con-
    vert text case.

Date Command   Insert, Date and Time

The Date command accesses the system date information stored during
the startup process and presents it in a format like 12/15/98 or December
15, 1998. The Insert, Date and Time command sequence displays a menu
of 13 available formats for dates and times (Figure 2.70).

When you are entering date and time information in your document,
you have a choice of entering it as text or as a field. When you enter the
date or time as text, it is static and does not change from session to session.
When you enter it as a field, Word will automatically update it when the

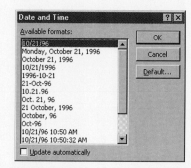

Figure 2.70
The various options available in
the Date and Time dialog box.

document is printed or opened (you must activate the Update automatically check box of the Date and Time dialog box for Word to do this).

The advantage of inserting a date as a field is that no matter when you print or open the document, the date and time will always be current. For example, if you type a document on December 15, 1998, and print it two days later, the printout will be dated December 17, 1998. This field update works automatically when you print the document.

Hands-On Exercise: Entering Dates

Rosa wants Isabel to show her how the date feature of Word functions.

1. **Close any documents and, if necessary, open a new document.**

2. **Insert today's date as text.**

Insert	Click to open the Insert menu.
Date and Time. . .	Click to open the Date and Time dialog box.
October 21, 1996	Click this format selection to indicate that the date should be entered in this manner as text (the actual date will be different).
OK	Click to close the dialog box and enter the date as text in the document.
(ENTER)	Press to move to the next line.

3. **Enter today's date as a field.**

Insert	Click to open the Insert menu.
Date and Time. . .	Click to open the Date and Time dialog box.
October 21, 1996	Click this format selection to indicate that the date should be entered in this manner (the actual date you see will be different).
Update Automatically	Click this check box to enter the date as a field.
OK	Click to close the dialog box and enter the date code in the document.
(ENTER)	Press to move to the next line. Your screen should now look similar to Figure 2.71. Unfortunately, you cannot easily tell which is the text and which is the field.

Figure 2.71
The document with the two dates entered.

4. **Select both lines.**

    CTRL + Click   Use this shortcut command to select both dates from the selection bar. You should see a screen like that shown in Figure 2.72. The text appears in black, and the field appears in gray.

5. **Exit without saving the document.**

Figure 2.72
When you select both dates, the text appears in black and the field appears in gray.

Reinforcing the Exercise

1. You can insert dates as either text or fields.
2. A date entered as a field changes to reflect the current date when you open the document.

SAVING AND BACKING UP FILES

As explained in Session 1 of Module 3: Common Features of Office 97 Applications, there are various ways of saving files and exiting Word. Clicking the Save button on the Standard toolbar is the easiest way to save a file periodically while you are working on it. The Close and Exit commands in the File menu let you save or discard the latest version of a file as you leave the file. If you do not save the screen version of the file, the original file on the disk will remain unaffected by your latest edits.

    The reason Word can exit without saving a document and without affecting the original file is that when you open a document, it is loaded into a **temporary file** in the computer's memory (RAM). Word never works directly on the stored file when you are editing, nor does it permanently save anything you type in a temporary file until you specifically tell Word to save it. When you save your document, this temporary file becomes permanent, replacing the old file on the disk (if there was one).

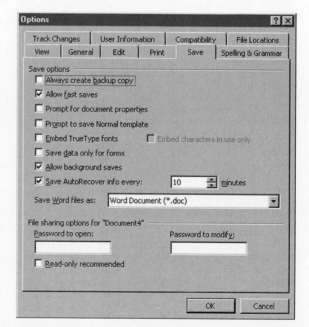

Figure 2.73
The Save tab of the Options dialog box.

Timed Backup Feature of Word

The timed backup feature of Word is a default option that is initially set to save your file every 10 minutes. If anything occurs (like a power outage), Word can use the backup file to allow you to restore your files. To change the amount of time between backups, issue the Tools, Options, Save command sequence. In the Save tab of the Options dialog box (Figure 2.73), you can then reset the time using the spin box.

Saving your file to disk at set intervals can save you a tremendous amount of mental distress and work if something goes wrong with the computer.

When using the automatic save feature of Word, it is best to use the fixed disk for saving documents; otherwise, you can waste a lot of time waiting for Word to save the document to a disk every 10 minutes.

SESSION REVIEW

The Word application window contains a number of hotspots that you can double-click to open dialog boxes you need to perform specific tasks.

Word provides a number of ways to view the document you are working with. Typically you use the Normal view for entering and editing a document. In Online Layout view, the screen is split, with the titles and headings of the document listed in the left pane and the complete document displayed in the right pane. You can use this view to jump to parts of the document quickly. The Page Layout view allows you to see special features, such as headers and footers, footnotes, and page numbers, that are hidden in Normal view.

Word allows you to establish indents for paragraphs by manipulating the indent handles on the ruler. You can create left indents, double indents, and hanging indents by using the indent handles. You can also use the Increase Indent and Decrease Indent buttons to create a left indent. Shortcut commands are also available for this purpose.

Word provides various ways to position or align data. The Tabs dialog box allows you to set tab stops like those on a typewriter and to create aligned columns of data. You can set tabs for text or numeric data. You can also create tab stops directly on the ruler by using the mouse. Tab leaders are dotted or solid lines that you can use to fill in blank space between tab stops.

Word gives you two ways to find text via the Find and Replace dialog box. Using the Find tab, you can simply locate text, which you can then manipulate or change in any way you please. Using the Replace tab, you can find the text and replace it with other text.

When you are editing a file using Word, you are not dealing directly with that file but rather with a temporary file that Word has copied from the original. Temporary files reside in RAM and enable easy error handling. If you really mess up the file that you are editing, all you have to do is issue the File, Close command sequence without saving the file. The original file remains intact, and the messed-up file is erased.

The timed backup feature of Word automatically saves your document to disk every 10 minutes. You can change this default time so that your document is saved more or less frequently by using the Save tab of the Options dialog box.

KEY TERMS AND CONCEPTS

alignment character　4-74	Normal view　4-48	tab leader　4-69
bar tab stop　4-69	Online Layout view　4-48	tab stop　4-68
decimal alignment　4-74	Outline view　4-50	temporary file　4-84
hanging indent　4-58	Page Layout view　4-49	view　4-48
hotspot　4-46	paragraph mark (¶)　4-76	

SESSION QUIZ

Multiple Choice

1. Which of the following commands cannot be performed from the expanded Replace tab?
   a. Replace All
   b. Find Next
   c. Find whole words only
   d. Search for embedded codes
   e. All of the above commands can be performed.

2. Which of the following statements about views is true?
   a. The Outline view is commonly used by the Word novice.
   b. The Normal view allows you to view headers and footers.
   c. The Page Layout view does not allow you to see columns.
   d. None of the above statements is true.

3. Which of the following is not a paragraph-related command?
   a. Format, Paragraph
   b. Align Left
   c. Hanging Indent
   d. Left Indentation
   e. All of the above are paragraph-related commands.

4. Which of the following is not a valid tab stop?
   a. decimal-align
   b. center-align
   c. column-align
   d. right-align
   e. All of the above are valid tab stops.

5. A tab leader has which of the following characteristics?
   a. It can place fill characters between two tab stops.
   b. It can be entered directly on the ruler.
   c. It can consist of dots, dashes, or underlines.
   d. A tab leader has all of the above characteristics.

True/False

6. If you really mess up a file that you are editing, the safest thing to do is to click the Close button without saving changes.

7. A major problem in using tabs is that the decimal points do not easily align in a straight column unless you define a decimal-align tab.

8. After you have exited the Find tab of the Find and Replace dialog box, you can find additional text by using the (SHIFT) + (F4) shortcut command.

9. Page Layout view can be used to view footnotes before a document is printed.

10. You can create indents directly on the ruler by dragging the indent handles to a new location.

SESSION REVIEW EXERCISES

1. Define or describe each of the following:
   a. temporary files
   b. tab leader
   c. hanging indent
   d. tab stops
   e. hotspots

2. The _____, _____ command sequence displays the ruler on the screen.

3. The _____ command lets you abandon a file being created or edited.

4. When you are working with large documents, it is a good idea to use the _____ _____ command, which by default, executes every 10 minutes.

5. If you are editing an existing file, the file that you are actually changing is a(n) _____ file in RAM.

6. A word *hotspot*, when double-clicked, opens a/an _____.

7. The _____ _____ or _____ dialog boxes can be used for resetting the right margin.

8. Click the _____ _____ button in the Tabs dialog box to clear all tabs from the ruler.

9. The _____-align tab stop is Word's default tab setting.

10. The _____ key is used to move the cursor to the next tab location.

11. The _____ -align tab stop is used when numeric information is being entered and directs Word to align the numbers on the decimal point.

12. The _____, _____ command sequence is used to insert the date into a Word document via the Date and Time dialog box.

13. The _____ view is typically used for entering or editing documents.

14. The shortcut command _____ + _____ can be used to delete indents from a paragraph.

15. Tab stops can be deleted from the ruler by _____ them off with the mouse.

16. A Replace All command can be reversed by clicking the _____ button on the Standard toolbar.

17. The periods or dots sometimes shown between two tab stops are known as a(n) _____ _____.

18. The shortcut command used to convert uppercase letters to lowercase letters and vice versa is _____ + _____.

19. The shortcut command _____ + _____ is the Find Next command.

20. The _____ button of the Find and Replace dialog box displays an expanded dialog box with options for locating and replacing Word data in a word document.

COMPUTER EXERCISES

1. Using the 4Ch2 Introduction to Word Processing document, perform the following tasks:
   a. Move to the beginning of the document. Using the Paragraph dialog box, set the left margin to 1.5 inches. Set the right margin to 0.8 inch.
   b. Move to the second paragraph of page 2. Indent the left margin two tab stops using the Increase Indent button.
   c. Reset the left margin of both paragraphs back to 1.25 inches and the right margin to 1.25 inches.
   d. Move to the second paragraph of page 3. Create a double indent.
   e. Click the Show/Hide ¶ button to examine the beginning of the second paragraph of page 2. Note the codes that have been embedded by Word. Set the document for double-spacing. Reset the margins to 2.5 inches for the left and 2.5 inches for the right. Use the Close command to exit the document. Do not save the file.

2. Clear the screen. Enter the document shown in Figure 2.74. Use the Center command to center the first two lines of text.
   a. Delete all tab stops from the ruler.
   b. Enter a left-align tab stop at 1.0 inch and a decimal-align tab stop at 5.0 inches.
   c. Enter the columns of data, the first column with the left alignment at 1.0 inch and the second column with decimal alignment at 5.0 inches.

   Notice how the decimals are now lined up. Save the document using the name M4Ch2 Exercise 2.

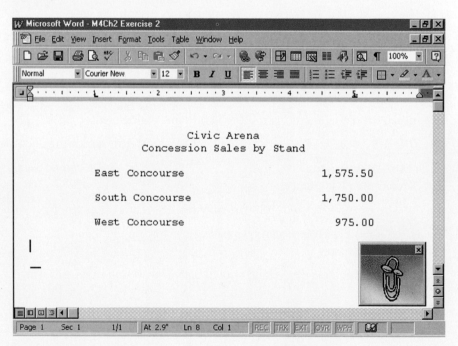

Figure 2.74
The M4Ch2 Exercise 2 document.

3. Clear the screen and, if necessary, open a new document. Enter the document shown in Figure 2.75.
   a. Delete all existing tab stops. Set a left-align tab stop at 0.5 inch and a decimal-align tab stop at 4.5 inches.
   b. Enter data
   c. Use the Insert Date command to insert the date in the letter as text.
   d. Print the document.
   e. Save the document using the name M4Ch2 Exercise 3.

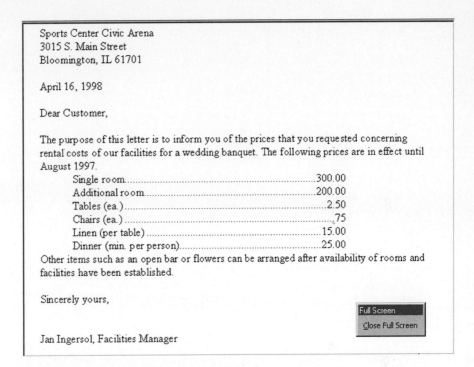

Figure 2.75
The M4Ch2 Exercise 3 document.

4. Clear the screen. Clear all tab stops.
   a. Set the font to Courier New 12 pt.
   b. Set a right-align tab stop at 0.5 inch.
   c. Set decimal-align tab stops at 2.4 inches, 4.0 inches, and 5.5 inches.
   d. Enter the document shown in Figure 2.76.
   e. Save the file to disk using the name M4Ch2 Exercise 4.
   f. Print the document.

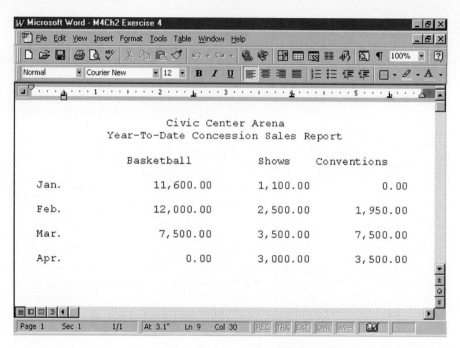

Figure 2.76
The M4Ch2 Exercise 4 document.

5. Clear the screen. Clear all tab stops. Enter the document shown in Figure 2.77.

   a. Set regular text tab stops at 2 inches, 4 inches, 5.0, and 5.4 inches.

   b. Use 12 pt for the heading and 10 pt for the vendor list.

   c. Enter the vendor list.

   d. Save the document using the name M4Ch2 Exercise 5.

   e. Print the document.

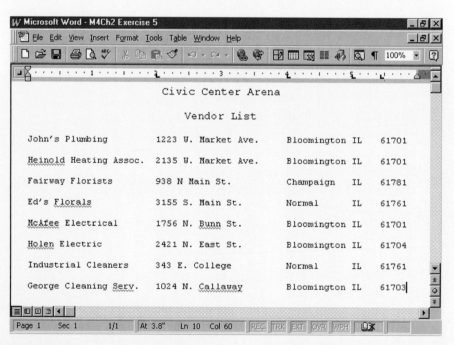

Figure 2.77
The M4Ch2 Exercise 5 document.

6. Clear the screen. Clear all tabs.
   a. Enter a right-align tab stop at 0.6 inch.
   b. Enter decimal-align tab stops at 2.0 inches, 3.5 inches, and 5.0 inches.
   c. Save the document to disk as M4Ch2 Exercise 6.
   d. Enter the document shown in Figure 2.78.
   e. Print the document.

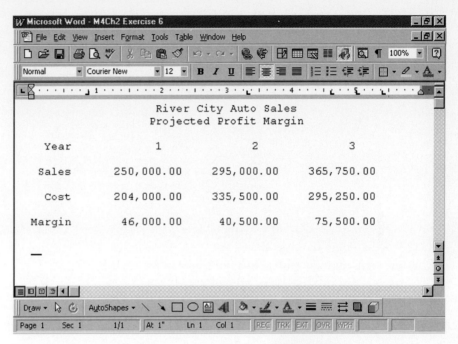

Figure 2.78
The M4Ch2 Exercise 6 document.

7. Clear the screen. Enter the bibliography shown in Figure 2.79.
   a. Include the appropriate underlining where it is indicated.
   b. Include the indicated indents.
   c. Save the document to disk as M4Ch2 Exercise 7.
   d. Print the document.

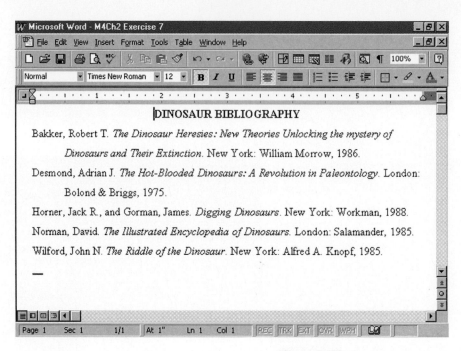

Figure 2.79
**The M4Ch2 Exercise 7 docu-
ment.**

8. Clear the screen. Delete all existing tabs.
  a. Set a left-align tab stop at 0.5 inch.
  b. Set a left-align tab stop with a dot leader at 5.0 inches.
  c. Set the font to 12 pt Times Roman.
  d. Save the document to disk as M4Ch2 Exercise 8.
  e. Enter the document shown in Figure 2.80.
  f. Print the document.

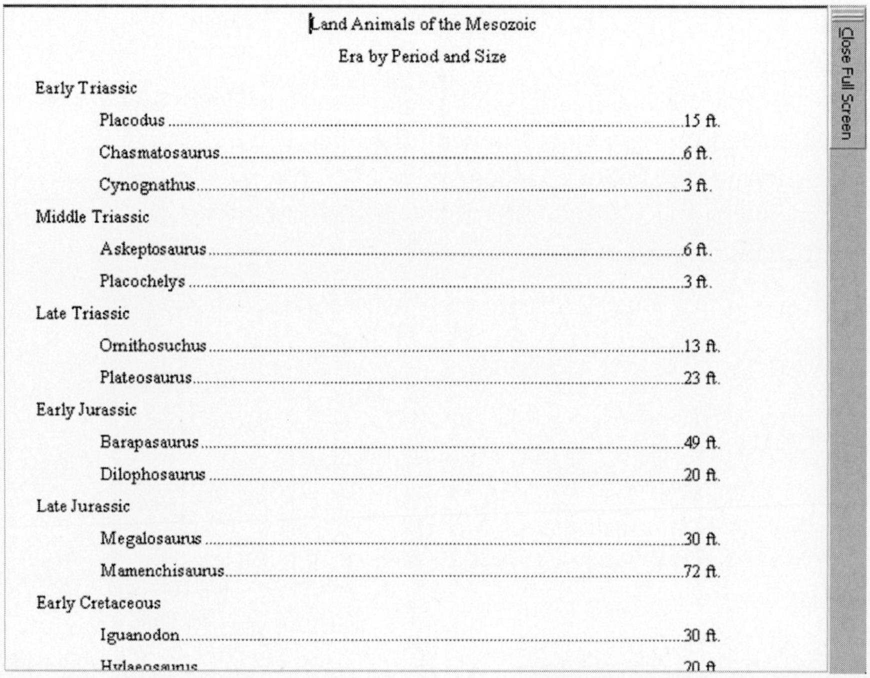

Land Animals of the Mesozoic
Era by Period and Size

Early Triassic
      Placodus ....15 ft.
      Chasmatosaurus...6 ft.
      Cynognathus...3 ft.
Middle Triassic
      Askeptosaurus...6 ft.
      Placochelys..3 ft.
Late Triassic
      Ornithosuchus...13 ft.
      Plateosaurus...23 ft.
Early Jurassic
      Barapasaurus..49 ft.
      Dilophosaurus...20 ft.
Late Jurassic
      Megalosaurus..30 ft.
      Mamenchisaurus..72 ft.
Early Cretaceous
      Iguanodon...30 ft.
      Hylaeosaurus..20 ft.

Close Full Screen

Figure 2.80
**The M4Ch2 Exercise 8 docu-
ment.**

9. Open the 4Ch2 Introduction to Word Processing document. Practice using the (SHIFT) + (F3) (Change Case) shortcut command on individual words as well as selected text.

10. Load the document named 4Ch2 Exercise 10 shown in Figure 2.81.

   a. Using the indicated Change Case commands, make the requested changes to the document.

   b. Print the document.

   c. Use a Save As command to save the changes to a document called M4Ch2 Exercise 10.

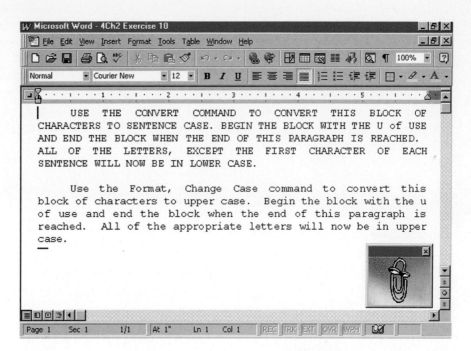

Figure 2.81
The 4Ch2 Exercise 10 document to be changed using the Format, Change Case command.

INTERNET EXERCISES

1. Get information about the World Wide Web from Microsoft.

   a. Access the Microsoft Web page with your browser (http://www.microsoft.com).

   b. Click the Search button at the top of the Web page to open the Search page.

   c. Enter the topic *World Wide Web* in the text box in step 1 on the Search page.

   d. Click the Support & Knowledge Base option in step 3 of the Search page.

   e. Click the Search Now! button.

   f. On the Search Results page that appears, look for links related to Office and the Web. Links may be on the 2nd, 3rd, 4th (and so forth) pages of the Search Results. Click the links at the bottom of the page labeled <u>1</u>, <u>2</u>, <u>3</u>, and so forth to view each page of Search results.

   g. Print a Web page related to Office and the Web.

 *On Your Own*

Word has a hyphenation feature that allows you to include hard or soft hyphens in a document. A **hard** hyphen always appears after it has been entered in text. Word controls a **soft hyphen** and, as text is changed in a document these soft hyphens may disappear and others appear elsewhere in the document.

Enter a hard hyphen, not by pressing the minus key ⊝, but by holding down the ⌈CTRL⌉ and ⌈SHIFT⌉ keys and then press the dash key on the main keyboard. Hard hyphens keep hyphenated words together on a line.

Use this option after you have finished your document. If you want to include the entire document, position to the beginning of the document before you invoke this feature. Soft hyphens are controlled using the command sequence Tools, Language, Hyphenation… This command sequence displays the Hyphenation dialog box. Select the desired options and hyphenation starts from your current location in the document.

SESSION 3

Word's Document Accent Features

After completing this session, you should be able to:

➤ Insert page numbers

➤ Use the Style Gallery

➤ Apply autoformatting

➤ Create bulleted and numbered lists

➤ Insert pictures

➤ Use the Borders and Shading commands

➤ Insert a picture and caption

➤ Create page headers and footers

➤ Insert footnotes and endnotes

➤ Insert symbols

➤ Link a Word document and an Excel worksheet

➤ Embed an Excel chart in a Word document

 Isabel's daughter, Rosa, is a high school student who has been assigned to write a term paper for her English composition class. For her paper, Rosa has selected the topic of ferrets as pets. She has written her paper on the family's home computer, which has a rather low-level word processor on it. Her word processing program, for instance, cannot place footnotes at the bottom of the page. Rosa also does not understand what some of the other features of word processing are that can be used to "dress up" her document to make it look better.

Rosa and Isabel have agreed that if Rosa can type the document into the computer and correct the grammar, Isabel will introduce her to Word and some of the commands that will give her document a more professional appearance.

While gathering her research, Rosa talked with Michael Dowd, the organizer for the Ferret Frolic, to get some information for her paper. He provided her with a picture of a ferret that she wants to include in her report to show the reader what a ferret's face looks like. Rosa also wants to include a ferret family tree graphic based on information that she found on the World Wide Web and recreated using a Paint program.

In addition to the term paper, Isabel also wants to use Word to prepare a progress report and provide financial data related to a loan that the Civic Arena has with Central Savings and Loan. Besides incorporating spreadsheet data in the report, Isabel also hopes to include a graph that she has embedded in the worksheet. This session provides all the information Isabel and her daughter need for their tasks.

In this session you will learn about commands that let you accent your document with page numbers, page headers and footers, embedded files to be used as figures, footnotes, or endnotes, and so forth. This session focuses on topics most useful to a beginning Word student and emphasizes the features that appear on the toolbar.

USING DOCUMENT ENHANCEMENT COMMANDS

You can use document enhancement commands to develop a more professional-looking document.

Adding Page Numbering Insert, Page Numbers

Word does not use page numbering unless you tell it to. To insert page numbers into a document that does not have headers or footers, issue the Insert, Page Numbers command sequence. This command displays the Page Numbers dialog box (Figure 3.1).

You can control whether or not a page number appears on the first page by making certain a check mark appears in the *Show number on first page* box in the lower-left corner of the dialog box. Click this option to get rid of the check mark if you don't want the page number to appear on the first page.

To change the format of page numbers, click the Format button to invoke the Page Number Format dialog box (Figure 3.2). The Number Format list box shown in Figure 3.3 offers several format options for page numbers, including Roman numerals and uppercase or lowercase letters. Word's default format is Arabic numerals—1, 2, 3, and so on.

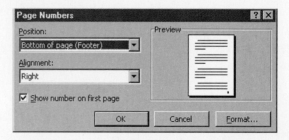

Figure 3.1
The Page Numbers dialog box.

For long documents, you may want page numbering to start over for each section. To do this, open the Page Numbering dialog box at the desired location in your document, and then open the Page Number Format dialog box. Enter a new starting page number in the Start at text box, or use the spin box to select the desired number. When you return to the document, the page numbering will be changed.

You can use this feature, for example, to number the front matter, such as the foreword, acknowledgments, and table of contents, of a document using lowercase Roman numerals, and then number the pages of the body of the document using Arabic numbers.

Figure 3.2
The Page Number Format dialog box, where you can change the page numbering format and set a new page number.

Hands-On Exercise: Using Page Numbering

All of the Hands-On Exercises for the first part of this session use Rosa's term paper document in the Student Data Disk for this text. To provide you with a backup copy, you will be saving the term paper document to a document containing your name. If you get into trouble and cannot recover, you will be able to start over with the original file.

Figure 3.3
The Number Format list box for selecting the number style to be used.

1. **Open the 4Ch3 Ferret Term Paper document.** Be sure to use the Open dialog box to change to the location where your student files are stored. The document should look like that shown in Figure 3.4.

2. **Use the Save As command to add your name to the document name.**

File   Click to open the File menu.

Save As. . .   Click to open the Save As dialog box.

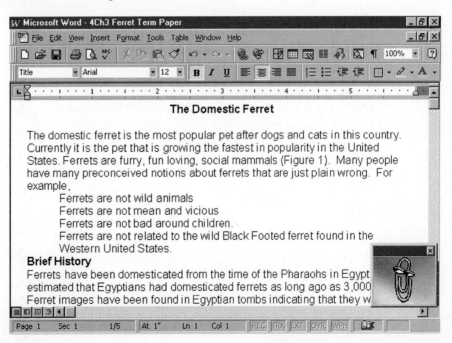

Figure 3.4
The 4Ch3 Ferret Term Paper document.

Click

Click at the end of the existing document name to reposition the insertion point.

Type: -**Your name**

Enter a space, a dash, and a space, and then type your name. The Save As dialog box should now look similar to Figure 3.5.

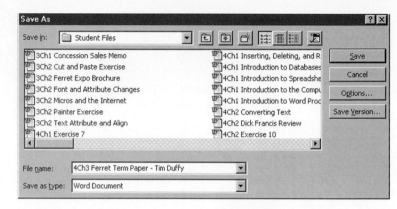

Figure 3.5
The completed dialog box for saving the term paper document to a file whose name incorporates your name.

3. **Use Print Preview to examine the document.**

 Click to open the Print Preview window. If necessary, click the One Page button. Your screen should look like Figure 3.6. Notice that no page numbers appear at the bottom of the page.

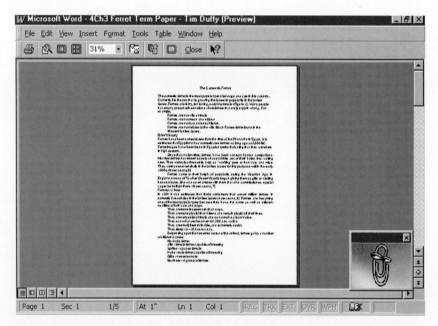

Figure 3.6
The Preview window for the term paper document.

(PGDN) Press to see if a page number appears at the bottom of the second page.

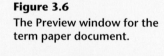 Click Return to the document.

4. **Include page numbers.**

Insert Click to open the Insert menu.

Page Numbers. . . Click to open the Page Numbers dialog box (Figure 3.7).

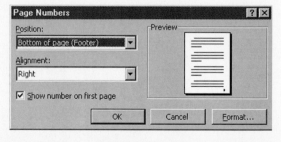

Figure 3.7
The Page Numbers dialog box.

5. Examine alternative positions for placing the page number.

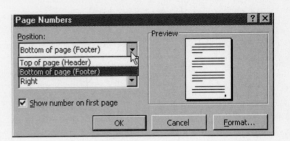

Position

Click the Position list box to see the options shown in Figure 3.8.

Bottom of page (Footer)

Click to place page numbers at the bottom of the page.

Figure 3.8
The Position list box allows you to place the page number at the top or bottom of the page.

Alignment

Click the Alignment list box to see the alternatives shown in Figure 3.9.

Center

Click to center the page number.

Show number on first page

Click to indicate that you do not want the page number to appear on the first page (the box should not be checked). The Page Numbers dialog box should now look like Figure 3.10.

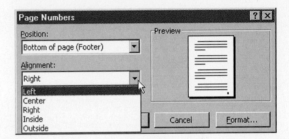

| OK |

Click to close the dialog box and return to the document.

Figure 3.9
The Alignment selection box alternatives.

6. Verify the appearance of the page numbers.

PGDN

Press five times to move to the bottom of the first page. There should be no page number in the bottom margin of this page.

PGDN

Press until you can see the page number at the bottom of the second page (Figure 3.11). Verify that the page numbers appear on successive pages.

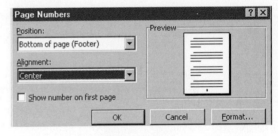

7. Close the document without saving any changes.

Figure 3.10
The completed Page Numbers dialog box.

T I M E L Y   T I P

Once you have inserted a page number, you may later want to delete it from your document. To delete a page number, follow these basic steps:

1. Activate Page Layout view.
2. Double-click the page number to activate the Header/Footer toolbar.
3. Select the page number with a click and drag operation.
4. Press DEL.
5. Click the Close button on the Header/Footer toolbar.

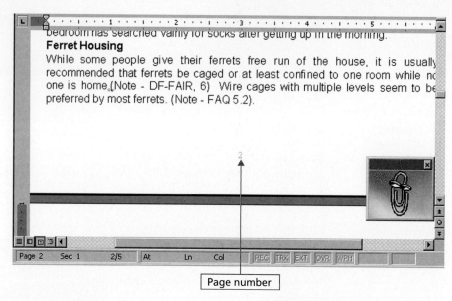

Ferret Housing
While some people give their ferrets free run of the house, it is usually
recommended that ferrets be caged or at least confined to one room while no
one is home.(Note - DF-FAIR, 6) Wire cages with multiple levels seem to be
preferred by most ferrets. (Note - FAQ 5.2).

Page number

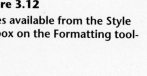

Figure 3.11
The page numbers are displayed very faintly at the bottom of the second and subsequent pages of the document.

Reinforcing the Exercise

1. You can insert page numbers using the Insert, Page Numbers command sequence.
2. You can place the page number at the top or bottom of a page.
3. You can align page numbers in a number of different ways.
4. You can restart page numbering within a document.
5. Word offers a variety of page numbering formats.

Using the Style Gallery

Each document that you create uses a template (the Normal template is the default). Each template contains a set of standard styles. A **style** is a collection of formatting options applied to selected text or to the entire document. A style, for example, might change the font type, size, boldfacing, and italics of a piece of selected text. You can access several standard styles by using the Style list box found in the Formatting toolbar (Figure 3.12). As you make changes to the document, more styles may appear.

Figure 3.12
Styles available from the Style list box on the Formatting toolbar.

Using AutoFormatting Format, AutoFormat

✔ *On Your Own*

Word's **AutoFormat feature** automatically formats your document, paragraph by paragraph, applying different formatting styles (font styles, tab settings, paragraph positioning, bullets, and so on). Any features that are applied are from the Normal template, unless you have specified some other template. Autoformat en-

Use the Format, Style Gallery command sequence to examine how you can apply styles to your document using the Style Gallery dialog box. Figure 3.13 shows the term paper with the Elegant Letter style applied to the document.

1. Try using several different formats with your term paper document.
2. Examine the effect of each style on your document in the Preview window.
3. Click the Cancel button to exit without making any of the changes.

sures that the formatting is consistent throughout a document.

To begin automatic formatting, you issue the Format, Auto-Format command sequence. The AutoFormat dialog box opens as shown in Figure 3.14, providing you with several options for reformatting a document. If you don't like the formatting changes you make by using the AutoFormat command, you can restore the document to its original condition by clicking the Undo button on the Standard toolbar.

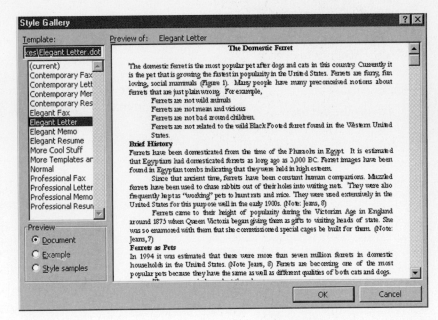

Figure 3.13
The Style Gallery dialog box, which makes a number of different styles available for use with a document.

Adding Bullets and Numbering

A bulleted or numbered list is a special type of list that is formatted with dots (bullets) or numbers. Figure 3.15 shows both bulleted and numbered lists. Bulleted lists have a **bullet,** or large dot, at the left margin, and numbered lists are numbered sequentially.

Bulleted and numbered lists can be created in one of two ways. You can create a bulleted or numbered list by pressing ⁅TAB⁆ before entering each item, without bullets or numbers, and then clicking the Bullets or Numbering button on the Formatting toolbar. Alternatively, you can enter text, again without bullets or numbers, select that text, and then click the Bullets or Numbering button.

To create a bulleted or numbered list from the menu, follow these steps:

1.   Place the cursor at the location where you want the list to appear.

Figure 3.14
The AutoFormat dialog box.

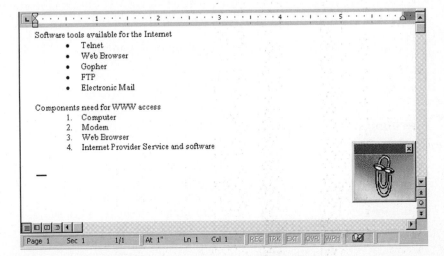

Figure 3.15
Examples of bulleted and numbered lists.

2. Issue the Format, Bullets and Numbering command sequence to open the Bullets and Numbering dialog box.

3. Click on the tab that builds the type of list you want to include in your document: Bullet, Numbered, or Outline Numbered.

4. Select the style of list you prefer. If none of the options is exactly what you want, choose the one that comes closest and then click the Customize Button to customize the option.

5. Click OK to begin the bulleting or numbering process. Each time you begin a new paragraph, Word formats the paragraph with either a bullet or a number.

6. To end a bulleted or numbered list, press Enter to add a bulleted or numbered blank line to the end of the formatted lines. Then issue the Format, Bullets and Numbering command sequence to display the dialog box, and click None to end the bulleted or numbered list.

✔ **On Your Own**

If you want multilevel bullets, you can use the Format, Bullets and Numbering command sequence to open the Bullets and Numbering dialog box shown in Figure 3.16. Use the Increase/Decrease Indent button when creating a document.

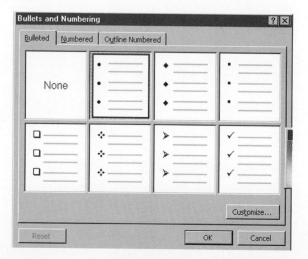

Figure 3.16
The Bullets and Numbering dialog box.

Hands-On Exercise: Using Styles, AutoFormat, and Lists

Rosa wants to make her report look more appealing by applying various styles and adding bulleted and numbered lists.

1. **Open your personalized copy of the 4Ch3 Ferret Term Paper document that you created earlier in this session.**

2. **Apply a Heading 1 style to the title of the term paper.**

 Click to return to Normal view.

The Domestic Ferret Select the report title.

 Click the down arrow of the Style list box to see the selections shown in Figure 3.17.

Heading 1 Click this selection to apply it to the report heading. The heading now moves to the left.

 Click the Center button on the Formatting toolbar to center the text. The document should now look like Figure 3.18.

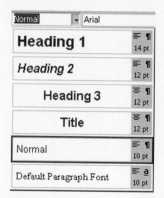

Figure 3.17
The displayed Style list box.

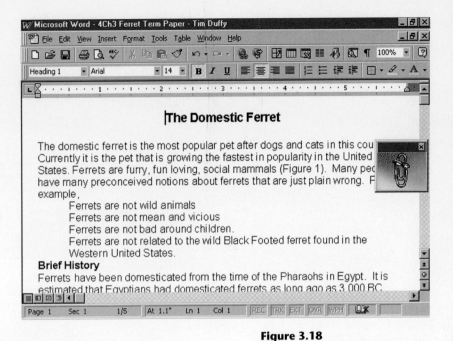

Figure 3.18
The new style applied to the re-port heading with the heading centered.

3. **Apply the same style to the heading at the end of the paper.**

CTRL + END   Use this shortcut command to move to the end of the document.

PGUP   Press until the title of the citations is visible.

Works Cited   Select this title.

       Click the down arrow of the Style box to open the selection box of available styles.

Heading 1   Apply this selection to the report heading. The heading now moves to the left.

       Click to center the text. The citation page should now look like Figure 3.19.

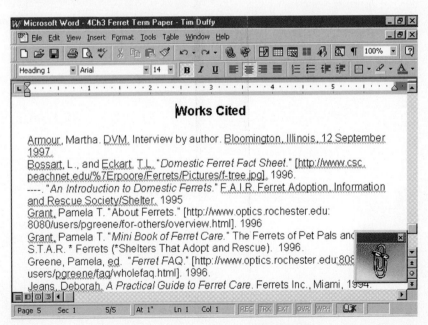

Figure 3.19
The new style applied to the ci-tation page.

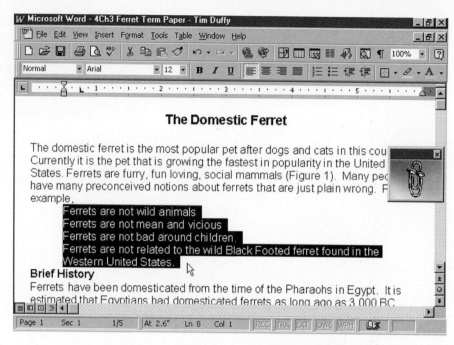

Figure 3.20
The text selected to become the first bulleted list.

4. Create the first bulleted list.

CTRL + HOME	Use this shortcut command to move to the beginning of the document.
Click and drag	Select the indented text as shown in Figure 3.20.
▤	Click the Bullets button on the Formatting toolbar to create the bulleted list.
Click	Click anywhere in the document to turn off the selection. Your document should now look like Figure 3.21.

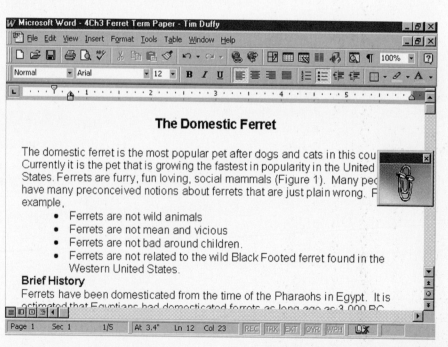

Figure 3.21
The paper with the bulleted list.

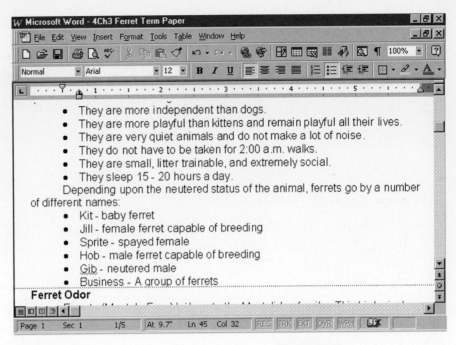

Figure 3.22

Two more bulleted lists created in the document.

5. **Use the commands described in step 4 to create the two bulleted lists shown in Figure 3.22.**

6. **Create the first numbered list.**

Click and drag

Select the indented text as shown in Figure 3.23.

Click the Numbering button on the Formatting toolbar to create the numbered list.

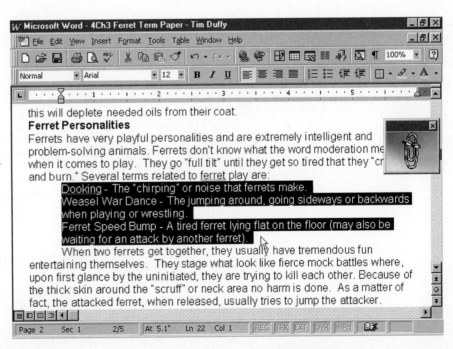

Figure 3.23

The text selected to become the first numbered list.

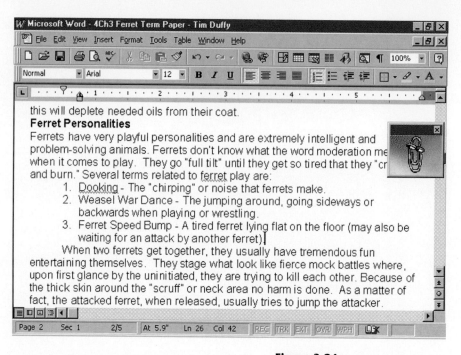

Figure 3.24
The paper with the first numbered list.

Click   Click anywhere in the document to turn off the selection. Your document should look like Figure 3.24.

7. **Use the commands described in step 6 to create the numbered list shown in Figure 3.25.**

8. **Use the AutoFormat command with the document.**

(CTRL) + (HOME)   Press to move to the beginning of the document.

Format   Click to open the Format menu.

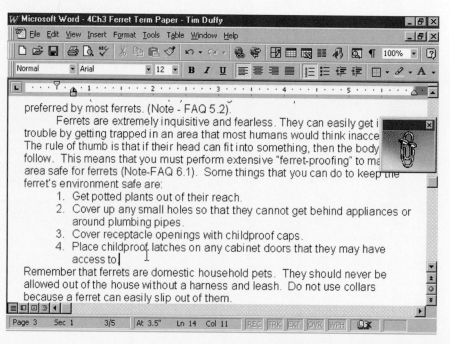

Figure 3.25
The second numbered list.

Autoformat. . .   Click to open the AutoFormat dialog box shown in Figure 3.26. Notice that the name of your document is at the top of the dialog box.

OK   Click to accept the default values. Your document should look like Figure 3.27.

9. Reverse the change.

Click to return the document to its prior condition. It should look like it did before you issued the AutoFormat command.

Figure 3.26
The AutoFormat dialog box.

Click to reformat the document again.

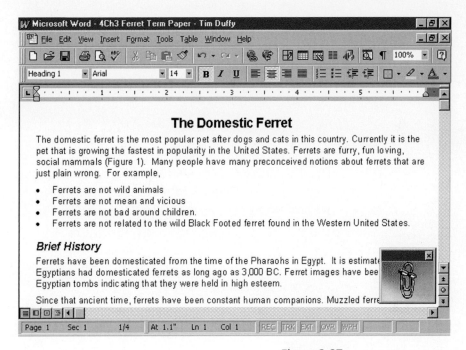

Figure 3.27
The document after AutoFormat has been applied to it.

10. Return the bulleted text to its original indented format.

Drag   Select each section of bulleted text. Drag the left tab stop on the ruler to the 0.6-inch location.

TIMELY TIP

Be certain that you do not have any text selected when you apply automatic formatting. If you do, the AutoFormat command will not execute. If the command won't execute, click anywhere in the document to turn off any selection, and then issue the Format, AutoFormat command sequence again.

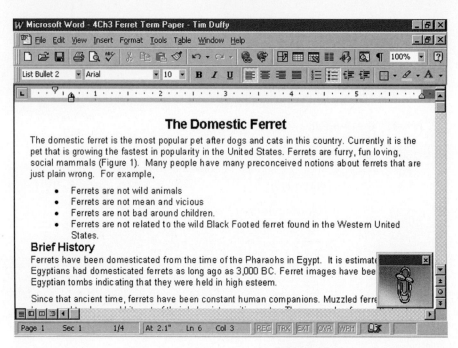

Figure 3.28
The changed bulleted text indented after the AutoFormat command has executed. Notice the location of the indent handles in the ruler.

Click on the square portion of the bottom indent handle and drag so that both handles appear at the 0.4-inch mark in the ruler. Figure 3.28 shows the first reformatted bulleted list on the changed ruler bar.

11. Save the document.

Click to save the document.

Reinforcing the Exercise

1. You can change the text in a document by using the Style box of the Formatting toolbar.

2. You can apply bullets and numbers to selected text.

3. AutoFormat changes the appearance of a document.

4. You can use the Undo command to reverse an AutoFormat, Bullet, or Numbering command.

Inserting a Picture

Inserting a graphic image in a document is a multistep process:

1. Select the image.

2. Determine where to place the image.

3. If necessary, resize the image.

4. Indicate how text is to flow around the image.

5. If desired, place a border around the image.

6. Create a text box for the caption to accompany the image.

7. If necessary, change the font for the caption text.

8. Indicate how text is to flow around the caption's text box.

9. Possibly reposition or resize the text box used for the caption.

   Once you have an image embedded in your document, the **Picture toolbar** appears in the window. The buttons of the toolbar are described in Table 3.1.

TIMELY TIP

You can create a style by using selected text that contains attributes that you want to apply to the style. Once the selection is made, issue the Format, Style... command sequence to invoke the Style dialog box. Click the New button and name the style.

If you want to make changes to an existing style, issue the Format, Style... command sequence to invoke the Style dialog box and click the Format button. A list of attributes appears. If, for example, you want to change the margins, select the Paragraph entry. To change the shading of text, select the Border option.

Table 3.1 Buttons of the Picture Toolbar

Button	Name	Function
	Insert Picture	Opens the Insert Picture dialog box used for selecting the image to be embedded in the document.
	Image Control	Displays a menu that allows you to control how the image will be displayed. The Watermark option allows you to create an image over which the rest of the document can appear, like a watermark on stationery.
	More Contrast	Increases the intensity of the colors of the image. Decreases the gray color.
	Less Contrast	Decreases the intensity of the colors of the image. Increases the gray color.
	More Brightness	Adds white to lighten the colors.
	Less Brightness	Adds black to darken the colors.
	Crop	Trims or restores portions of a picture. Click the crop button, then use the resize handles of the selected image.
	Line Style	Displays a menu of line sizes.
	Text Wrapping	Displays a menu you can use to determine how text should wrap around the selected image.
	Format Picture	Displays the Format Picture dialog box.
	Set Transparent Color	Allows you to change the color of the selected object to make it transparent.
	Reset Picture	Removes any changes made on the selected image and returns it to its original appearance.

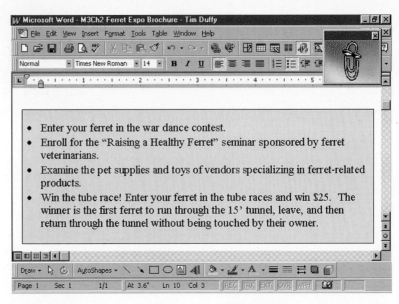

Figure 3.29
A document with a border and shading.

Creating Borders and Shading Paragraphs

A **border** is a box or a line that surrounds a paragraph or paragraphs. You can add **shading** to an area surrounded with a border to give special emphasis to a paragraph, as shown in Figure 3.29. You can apply borders to any text that is followed by a paragraph mark (¶). (Click the Show/Hide ¶ button on the Standard toolbar to see the nonprinting paragraph marks that Word has embedded in the document.

To add border lines around a paragraph, select the material for which you want to create a box or a line, and issue the Format, Borders and Shading command sequence to open the Borders and Shading dialog box (Figure 3.30). The Borders tab is activated by default. Click the desired Setting option to choose the desired bordertype. To change the type of line used in the border, choose an option from the Style list box (Figure 3.30). To change the width of the borderline, you can select an option from the Width list box (Figure 3.31). If you want to change the amount of shading,

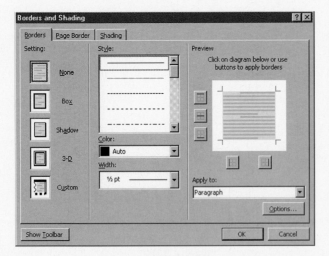

Figure 3.30
The Borders tab of the Borders and Shading dialog box.

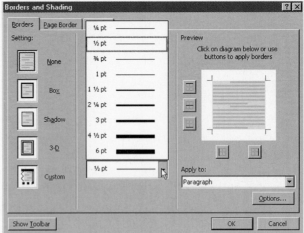

Figure 3.31
The options of the Width list.

click the Shading tab and then click the down arrow in the Style list box to see a list of shading options (Figure 3.32).

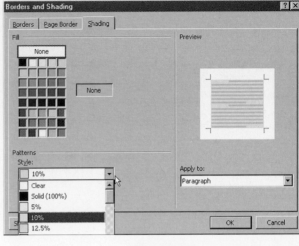

Figure 3.32
The options of the Style list box
allow you to control the amount
of shading used in a bordered
box.

Hands-On Exercise: Inserting Borders and Pictures

Rosa has a picture of a ferret that she wants to add
to her paper.

1. **If necessary, open your personalized copy of
   the 4Ch3 Ferret Term Paper.**

2. **Apply a border and shading to the paper title.
   You should be at the beginning of the document.**

Click   Place the mouse pointer in the selection bar and click to
                      select the title line (Figure 3.33).

Figure 3.33
The title line selected.

Format	Click to open the Border menu.
Borders and Shading. . .	Click to open the Borders and Shading dialog box.
Box	Click this option in the Setting portion of the Borders tabs to place a border around the text.
Shading	Click this tab.
Style:	Click to display the Style options (Figure 3.34).
	Click this entry to establish the amount of shading.

TIMELY TIP

If you want to apply
borders only, you can
click the Border button
on the Formatting tool-
bar and then select the
border type.

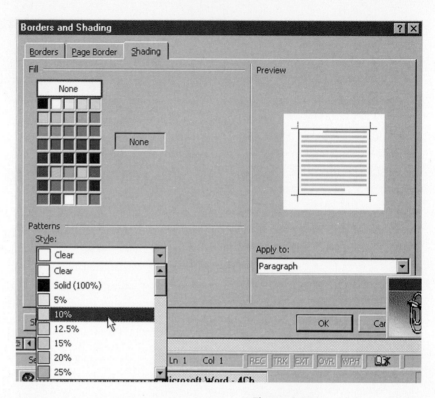

Figure 3.34
The Style list box.

OK	Click to close the dialog box and return to the document.
Click	Click anywhere to turn off the selection. Your shaded, bordered title should appear as shown in Figure 3.35.

3. Insert the first picture. Position the insertion point at the end of the first bulleted line.

Insert	Click to open the Insert menu.
Picture	Click to open the Picture menu.
From File. . .	Click to open the Insert Picture dialog box. Use the Look in box to change to the location containing your student files. Two images are listed (Figure 3.36).

Figure 3.35
The paper title with the shading and border applied.

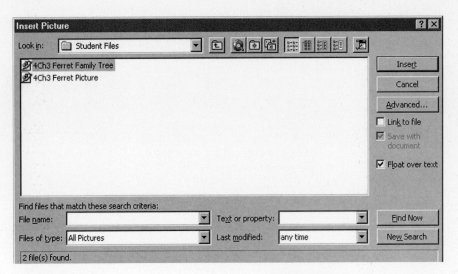

Figure 3.36
The images to be used in this project.

4Ch3 Ferret Picture   Double-click this picture name to load it. The picture appears in your document at the insertion point location, and the document has been placed in Page Layout view.

Drag   Drag the picture to the end of the first bulleted line. Your document should now look like Figure 3.37. Notice that text does not appear to the left of the inserted picture and that the Picture toolbar is displayed.

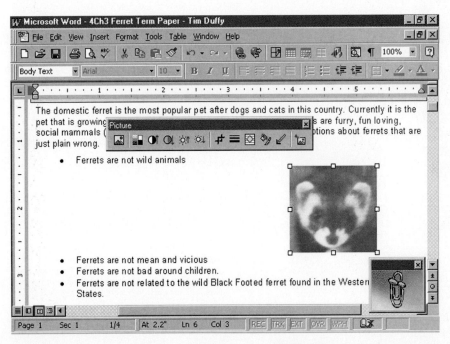

Figure 3.37
The document with the ferret picture added.

4. Change how text flows around the image.

 Click to open the Format Picture dialog box.

Wrapping Click to open the Wrapping tab (Figure 3.38).

Square Click this option of the Wrapping style portion of the tab.

Left Click this option of the Wrap to portion of the tab.

OK Click to close the dialog box and make the changes to the document, which now appears as shown in Figure 3.39.

5. Move and resize the image.

Drag Move and resize the image until it appears like Figure 3.40.

6. Place a border around the image.

 Click to open the Format Picture dialog box.

Colors and Lines Click to open this tab.

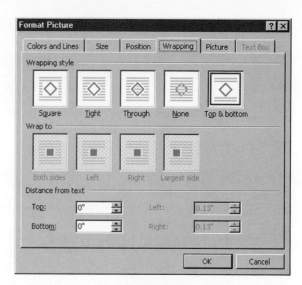

Figure 3.38
The Wrapping tab controls how text wraps around an embedded image.

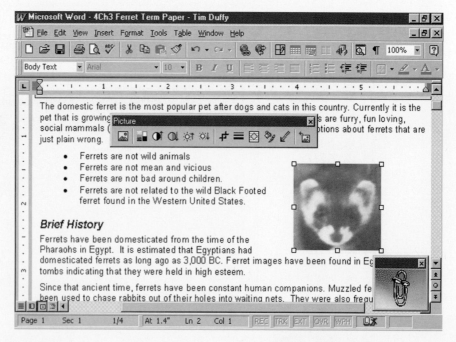

Figure 3.39
Text now wraps to the left of the image.

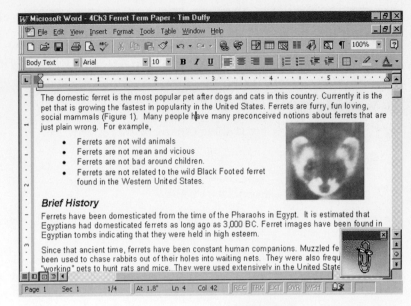

Figure 3.40
The image properly positioned and resized.

TIMELY TIP

If you make a mistake and something appears incorrectly, click the Undo button and try to enter the command correctly.

Color	Click this list box in the Line portion of the tab. A color palette appears as shown in Figure 3.41.
Black	Click this color. The Lines portion of the tab should now look like Figure 3.42.
OK	Click to make the change and return to the document.

7. **Add the caption. Make certain the image is still selected with the resizing handles around it.**

Insert	Click to open the Insert menu.
Caption. . .	Click to open the Caption dialog box (Figure 3.43).

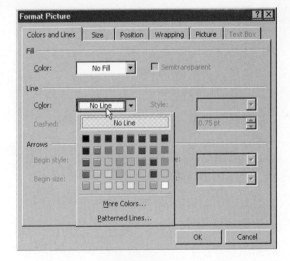

Figure 3.41
The line color palette.

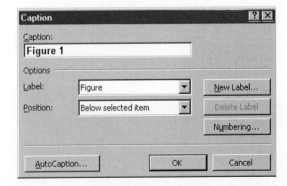

Figure 3.43
The Caption dialog box for inserting explanatory text under a figure.

Figure 3.42
The Line portion of the Colors and Lines tab.

Type: **-A typical domestic ferret**   Be sure to enter a space before the dash.

OK	Click to insert the caption in the document beneath the picture (Figure 3.44). Notice, however, that all of the text is not present.

8. Modify the caption text.

Drag   Select all of the text (try to drag downward).

10   Click to display the Font Size menu.

8   Click on the 8 pt option.

             Click to center the caption under the picture to give it a more balanced appearance.

Click   Click the caption text to turn off the selection. Your image and caption should now look like Figure 3.45. Change the font for the remaining text.

9. Flow the text around the caption.

Format   Click to open the Format menu.

Text Box...   Click to open the Text Box dialog box.

Wrapping   Click the Wrapping tab.

Square   Click the Square option of the Wrapping style portion of the tab.

Left   Click the Left option of the Wrapping tab.

OK   Click to apply these settings to the document.

Click   Click anywhere to turn off the selection. Your document should now look Figure 3.46.

10. Insert a drop cap at the beginning of the paper.

Click   Move the insertion point to the left of the word *The* in the first line of the document.

Format   Click to open the Format menu.

Figure 3.44
The image with the caption and some of its text.

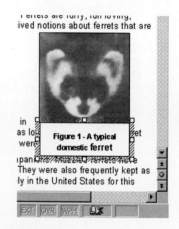

Figure 3.45
The caption text resized and centered.

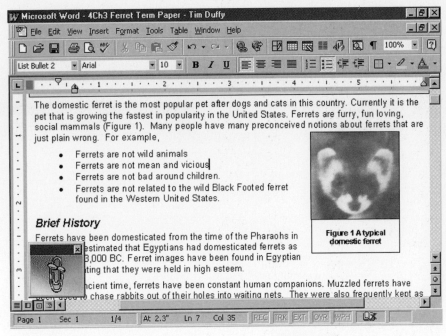

Figure 3.46
The completed picture and caption.

Drop Cap. . .	Click to open the Drop Cap dialog box (Figure 3.47).
Dropped	Double-click the Dropped option in the Position portion of the dialog box. You return to the document.
Click	Click anywhere to get rid of the selection. Your document should now look like Figure 3.48.

11. Add the second graphic image (the ferret family tree).

Click	Move to the end of the second paragraph on the second page and click.
	Click the Close button on the Office Assistant to turn off this feature.
(ENTER)	Press twice to insert two blank lines for the image.
Click	Place the insertion point at the left margin on the blank line following the paragraph and click.
Insert	Click to open the Insert menu.
Picture. . .	Click to open the Picture menu.
From File. . .	Click to open the Insert Picture dialog box. The previously set location should still be in effect.

12. Load the picture.

4Ch3 Ferret Family Tree	Double-click this picture name to load it. Your document should look like Figure 3.49. You may have to reposition the image. Click the image to select it.

13. Add a border.

	Click to open the Format Picture dialog box.

Figure 3.47
The Drop Cap dialog box for creating a dropped capital letter.

Figure 3.48
The document with the drop cap added at the beginning.

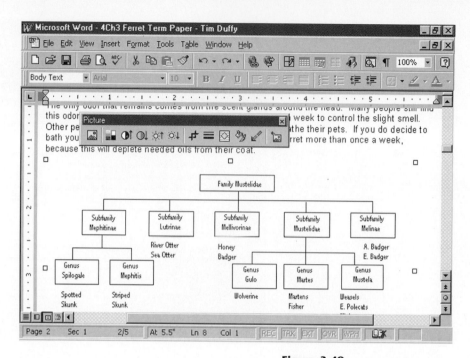

Figure 3.49
The document with the 4Ch3
Ferret Family Tree image added.

Colors and Lines Click to open this tab.

Color Click this box in the Line portion of the tab. A color palette appears.

Black Click this color.

OK Click to make the changes. Your document should look like Figure 3.50.

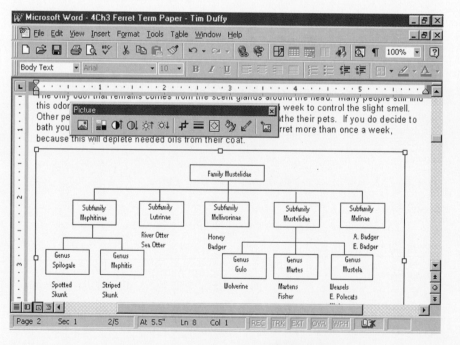

Figure 3.50
The image with the added border.

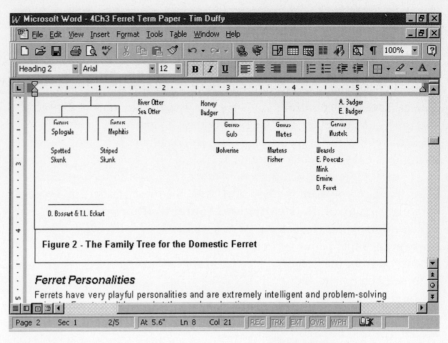

Figure 3.51
The term paper with the second graphic and caption entered.

14. **Add the caption.**

Insert   Click to open the Insert menu.

Caption. . .   Click to open the Caption dialog box.

Type: **-The Family Tree for the Domestic Ferret**   Be sure to enter a space
                        before the dash.

OK   Click to insert the caption beneath the picture.

Click   Click anywhere to turn off the selection. Your document
                        should now look like Figure 3.51.

15. **Save the document.**

Reinforcing the Exercise

1. You can use the Format Picture dialog box to add borders around selected paragraphs.

2. You can also use the Borders toolbar to shade selected paragraphs.

3. When you embed an image into a document, text initially appears above and below the image but cannot wrap around it.

4. The Format Picture dialog box controls how text wraps around an embedded image.

5. Once you have inserted a picture, you can add a caption to it.

Adding Headers and Footers   <u>V</u>iew, Header and Footer

Headers and **footers** are lines of identifying text printed below the top and above the bottom margins of multiple pages in a document, such as the document title, page number, time, or date. You can add headers and footers to a document by issuing the View, Header and Footer command sequence. Enter this command sequence only once, at the start of the file, and the header or footer will be printed on each page. You can also change headers and footers for each section of your document. By default, Word documents have no header or footer.

To create headers and footers, first move the cursor to the top of the page on which you want them to start. Issue the View, Header and Footer command sequence. The **Header and Footer toolbar** appears, and your screen will look like Figure 3.52. Word switches to Page Layout view and displays an empty pane where you enter the header or footer. The Header and Footer toolbar is displayed below the pane. Its buttons are summarized in Table 3.2. If you click the fourth toolbar button from the right, you will find that you toggle between the header and footer.

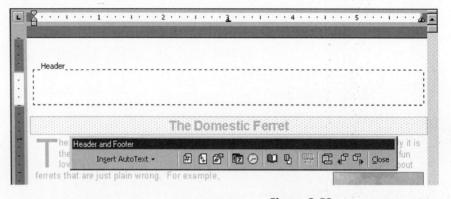

Figure 3.52
The term paper document in Page Layout view with the Header and Footer toolbar and a pane for the header displayed.

If you want a different header or footer on the first page, click the Page Setup button, click the Layout tab of the Page Setup dialog box, and select the Different First Page option. You can also indicate different headers or footers for odd and even pages.

When you are finished entering the header or footer, click the Close button on the Header and Footer toolbar. To see the placement of headers and footers as they will appear when printed, click the Page Layout button.

If the user does not specify position, by default Word prints headers in the top margin of the page, one-half inch from the edge of the paper. After the header is printed, any space left over from the header falls between the header and the document text. The last line of a footer is printed at the bottom margin of the printed page, one-half inch from the edge of the paper. Any space left over from the footer falls between the footer and document text.

If you discover an error in a header or footer or you simply want to change a header or footer, issue the View, Header and Footer command sequence. In Page Layout view, you can double-click the header or footer you want to edit.

You may not want to have a header on the first page of a document, but you may want a footer to print there. In this case, you must click the Different First Page option on the Layout tab of the Page Setup dialog box. Enter the footer for the first page. Then enter the desired footer and header on the second page.

Table 3.2 Header and Footer Toolbar Buttons

Button	Name	Function
Insert AutoText ▾	Insert AutoText	Displays a menu of options for embedding text and codes in a header or footer.
	Insert Page Number	Inserts a page number field in the header or footer.
	Insert Number of Pages	Prints the total number of pages in the document so that an entry like "Page 2 of 12" can be inserted.
	Format Page Number	Displays the Page Number Format dialog box to format the page numbers in the section or document.
	Insert Date	Inserts a date field in the header or footer.
	Insert Time	Inserts a time field in the header or footer.
	Page Setup	Changes the page setup of the selected sections.
	Show/Hide Document Text	Toggles between making the document text visible and not visible.
	Same as Previous	Makes the header or footer for this section the same as that for the previous section.
	Switch Between Header and Footer	Jumps between the header and the footer.
	Show Previous	Shows the header or footer for the previous section of the document.
	Show Next	Shows the header or footer for the next section of the document.
Close	Close	Returns to the document text.

Hands-On Exercise: Inserting a Header and Footer

Properly positioned headers and footers will make Rosa's paper look more polished.

1. **If necessary, load your personalized version of the 4Ch3 Ferret Term Paper document.** You should also be positioned at the beginning of the document.

2. **Enter the footer for the first page.**

View — Click to open the View menu.

Header and Footer — Click to open the Header and Footer toolbar and place the document in Page Layout view.

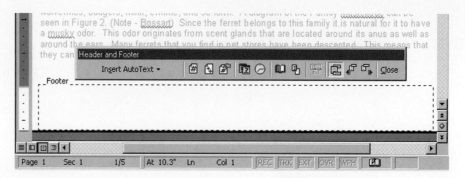

Figure 3.53
The document ready for a footer.

 Click this toolbar button to switch to the footer (Figure 3.53). Notice the tab stops for the footer in the ruler.

Type the footer text: ***Your Name - Term Paper***

 (TAB) Press twice to move to the end of the footer where the right-align tab is located.

Type: **Page -** Be sure to end with one space.

 Click this toolbar button to insert the page number as part of the footer.

3. Enter a borderline for the footer.

Click Position the mouse in the selection bar to the left of the footer and click. The entire line should be selected.

 Click the down arrow of the Border button on the Formatting toolbar. A number of boxes appear indicating where the line will be formed.

 Click this button to draw the borderline.

T I M E L Y   T I P

When you are inserting headers and footers, the toolbar may appear over the header or footer area in the document. In such a situation, you can position the pointer in the title bar and use a drag operation to move the toolbar to another area on the screen.

T I M E L Y   T I P

Word allows you to have different headers and footers for odd or even pages. To accomplish this, position the insertion point to the point in the document where you want this feature to take effect. Issue the command sequence File, Page Setup… to invoke the Page Setup dialog box. Invoke the Layout tab. Click the Different Odd and Even choice in the Headers and Footers area. Click the OK button to finish this portion of the task.

Now when you issue the View, Header and Footer command sequence, instead of seeing just header and footer boxes at the top and bottom of the page, you see Odd Page Header or Even Page Header text boxes when dealing with a header. When you see the footer, you now see Odd Page Footer or Even Page Footer text boxes. You can now enter distinct header/footer text for odd or even pages.

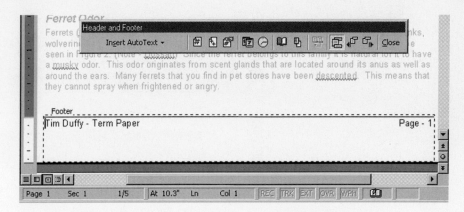

Figure 3.54
The completed footer.

4. **Copy the first page's footer text to the clipboard. Select the footer text.**

Click the Copy button to copy the footer.

Click — Click anywhere to turn off the selection. Your footer should now look like Figure 3.54.

5. **Control the display of the header.**

Click this button on the Header and Footer toolbar to open the Page Setup dialog box.

Layout — Click the Layout tab if it is not selected.

Different First Page — Click this option so that no header will print on the first page (Figure 3.55).

OK — Click to return to the document.

Copy the previous footer text to the footer pane for the first page.

6. **Enter the header for subsequent pages.**

(PGDN) — Move to the second page of the paper.

(TAB) (twice) — Move to the right-justify tab stop.

Type the header text: **The Domestic Ferret**

7. **Create a borderline beneath the header.**

Click — Position the cursor in the selection bar, and click to select the header line.

Click the down arrow portion of the Border button on the Formatting toolbar.

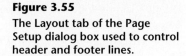

Figure 3.55
The Layout tab of the Page Setup dialog box used to control header and footer lines.

 Click to draw the borderline.

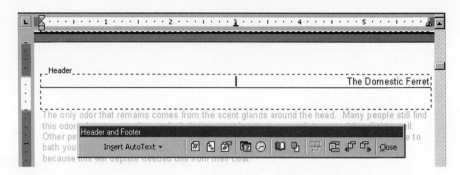

Figure 3.56
The header to be used in the document.

Click   Click anywhere to clear the selection. Your header should now look like Figure 3.56.

8. Check the changes.

Click the Close button on the Header and Footer toolbar to close the panes and toolbar and return to the document. If you are no longer in Page Layout view, click that icon to activate it.

9. Examine the document using the Print Preview feature.

10. Save the document.

Reinforcing the Exercise

1. You can create headers and footers by using the View, Headers and Footers command sequence.

2. You can use the Borders button with a header or footer.

3. The Header and Footer toolbar buttons allow you to move from one pane to another and to insert the page number, date, or time in a pane.

4. You can edit a header or footer by double-clicking it in Page Layout view.

5. You can use the Layout tab of the Page Setup dialog box to control the appearance of headers and footers in a document.

Adding Footnotes and Endnotes <u>I</u>nsert, Foo<u>t</u>note

One concern to anyone who wants to create a scholarly document is page size when **footnotes** (citations indicating the source of material used) are placed at the bottom of each page. How many lines of text should be placed on a particular page? How many footnotes can occur on a page? How many lines of print are needed for the footnotes? If you are using a typewriter, these are critical concerns, and a wrong decision means you have to retype the entire page. One solution often used to avoid these problems is to place the notes at the end of the document as **endnotes**.

Word takes care of creating footnotes and endnotes automatically and provides a professional-looking printed page. It keeps track of numbering, inserts the footnote or endnote in the proper position, and automatically calculates the number of text and footnote lines to print on each page.

To create footnotes or endnotes, you position the cursor at the appropriate location in the text and issue the Insert, Footnote command sequence. The Footnote and Endnote dialog box opens (Figure 3.57), with two Insert options, Footnote and Endnote, and two Numbering options, AutoNumber and Custom Mark. Additional options are the Options and Symbol command buttons.

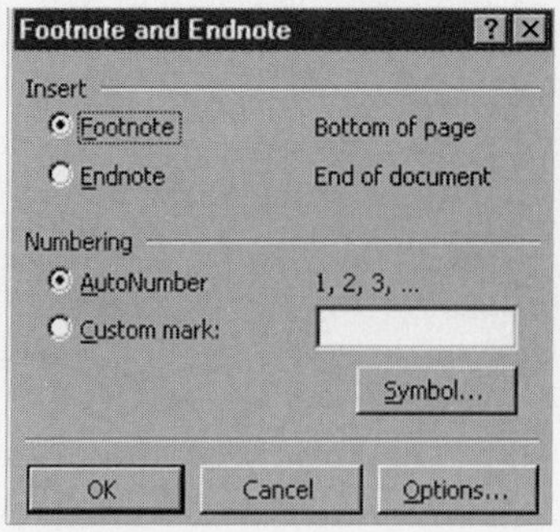

Footnote
Choose the Footnote option if you want the reference to appear at the bottom of the page.

Endnote
Choose the Endnote option if you want the reference to appear at the end of the paper.

AutoNumber
Select the AutoNumber option to have Word number the footnotes. Word will automatically insert the proper footnote number within the document. When you use this option, all footnotes are renumbered whenever a footnote is added, deleted, copied, or moved.

Options
The Options button of the Footnote and Endnote dialog box opens the Note Options dialog box (Figure 3.58). The All Footnotes tab in this dialog box controls the placement and numbering of footnotes. It also provides three numbering options. The Convert button allows you to convert footnotes to endnotes.

Remember, Word automatically inserts the footnote or endnote number, so do not try to enter the number.

Figure 3.57
The Footnote and Endnote dialog box.

Figure 3.58
The Note Options dialog box allows you to perform a number of tasks related to footnotes and endnotes.

Hands-On Exercise: Inserting Footnotes

In this exercise, you create footnotes for your personalized version of Rosa's 4Ch3 Ferret Term Paper. As you enter the footnotes, remove the text with parenthetical reminders.

1. **If necessary, load your personalized copy of the term paper.** Make certain that you are in Page Layout view.

2. **Move to the end of the second paragraph under the *Brief History* subtitle.** Erase the reminder note.

Click and drag   Include the text in the reminder.

DEL   Press to delete the selection.

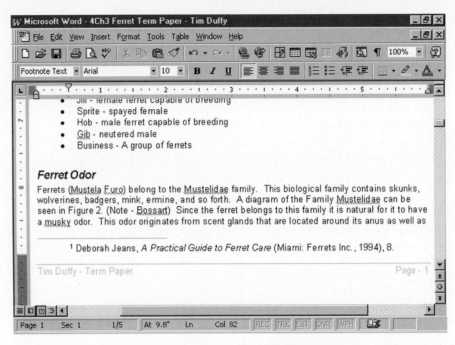

Figure 3.59
The text for the first footnote.

3. **Create the first footnote. Be sure to delete the reminder text in paren-theses before proceeding.**

Insert   Click to open the Insert menu.

Footnote. . .   Click to open the Footnote and Endnote dialog box.

AutoNumber   Check to make sure this default option is selected. If it isn't, click to have Word number the footnote.

[OK]   Click to accept the command. The insertion point is now in the footnote area at the bottom of the page.

4. **Drag the first line indent handle of the ruler to the location shown in Figure 3.59.**

5. **Enter the text of the footnote shown in Figure 3.59.**

6. **Using Figure 3.60 to Figure 3.63, enter the footnotes for the remainder of the paper. Repeat steps 2 and 3.**

7. **Print the document.**

                        Click to print the document.

8. **Save the document. Close the document.**

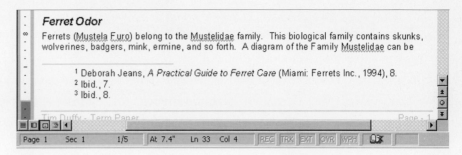

Figure 3.60
The footnotes for the first page.

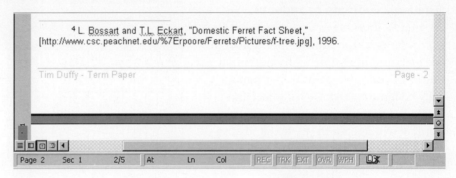

Figure 3.61
The footnote for the second page.

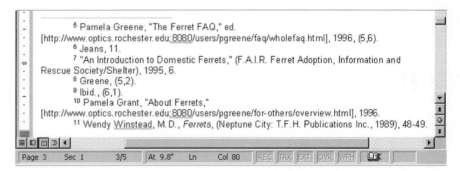

Figure 3.62
The footnotes for the third page.

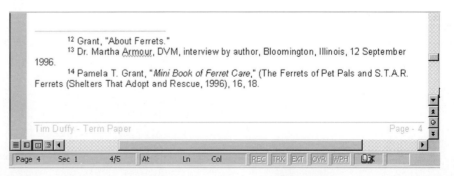

Figure 3.63
The footnotes for the fourth page.

Reinforcing the Exercise

1. You can enter notes as footnotes or endnotes.

2. Use the Insert, Footnote command sequence to enter a footnote or endnote.

3. When you use Page Layout view, notes are entered at the bottom of the page.

4. Word automatically numbers footnotes and changes numbers as footnotes are added, deleted, moved, or copied.

5. You can change footnotes to endnotes by using the Convert option in the Note Options dialog box.

Deleting a Footnote or Endnote

To delete a footnote or endnote, select the note reference (the superscript number in the text) and press (DEL). Any notes that follow in your document will automatically be renumbered. *Do not* select and delete the footnote text, or the reference number will remain in the text and automatic renumbering will not occur.

If you are in Page Layout view, you can edit footnotes or endnotes like any other text; simply move the insertion point to the footnote and make the changes.

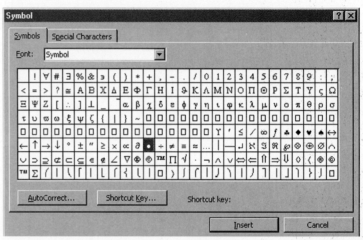

Figure 3.64
The Symbol dialog box for embedding special characters.

Inserting Symbols Insert, Symbol

Word lets you embed many special characters in a document that are not shown on the normal keyboard. Issue the Insert, Symbol command sequence to open the Symbol dialog box (Figure 3.64). The default font is the Symbol font. If you want to change to another font, click the down arrow in the Font list box to display the list of fonts (Figure 3.65), and then click the desired font.

To insert special characters such as the copyright or trademark symbol, click the Special Characters tab of the Symbol dialog box. Figure 3.66 displays all of the special characters available in Word.

To embed a character from either tab of the Symbol dialog box, double-click the desired character.

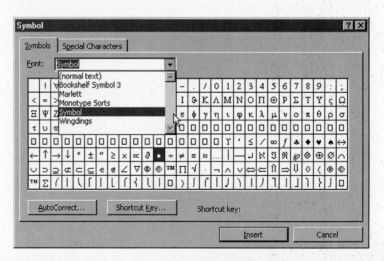

Figure 3.65
The Font list box.

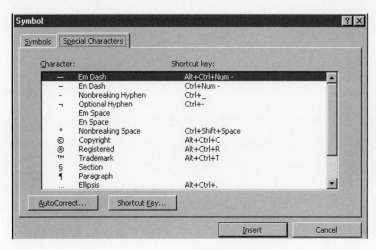

Figure 3.66
The Special Characters tab of the Symbol dialog box.

EMBEDDING AND LINKING TO OTHER APPLICATION FILES

This section requires some general familiarity with spreadsheet software. If you are completely unfamiliar with spreadsheets, you may want to come back to this section after you've learned something about them in Module 5: Microsoft Excel 97 for Windows.

Word can either embed or link data between applications that support object linking and embedding (OLE). This means you can access any Microsoft Windows application program that performs this function and embed or link to a worksheet, document, chart, or picture from another open Windows application program.

Embedding a Worksheet in a Document

You can **embed** an Excel worksheet, such as that shown in Figure 3.67, by using an Insert operation. You tell Word to import a work-

		This Year	Last Year	Change	% Change	
1	Arena Sales					
2		The Sports Center				
3						
4	Category	This Year	Last Year	Change	% Change	
5						
6	Candy	1,500.00	1,100.00	400.00	27%	
7	Popcorn	700.00	575.00	125.00	18%	
8	Sandwiches	2,875.00	2,900.00	(25.00)	-1%	
9	Soft Drinks	1,475.00	1,400.00	75.00	5%	
10	Beer/Wine	1,500.00	1,410.00	90.00	6%	
11				-		
12	Grand Total	8,050.00	7,385.00	665.00	8%	
13						
14						
15						

Figure 3.67
The 4Ch3 Arena Sales Excel worksheet, which can be embedded in a Word document.

sheet as an object, which causes Word to convert the worksheet into a table
that is automatically placed in your document, graphically illustrating the
rows and columns.

Hands-On Exercise: Embedding a Worksheet as a Table

Isabel now wants to turn her attention to preparing a progress report for her
bank. This exercise requires the Word 4Ch3 Bank Letter document and the
Excel 4Ch3 Arena Sales worksheet file, which are on your Student Data
Disk.

1. **If necessary, clear the Word screen.**

2. **Open the 4Ch3 Bank Letter document (Figure 3.68).**

3. **Use the Save As command to save the document using the name
   M4Ch3 Sample 1.**

4. **Position the insertion point at the beginning of the second blank line
   beneath the first paragraph.**

5. **Insert the 4Ch3 Arena Sales worksheet.**

Insert   Click to open the Insert menu.

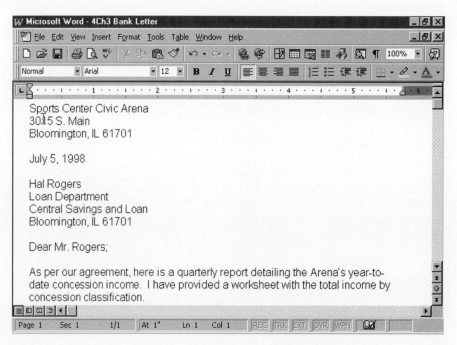

Figure 3.68
The 4Ch3 Bank Letter.

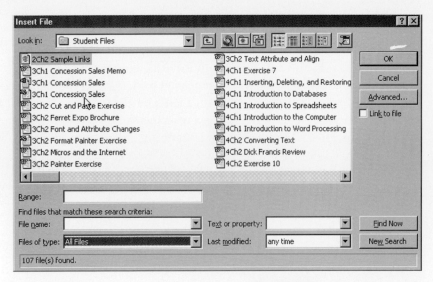

Figure 3.69
The Insert File dialog box.

Fi̱le. . .	Click to open the Insert File dialog box.
Files of t̲ype	Click to open this list box.
All Files	Click to indicate that all files are to be displayed in the dialog box. Your dialog box should look like Figure 3.69.

6. **Select the worksheet file.**

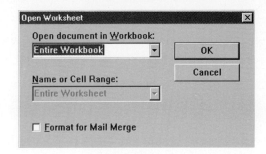

Figure 3.70
The Open Worksheet dialog box.

4Ch3 Arena Sales	Double-click this Excel file name to open the Open Worksheet dialog box (Figure 3.70).
	Click to insert the entire worksheet in the Word document. After repositioning the worksheet, your screen should look like Figure 3.71.

7. **Save the document.**

8. **Close the document.**

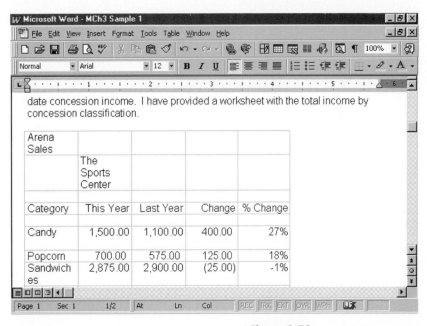

Figure 3.71
The 4Ch3 Bank Letter with the embedded 4Ch3 Arena Sales worksheet data.

Linking a Worksheet with a Document

In the previous Hands-On Exercise, the worksheet you embedded in a Word document was static text. If you were to make a change in the original worksheet, that change would not be reflected in the imported worksheet. You can, however, tell Word to establish a **link** between a worksheet and a document. Such a link lets you change a worksheet and have that change automatically reflected in a document containing linked material.

Use the Edit, Paste Special command sequence to create an automatic link. When you update the worksheet, the imported data in Word is also updated. However, this updating process can be time-consuming if you have many updates and a slow computer.

Hands-On Exercise: Linking to a Worksheet

To ensure that her report is current and accurate, Isabel wants to link her letter to an Excel worksheet. This exercise uses the Word 4Ch3 Bank Letter document and the Excel 4Ch3 Arena Sales worksheet.

1. **If necessary, clear the Word window.**

2. **Open the 4Ch3 Bank Letter document.**

3. **Use the Save As command to save the document under the name M4Ch3 Sample 2.**

4. **Position the insertion point at the beginning of the second blank line, beneath the first paragraph.**

5. **Open Excel and the 4Ch3 Arena Sales worksheet.**

   Click to open the Start menu.

   Click to open the Programs menu. If you have an Office 97 option, click that entry.

   Click to start Microsoft Excel.

   Click to open the Open dialog box. Indicate the location of your student files.

4Ch3 Arena Sales   Double-click to open the worksheet (Figure 3.72).

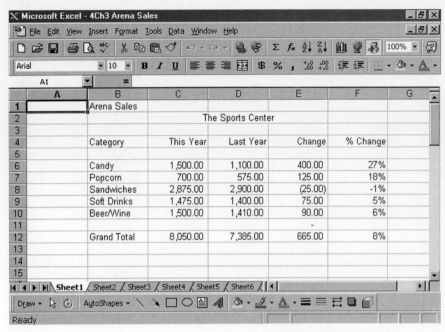

Figure 3.72
The 4Ch3 Arena Sales worksheet to be linked to the 4Ch3 Bank Letter document.

6. Select what is to be copied.

Click and drag

Using a click-and-drag operation, create the selection shown in Figure 3.73.

Click the Copy button on the Standard toolbar to copy the selected portion of the worksheet.

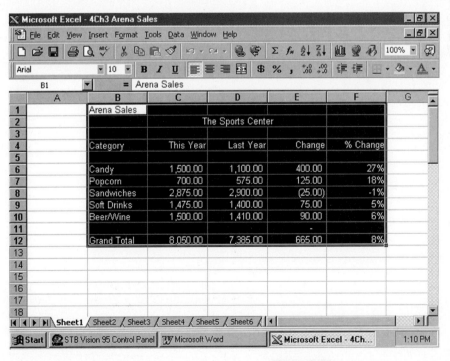

Figure 3.73
The portion of the worksheet to be copied.

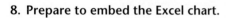 Click this application button in the taskbar to return to Word and the letter.

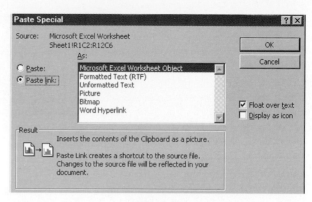

Figure 3.74
The completed Paste Special dialog box.

7. Embed the linked worksheet.

Edit   Click to open the Edit menu.

Paste Special. . .   Click to open the Paste Special dialog box shown in Figure 3.74.

O Paste link: Click to activate the link.

Microsoft Excel Worksheet Object   Click this entry to select it. The Paste Special dialog box should look like Figure 3.74.

OK   Click to complete the link. Your document should look like Figure 3.75. You can open Excel with this worksheet any time by double-clicking on one of the cells. Any time that the mouse pointer is positioned above a cell, it appears as a four-headed arrow.

8. Prepare to embed the Excel chart.

Click   Move the insertion point to the top of the second page and click.

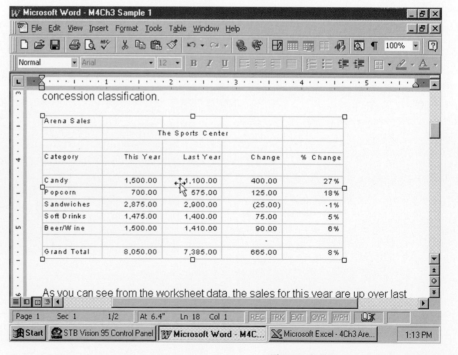

Figure 3.75
The letter with the linked worksheet.

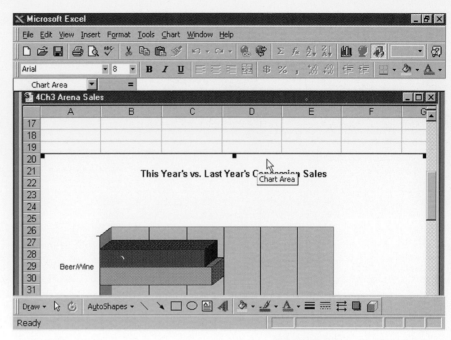

Figure 3.76
The chart selected for the link operation.

Microsoft Excel	Click this application button on the taskbar to display the Excel window.
(PGDN)	Scroll down the worksheet page to see the chart.
Click	Click anywhere on the top border of the chart to establish a selection (Figure 3.76). You should be able to see the selection handles.
	Click the Copy button of the toolbar to copy the chart to the clipboard.

9. Embed the chart.

Microsoft Word - 4(	Click to return to the Word application window.
Edit	Click to open the Edit menu.
Paste Special. . .	Click to open the Paste Special dialog box.
O Paste link	Click to activate the link. The Paste Special dialog box should look like Figure 3.77.

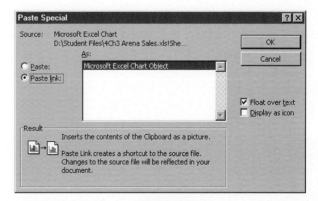

Figure 3.77
The completed Paste Special dialog box for embedding a chart.

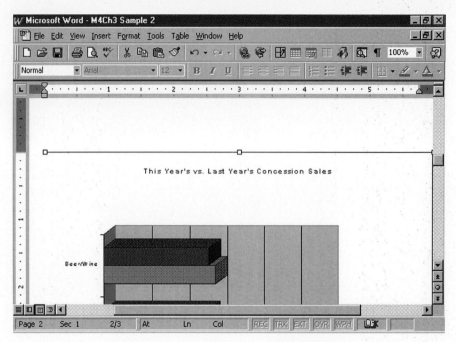

Figure 3.78
The Chart embedded in the letter.

     Click to return to the document, which has the chart embedded as shown in Figure 3.78.

10. **Print the document.**

11. **Save the document.**

12. **Close all open applications.**

Reinforcing the Exercise

1. You can embed worksheets in a document as text in a table. Embedded worksheets cannot be updated.

2. You create embedded tables by using the Insert, File command sequence.

3. You can embed a worksheet by using a Copy, Paste Special command sequence. If the Paste link option is activated, the link is established, and the worksheet can be updated.

4. You can delete an embedded object by clicking it and then pressing (DEL).

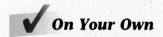 *On Your Own*

Connect to the Help feature, and then get information about the following topics.

• Examine how to create a hyperlink in a document.
• Examine how to create a Web document using Microsoft Word or other Office 97 software application.

SESSION REVIEW

Word lets you control how information appears on the page and provides flexibility in how the document is printed. These commands let you control page numbering, add bullets and numbers, and apply borders and shading. Other Word commands allow you to insert headers and footers, special symbols, footnotes and endnotes, and graphic images. You can also establish links to other applications, such as Excel worksheets.

You can also have control over how the document is formatted. If you want to Use Word defaults, the AutoFormat command will format the document. The Style gallery allows you to select from a number of stored formats that can be applied to your document.

KEY TERMS AND CONCEPTS

AutoFormat feature   4-98
border   4-108
bullet   4-99
embed   4-127
endnote   4-122

footer   4-118
footnote   4-122
header   4-118
Header and Footer toolbar   4-118
link   4-130

Picture toolbar   4-107
shading   4-108
style   4-98

SESSION QUIZ

Multiple Choice

1. Which is the default page numbering format?
   a. bottom center of every page
   b. no page numbers
   c. top alternating left and right
   d. none of the above

2. Which of the following statements concerning footnotes is false?
   a. You enter footnotes in a separate file and then combine them with your document file at print time.
   b. You can edit footnotes.
   c. In Page Layout view, you enter the footnote at the bottom of the page.

3. Which command sequence allows you to see a footer or header in Normal view?
   a. Format, Font
   b. Insert, Header and Footer
   c. Insert, Page Numbers
   d. Format, Style
   e. View, Header and Footer

4. Which of the following statements about linked worksheets is true?
   a. A worksheet can be embedded as a table in a Word document without link capabilities.
   b. The Copy and Paste commands sequence can be used to incorporate a linked worksheet in a Word document.
   c. You can open Excel by double-clicking a worksheet embedded as a text table.
   d. All of the above are true statements.

5. The commands or command sequence used to place an Excel chart in a Word document is:
   a. Copy and Paste Special
   b. Insert, Chart
   c. Layout, Chart
   d. View, Chart

True/False

6. If you want the header on the first page of a document to be blank, select the Different First Page option in the Page Setup dialog box and leave the first header blank.

7. You can see text of footnotes in Normal view.

8. Word does not allow you to change a header; rather, you must first delete the header and then reenter it.

9. Word can automatically renumber footnotes when you insert or delete a note.

10. The easiest way to include the page number in a header or footer is to click the Insert Page Numbers button of the Header and Footer toolbar.

SESSION REVIEW EXERCISES

1. Define or describe each of the following:
   a. linked worksheet
   b. header
   c. footer
   d. footnote

2. Page numbers are inserted in a document using the _____ , _____ command sequence.

3. The _____ command sequence opens the Symbol dialog box.

4. When you click the _____ option of the Insert Page Numbers dialog box, the page number does not print on the first page.

5. If you want to insert the page number into the header or footer, use the _____ button of the Header and Footer toolbar.

6. When a document is in Page Layout view, you can edit the footer or header by _____ -clicking the desired header or footer.

7. You must be in _____ _____ view when working with pictures.

8. The _____ _____ is used to control how text flows around an embedded graphic image.

9. Notes that appear at the end of the document are called _____ .

10. The _____ button of the Formatting toolbar can be used to incorporate lines in headers or footers.

11. You can open the Page Setup dialog box by clicking the _____ button on the Header and Footer toolbar.

12. A/an _____ can be placed below on embedded graphic to give that graphic some added meaning.

13. Use the _____ , _____ command sequence to view a header or footer.

14. When you first embed a picture in a document, the text appears _____ and _____ the image.

15. Clicking the _____ button on the Standard toolbar opens a list box that you can use to change the appearance of text in a document.

16. The _____ button on the Formatting toolbar opens a menu that allows you to include lines for selected text in a document.

17. The _____ button on the Standard toolbar embeds numbers in front of each paragraph included in a text selection.

18. Word's _____ feature allows you to place a dot character at the beginning of each indented line in a document.

19. You can include lines around one or more paragraphs of your document via the _____ and _____ dialog box.

20. The _____ command is used to reformat an entire document to standard styles and formats used by Word.

COMPUTER EXERCISES

1. Open the 4Ch3 Exercise 1 document (Figure 3.79). Use the Save As command to save it as M4Ch3 Exercise 1. Perform the following tasks on the newly named document:
   a. Insert the 4Ch3 Exercise 1 Excel worksheet shown in Figure 3.80 as a nonlinked table after the first paragraph.
   b. Print the document.
   c. Save the document.

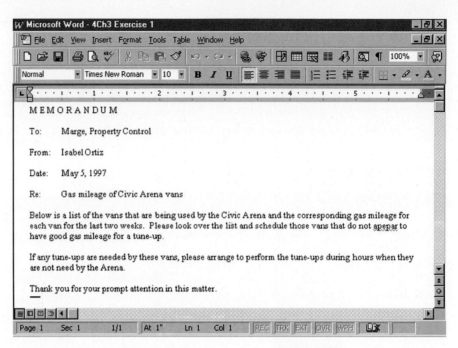

Figure 3.79
The memo in the 4Ch3 Exercise 1 document.

2. Open the 4Ch3 Exercise 1 document (Figure 3.79). Use the Save As command to save it as M4Ch3 Exercise 2. Perform the following tasks on the newly named document:

   a. Insert the 4Ch3 Exercise 1 Excel worksheet depicted in Figure 3.80 as a linked worksheet after the first paragraph using the Copy and Paste commands.

   b. Insert the chart contained in the worksheet file shown in Figure 3.81 on a new page.

   c. Print the document.

   d. Save the document.

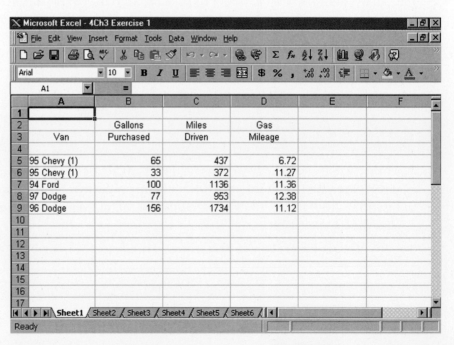

Figure 3.80
The 4Ch3 Exercise 1 worksheet.

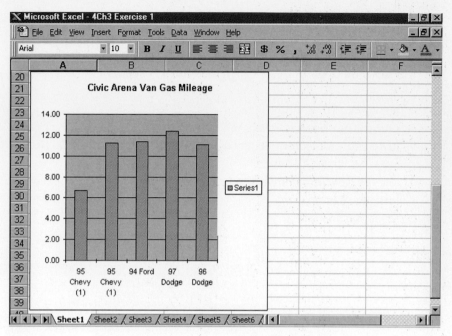

Figure 3.81
The embedded worksheet chart.

3. Open the 4Ch2 Introduction to Word Processing document. Use the Save As command to save it as M4Ch3 Exercise 3. Perform the following tasks on the newly named document:

   a. Insert a page number and center the page number at the bottom of each page. (Use the Word command that will not print the number on page 1.) Print the document.

   b. Change to Page Layout view. Select and delete the page-numbering code.

   c. Create the following header: Word Processing Report. Include this header at the top of each page.

   d. Create a footer that prints the word "Page" followed by the current page number (don't print the first page number). Print the document, and compare this printout with that from Step a.

   e. Tell Word to use 5 as the beginning page number. Print the document. Is the new numbering in effect?

   f. Save the document.

4. Clear the screen. Open the 4Ch3 Exercise 4 document. Use the Save As command to save the document as M4Ch3 Exercise 4. Perform the following tasks:

   a. Select the table title at the bottom of the page.

   b. Open the Paragraph dialog box and choose the Text Flow tab.

   c. Click the Page Break Before option. This will keep this table together so that it doesn't break at the end of the page.

   d. Print the document.

   e. Close and save the document.

5. Clear the screen. Open the M4Ch3 Exercise 3 document. Perform the following tasks:

   a. Enclose the title in a border.

   b. Shade the title box.

   c. Enclose the second and third paragraphs with a border, using a line width of 1½ points.

   d. Print the document.

   e. Close the document without saving it.

6. Clear the screen. Open the 4Ch3 Exercise 4 document.

    a. Left-justify the items in the table.

    b. Select the accounting package names.

    c. Place a number in front of each accounting package name by creating a numbered list.

    d. Place a border around the table.

    e. In the Line and Page Breaks tab of the Paragraph dialog box, choose Keep with Next to keep the table from being broken by a page break. Your document should now look like Figure 3.82.

    f. Use the Save As command to save the document as M4Ch3 Exercise 6.

    g. Print the document.

    h. Close the document.

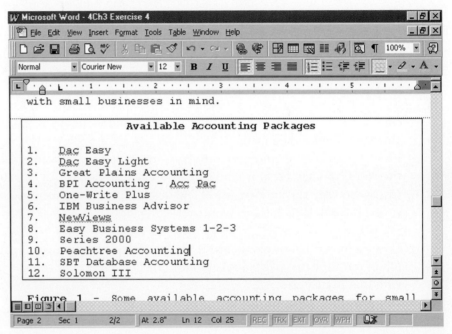

Figure 3.82
The changed table with a border.

7. Open the 4Ch3 Exercise 7 document shown in Figure 3.83. Perform the following tasks:

    a. Change the first group of indented lines to a bulleted indented list.

    b. Change the second group of indented lines to a numbered list.

    c. Use a Save As command to save the document using the name M4Ch3 Exercise 7.

    d. Print the document.

    e. Close the document.

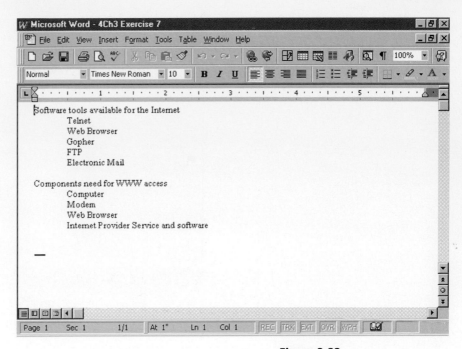

Figure 3.83
The 4Ch3 Exercise 7 document.

8. Open the document called 4Ch3 Exercise 8. Perform the following tasks on the document:

a. Open Page Layout view.

b. Create a footnote like that shown in Figure 3.84.

c. Print the document.

d. Use the Save As command to save the document as M4Ch3 Exercise 8.

e. Select the in-text footnote reference number, and press DEL. Does the footnote disappear from the bottom of the page?

f. Reverse the previous change by clicking the Undo button.

g. Close the document without saving any changes.

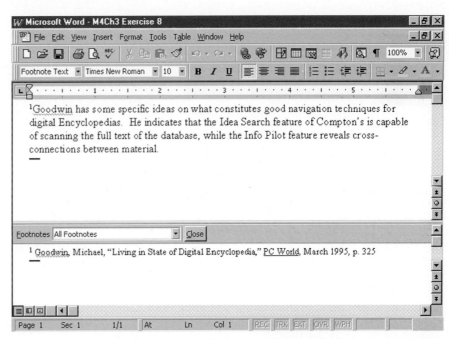

Figure 3.84
The 4Ch3 Exercise 8 document with the footnote to be inserted.

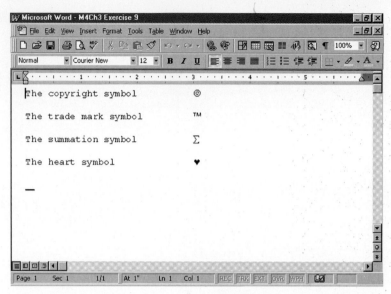

Figure 3.85
The document created using the Symbol font of the Symbol dialog box.

9. Open a blank document, and then create the document shown in Figure 3.85.
   a. Set the font to 12 pt Courier New.
   b. Use the Insert, Symbol command sequence to insert the four symbols.
   c. Print the document.
   d. Save the document as M4Ch3 Exercise 9.

10. Open the 4Ch1 Introduction to Computers document. Create a hyperlink that opens the 4Purchasing a Computer document.

INTERNET EXERCISES

1. Find out how to create a watermark in a Word document.
   a. Access the Microsoft Web page with your browser (http://www.microsoft.com).
   b. Click the Search button at the top of the Web page to open the Search page.
   c. Enter the topic *watermark* in the text box in step 1 of the Search page.
   d. Click the Support & the Knowledge Base option in step 3 of the Search page.
   e. Click the Search Now! button.
   f. On the Search Results page, click a link related to creating a watermark in Word.
   g. Use the information displayed to create a Word document with a watermark.

2. Find out how to embed a hyperlink in a Word document.
   a. Access the Microsoft Web page with your browser.
   b. Click the Search button at the top of the Web page to open the Search page.
   c. Enter the topic *create hyperlink* in the Search text box, click the Support & the Knowledge Base option, and click the Search Now! button.
   d. Look for a link related to using hyperlinks in Word97, such as WD97: General Information About Hyperlinks in Word. Such links may appear on the 2nd or 3rd pages of Search Results.
   e. Print the Web page.

Advanced Document Features of Word

After completing this session, you should be able to:

➤ Use the Columns command

➤ Use the Table feature

➤ Use the Sort feature

➤ Use the Macros feature

 Isabel's son John is a sophomore at the state university. He is majoring in information systems and wants to put together the first part of a newsletter for the Business Information Systems (BIS) club. He has two files that others have entered for the first part of the newsletter. John also wants to incorporate some clip art that comes with the Microsoft Office software suite.

Isabel wants to prepare a handout for her community college class covering a number of software suites and their corresponding application packages. She wants to include this information in a table to make it easy for her students to read.

Isabel also has two projects that she wants to accomplish related to her work with the Civic Arena. She wants to show one of the secretaries how to sort some membership information. Isabel also wants to create a macro that she can use to generate some letterhead stationery that she can use for day-to-day correspondence.

This session introduces a number of advanced document features of Word: columns, tables, sorting, and macros. These features provide tremendous flexibility and power for many tasks, such as creating reports, lists, and tables. You will learn how to use these features as you complete the exercises in this session.

USING THE COLUMNS COMMAND

Format, Columns or

Word can create two types of columns: newspaper and parallel. **Newspaper columns** are the type you find in newspapers and newsletters, where the text "snakes" from the top of a column to the bottom of the column and then back to the top of the next column. **Parallel columns** are best used for lists, tables, or any text or numbers that you want to keep aligned. These types of columns are discussed in more detail in the section on tables later in this session. The discussion in this section focuses on newspaper columns.

Newspaper columns are most frequently used for club or organization newsletters. Word's Columns feature allows text to flow from one column to the next on a page.

The Format, Columns command sequence opens the Columns dialog box shown in Figure 4.1. The dialog box has seven option areas: Presets, Number of columns, Line between, Width and spacing, Equal column width, Apply to (Whole document or This point forward), and Start new column. The Preview box shows the effects the selected options have on your document.

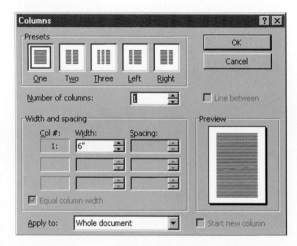

Figure 4.1
The Columns dialog box.

Editing Columnar Text

Editing columnar text requires cursor movement within and between columns. Use regular cursor movement commands to move the cursor within a column. To move most easily from one column to the next, use the mouse and any applicable scroll bar.

TIMELY TIP

Although you can also use the Columns button of the Standard toolbar to create columns, this command does not enable you to start columns at a specific location in the document. Instead, it places the entire document in columnar format.

Hands-On Exercise: Creating a Newsletter

For this exercise, you will help John create the newsletter shown in Figure 4.2. Others who have worked on the newsletter have placed some introductory information in a file called 4Ch4 Newsletter Introduction and the information for the first article in the file 4Ch4 Newsletter Text. Your responsibility is to take these two documents and create the newsletter. You will insert the text of the first document and then define columns and insert the text of the second document. Start this exercise using a blank Word document.

The text contained in the 4Ch4 Newsletter Text document is from the original 4Ch2 Introduction to Word Processing document. The Format, Paragraph command sequence has been used to make several changes to this document for this application:

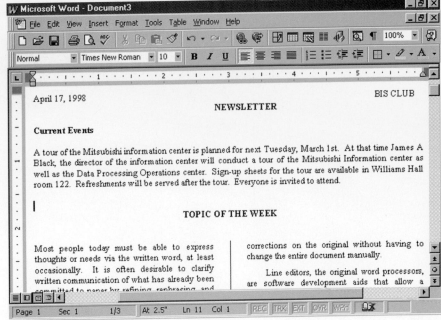

Figure 4.2
The Newsletter to be created.

- The title has been deleted.

- The Paragraph headings have been deleted.

- The font and type size have been changed to Times Roman 10 pt.

- A 6 pt line has been placed after each paragraph.

- Except for the first paragraph, each paragraph has been indented 0.3 inch.

- The alignment has been changed to justified.

1. **Insert the 4Ch4 Newsletter Introduction document from your student data files.** You will be using an Insert, File command to leave the original file unchanged. Start with a blank document on the screen in Normal view.

Insert   Click to open the Insert menu.

File . . .   Click to open the Insert File dialog box (Figure 4.3), which lists the titles you have given the files you have saved. Indicate the location of your student data files.

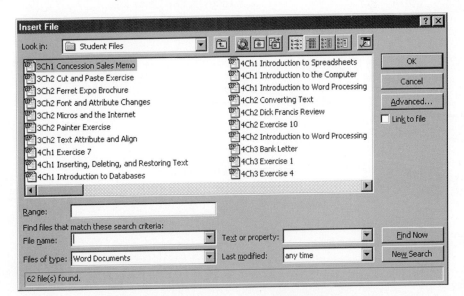

Figure 4.3
The Insert File dialog box.

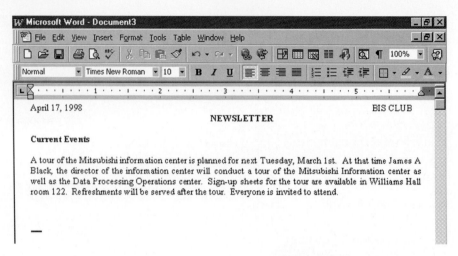

Figure 4.4
The introduction to the newsletter opened and inserted.

4Ch4 Newsletter Introduction	Double-click the file to load it into the blank document (Figure 4.4). The insertion point should be at the end of the inserted document.
	Click to center the line you are about to create.
B	Click to turn on boldfacing.

Type the heading: **TOPIC OF THE WEEK**

B	Click again to turn off boldfacing.
(ENTER)	Press three times to insert two blank lines.
≡	Click to turn on full justification.

2. **Create the columns.**

Format	Click to open the Format menu.
Columns. . .	Click to open the Columns dialog box (Figure 4.5).
Two	Click this item under the Presets option to create two columns in the newsletter.
Line between	Click to insert a vertical line between columns.
Apply to:	Click this list box or its down arrow to display the options.

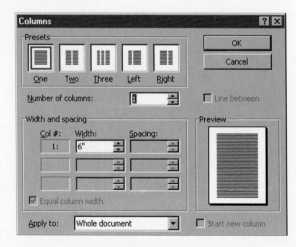

Figure 4.5
The Columns dialog box.

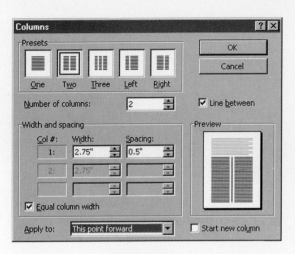

Figure 4.6
The completed dialog box for creating the newsletter columns.

This point forward	Click this option. Your Columns dialog box should now look like Figure 4.6.
OK	Click to return to the document. Word has now switched to Page Layout view. The columns are on, and the cursor is at the bottom of the document (Figure 4.7). Notice the rulers and the defined column entries.

3. **Insert the 4Ch4 Newsletter Text file into the document.**

Insert	Click to open the Insert menu.
File . . .	Click to open the File dialog box.
4Ch4 Newsletter Text	Double-click to insert the file. You are now positioned at the end of the document. You should see just one column of text (Figure 4.8). Notice that the ruler shows the columns.

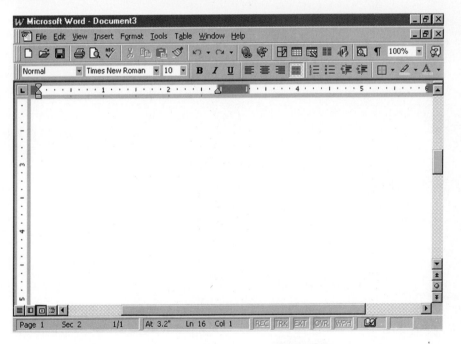

Figure 4.7
The Newsletter with the columns set up and ready to receive the 4Ch4 Newsletter Text document.

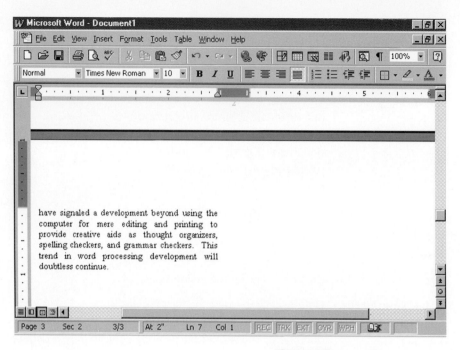

Figure 4.8
The newsletter after inserting
the text.

TIMELY TIP

If you incorrectly define your columns and your document is now a mess, click the Undo button get rid of the columns.

4. **Examine the newsletter.**

     CTRL + HOME   Press to move the insertion point to the beginning of the document.

     ↓   Press the down arrow key until the screen looks like Figure 4.9.

     CTRL + END   Press to move to the end of the document.

     PGUP   Press to move to the top of the last page. Notice that there are no lines in the second column (Figure 4.10).

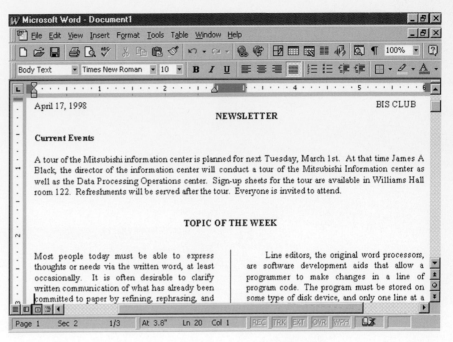

Figure 4.9
The beginning of the newsletter.

5. **Balance the length of the two columns.**

    CTRL + END   Press to go to the bottom of the newsletter.

Insert   Click to open the Insert menu.

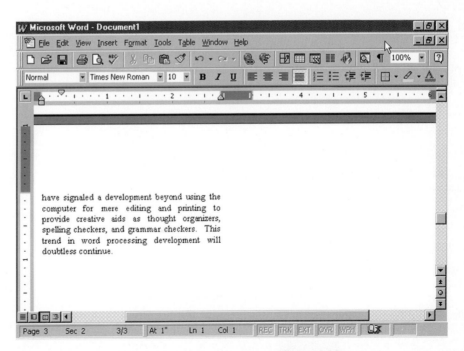

Figure 4.10
The last page of the newsletter
with an unequal number of lines
in the two columns.

Break . . .   Click to open the Break dialog box (Figure 4.11).

Continuous   Click to specify a continuous section break.

OK   Click to make the change. The newsletter should now look like Figure 4.12.

Figure 4.11
The Break dialog box for controlling the flow of text on a page.

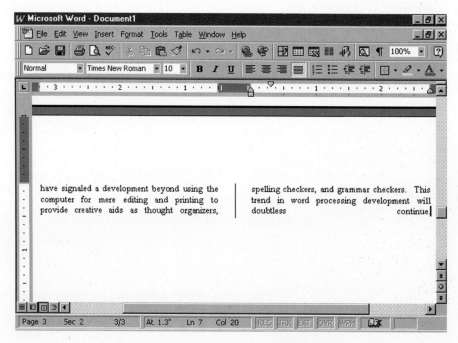

Figure 4.12
The columns at the end of the document are now equal in length.

Reinforcing the Exercise

1. The Format, Columns command sequence allows you to start a table anywhere, whereas the Columns button does not provide this type of control.

2. The Presets options in the Columns dialog box make it easier to insert a number of different column types.

3. You use Page Layout view to see the document with the text columns visible.

4. You can place lines between text columns.

5. You can use the Insert, Break command sequence to control how text aligns at the end of columns.

Adding Clip Art

Office contains a library of graphics called **clip art** that you can access and place in a document. Like the pictures you used in the previous session, you can add clip art to a document and have text flow around it. You access clip art through the Microsoft Clip Gallery 3.0 dialog box, which is available to every Office application program via the Insert, Picture, Clip Art command sequence.

Hands-On Exercise: Accessing and Manipulating Clip Art

1. **Insert a piece of clip art from the Office Clip Art Gallery.**

`CTRL` + `HOME`	Press to move to the beginning of the document.
`PGDN`	Press this key twice to reposition the insertion point.
Insert	Click to open the Insert menu.
Picture	Click this option from the Insert menu.
Clip Art. . .	Click to open the Microsoft Clip Gallery 3.0 dialog box (Figure 4.13). If necessary, click the Clip Art tab.
Academic	Click this clip art category in the list box on the left side of the dialog box.
Click	Scroll down the box of clip art until the Hand Writing piece shown in Figure 4.14 is visible.

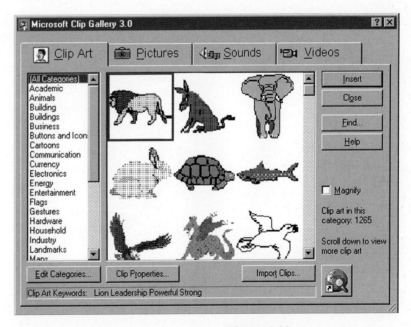

Figure 4.13
The Microsoft Clip Gallery 3.0 dialog box with the Clip Art tab activated. Yours may look different.

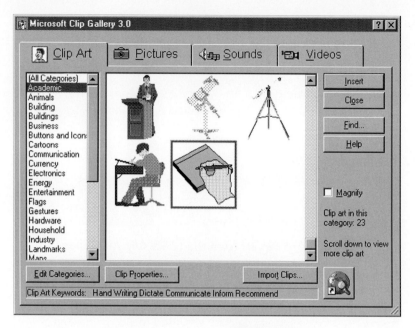

Figure 4.14
The Academic clip art category
with the desired figure visible.

Double-click

Double-click the Hand Writing clip art to insert it in the
document (Figure 4.15). Notice that the Picture toolbar is
displayed. You can drag this toolbar out of your way if
necessary.

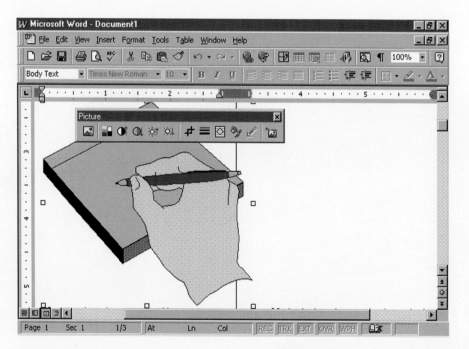

Figure 4.15
The inserted Hand Writing piece
of clip art.

2. **Reposition and resize the clip art in your document.**

Drag

Use the resize handles to resize and position the piece of clip art to the location shown in Figure 4.16.

3. **Change the text flow.**

Click this button of the Picture toolbar to open the Format Picture dialog box.

Wrapping

Click to open the Wrapping tab.

Square

Click the Square option of the Wrapping Style portion of the dialog box.

Left

Click the Left option of the Wrap to portion of the dialog box.

OK

Click to make the changes. Your document should look like Figure 4.17.

4. **Enter the caption for the clip art.** Make certain that the image is still selected.

Insert

Click to open the Insert menu.

Caption. . .

Click to open the Caption dialog box (Figure 4.18).

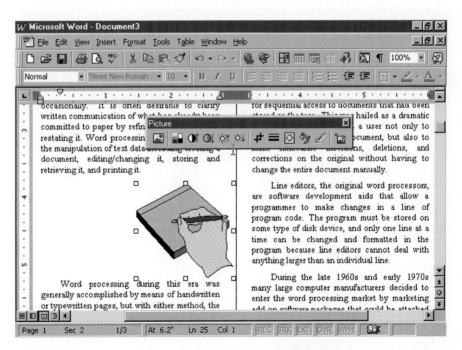

Figure 4.16
The Hand Writing clip art resized and repositioned in the document.

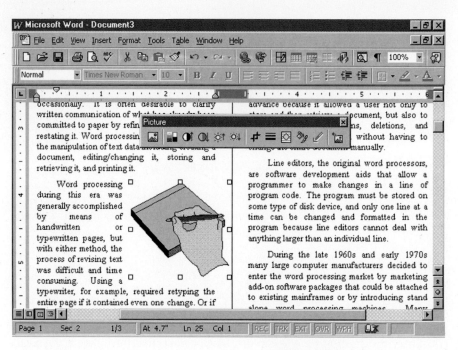

Figure 4.17
The text adjusted to flow around the piece of clip art.

Type: -**Word processing originally involved the use of pencil and paper.**
                          Enter the caption text. Be sure to place a space before
                          and after the leading dash. Insert the caption.

OK   Click to return to the document. All of the text does not
                          fit in the caption box.

Drag   Drag the lower-middle resize handle down until all of the
                          text fits. Your newsletter, with text under the caption,
                          should look like Figure 4.19. If necessary move the cap-
                          tion box.

5. **Change the flow of text around the caption.**

Format   Click to open the Format menu.

Text Box. . .   Click to open the Format Text Box dialog
                          box.

Wrapping   Click to open the Wrapping tab.

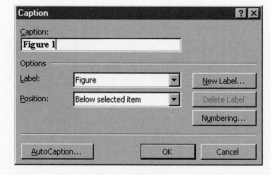

Figure 4.18
The Caption dialog box.

Square   Click the Square option of the Wrapping
                          Style portion of the dialog box.

Left   Click the Left option of the Wrap to portion of the
                          dialog box.

OK   Adjust the text.

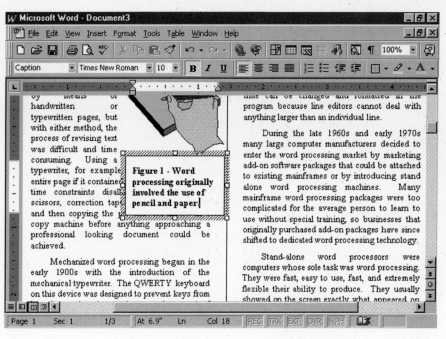

Figure 4.19
The figure with the embedded caption. Notice that text still lies under it.

Click — Click anywhere to turn off the selection. Your document should look like Figure 4.20.

6. Embed the second piece of clip art.

PGDN — Press this key four times to move through the document.

Click — Click at the beginning of the paragraph that begins *Until the 1980s.*

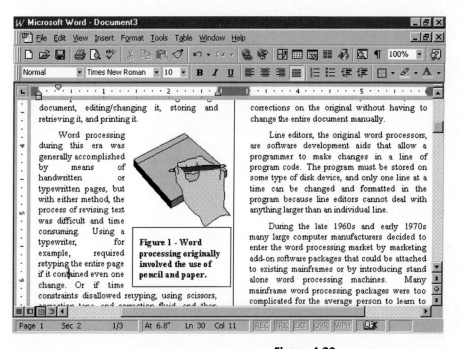

Figure 4.20
The text adjusted to flow around the caption.

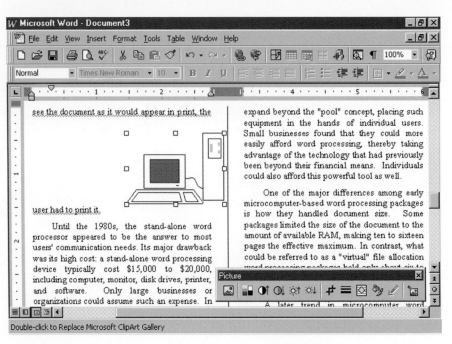

Figure 4.21
The document with the Generic Computer 2 positioned and re-sized.

7. **Repeat steps 1 and 2 to embed the Generic Computer 2 clip art found in the** *Science and Technology* **section in the document and resize it.** Your document should look like Figure 4.21.

8. **Repeat step 3 to change the flow of text around the picture.**

9. Type the caption: - **Computers have made word processing more efficient.**

   Flow the text around the caption. If necessary move the caption box. Your final product should look like Figure 4.22.

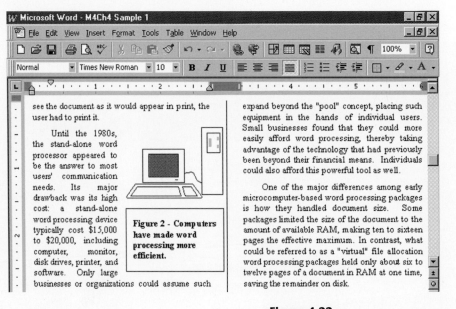

Figure 4.22
The second clip art figure with the embedded caption.

10. **Turn off the Columns feature.**

`CTRL` + `END`   Press to position the insertion point after the section break.

Format   Click to open the Format menu.

Columns. . .   Click to open the Columns dialog box.

One   Click this Presets option.

`OK`   Click to return to the document. You can now continue entering the newsletter in single-column mode.

11. **Save the document as M4Ch4 Sample 1.**

12. **Print the newsletter.**

13. **Close the document.**

 **On Your Own**

Create a small quotation that can be placed in a text box in the newsletter.

- Type a line or two of text related to word processing.
- Save it to disk.
- Create a text box at an appropriate place in the newsletter.
- Use the Insert, File command sequence to load the document into the text box.

Reinforcing the Exercise

1. Clip art is a library of graphics you can access within any Office application.

2. You access clip art by issuing the Insert, Picture, Clip Art command sequence.

3. The Microsoft Clip Gallery 3.0 dialog box is the source for Office clip art, which is organized in several different categories, such as Academic, Business, and Maps.

4. After you add a piece of clip art, the Picture toolbar appears on the screen. You can use the Format Picture button on the Picture toolbar to change the flow of text around clip art.

5. To add a caption under a clip art piece, the image must be selected.

USING THE TABLE FEATURE   <u>T</u>able, <u>I</u>nsert Table or

Microsoft Word allows you to organize data in tabular format (see Session 2 of this module) and in columnar format. You can use tables to display text horizontally, that is, side by side in parallel columns.

A **table** is a grid of rows and columns. You can use a table for price lists, inventory lists, income statements, sales forecasts, budgets, or almost anything that can be constructed by a spreadsheet such as Microsoft Excel.

Word's **Table feature** lets you create columns to enter text that aligns with parallel columns across the page. Unlike text in newspaper columns, which snakes from the bottom of one column to the top of the next, text in a table format continues to flow down the same column, even if that column extends onto another page.

Figure 4.23 shows the table that Isabel wants to create for her class. This table uses four columns to compare different software suites that were available for the Windows environment in early 1996. The first column contains the name of the software suite, the second contains the manufacturer's name, the third contains the names of the different modules, and the fourth contains the bit sizes of the software. (As a general rule, the bit size indicates whether or not the software is capable of supporting all of the features available in the Windows 97 environment.)

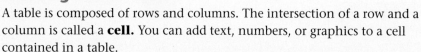

Some Common Software Suites Available in Early 1996			
Software Suite	Manufacturer	Application Modules	Bit Size of Software
Office 95	Microsoft	Excel 7.0	32 bit
		Word 7.0	32 bit
		PowerPoint 7.0	32 bit
		Access 7.0	32 bit
		Schedule +	32 bit
		Exchange 4.0	32 bit
Office Pro 4.3	Microsoft	Excel 5.0	16 bit
		Word 6.0	16 bit
		PowerPoint 4.0	16 bit
		Access 2.0	16 bit
Perfect Office	Novell	Quattro Pro 5.0	16 bit
		WordPerfect 6.0	16 bit
		Presentations	16 bit
		Envoy	16 bit
		InfoCentral	16 bit
		GroupWise	16 bit
SmartSuite 96	Lotus Corporation	Lotus 1-2-3 Release 5	16 bit
		Word Pro	32 bit
		Freelance Graphics 96	32 bit
		Organizer 2.1	16 bit
		Approach 96	32 bit

Figure 4.23
The table containing the software suites comparison.

Creating Tables

A table is composed of rows and columns. The intersection of a row and a column is called a **cell.** You can add text, numbers, or graphics to a cell contained in a table.

Using the Insert Table button on the Standard toolbar is the easiest way to create a table because the column widths are set automatically.

Entering Data in a Table

As you enter text in a cell that extends beyond the right margin, the text wraps to the next line in the cell. The cell expands downward to accommodate the text.

When you have finished entering text or numbers in one cell and wish to enter information in the next cell, press (TAB) to move to the next cell. To move backward through the cells, press (SHIFT) + (TAB). To begin a new line in a cell, press (ENTER).

Enhancing and Editing the Appearance of a Table

To produce professional-looking tables, you can format the text and the cells within a

TIMELY   TIP

Once you have inserted a table in your document, you can resize the column width by placing the mouse pointer over the column border until it becomes a double-arrow shape and then dragging the column border to the desired width.

table just as you format text in the body of a document. The AutoFormat entry of the Table menu allows you to apply a number of standard Word formats to your table. You can also use the Borders toolbar button to add lines. To use the Borders command, you first need to select the cells, rows, or columns you want affected.

T I M E L Y   T I P

You can use the mouse to click the cell where you want the insertion point to appear. If you need to add a row at the end of the table, press TAB after reaching the last cell in the table (the lower-right cell).

Hands-On Exercise: Using the Table Feature

For her class, Isabel wants to create the table shown in Figure 4.23. If necessary, first clear the screen and then set the font to 10 pt Times Roman.

1. Enter the title.

                                Click to issue the Center command.

Type the title: **Some Common Software Suites Available in Early 1996**

ENTER   Press twice to insert a blank line.

                                Click to return to left alignment.

2. Create a table.

                                Click this button on the Standard toolbar to display the object menu shown in Figure 4.24.

Click   Click the button that gives you four columns and four rows. The table is now created (Figure 4.25). Notice that lines appear around the cells. These lines will appear when the table prints. Once you insert a table and place the insertion point in it, the Insert Table button changes to an Insert Rows button.

                                Click to insert the needed fifth row in the table.

Figure 4.24
The menu displayed when you click the Insert Table button of the toolbar.

3. Enter the text for the column headings in row 1.

Click   Click the first cell to turn off the selection.

Type the column title: **Software Suite**

TAB   Press to move to column 2.

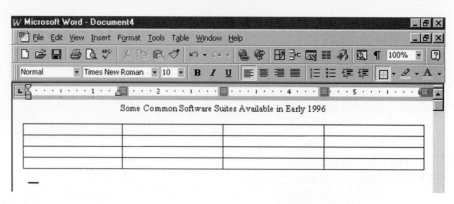

Figure 4.25
The empty 4x4 table.

Type: **Manufacturer**

TAB   Press to move to column 3.

Type: **Application Modules**

TAB   Press to move to column 4.

Type: **Bit Size of Software**

TAB   Press to go to the first cell of the next row.

4. **Using Figure 4.23 as a guide, enter the rest of the table text.** Be sure to press TAB to move to the next column. If you need to return to a previous column, press SHIFT + TAB. Press ENTER to go to the next line within a cell. Remember to press TAB when the insertion point is in the last cell of the table when you want to begin a new row.

5. **Use the Save As command to save the table as M4Ch4 Sample 2.**

6. **Your table should now look like that shown in Figure 4.26.** Notice that the special visual enhancements shown in Figure 4.23 still remain to be added.

7. **Print the table.** Notice that the lines do appear around the cells of the table.

8. **Format the appearance of the table.** Make certain that the insertion point is positioned in a table cell.

Table   Click to open the Table menu.

T I M E L Y   T I P

If you inadvertently press ENTER instead of TAB in a cell, a blank line is embedded in that table row. To delete this blank line, press BKSP.

Some Common Software Suites Available in Early 1996			
Software Suite	Manufacturer	Application Modules	Bit Size of Software
Office 95	Microsoft	Excel 7.0	32 bit
		Word 7.0	32 bit
		PowerPoint 7.0	32 bit
		Access 7.0	32 bit
		Schedule +	32 bit
		Exchange 4.0	32 bit
Office Pro 4.3	Microsoft	Excel 5.0	16 bit
		Word 6.0	16 bit
		PowerPoint 4.0	16 bit
		Access 2.0	16 bit
Perfect Office	Novell	Quattro Pro 5.0	16 bit
		WordPerfect 6.0	16 bit
		Presentations	16 bit
		Envoy	16 bit
		InfoCentral	16 bit
		GroupWise	16 bit
SmartSuite 96	Lotus Corporation	Lotus 1-2-3 Release 5	16 bit
		Word Pro	32 bit
		Freelance Graphics 96	32 bit
		Organizer 2.1	16 bit
		Approach 96	32 bit

Figure 4.26
The completed text for the table.

Table AutoFormat. . . Click to open the Table AutoFormat dialog box (Figure 4.27). Notice that it defaults to Simple 1 (which is how your table was built).

Classic 2 Click this format from the Formats list (Figure 4.28). Notice that a sample table appears in the Preview box.

OK Click to complete the command and return to the document. Your table should now look like that shown in Figure 4.29.

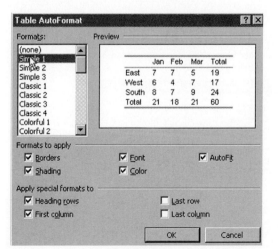

Figure 4.27
The Table AutoFormat dialog box for controlling the appearance of your table.

TIMELY TIP

The Table and Borders toolbar (activated using the View, Toolbars, Tables and Borders command sequence) provide for additional formatting of tables. For instance, the Align Top, Center Vertically, and Align Bottom buttons provide you with better control over how text appears within a cell. The Change Text Direction rotates text 90 degrees in a selected cell(s).

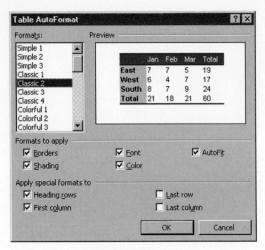

Figure 4.28
The Classic 2 table format.

TIMELY TIP

You can merge the contents of selected table cells to the upper-left-hand cell of the selection by taking the Merge Cells command from the Table pull-down menu.

You can also use the Cell Height and Width option of this menu to control the height and width of table rows and columns. This command is especially helpful because it allows you to shrink the height of table rows that must be contained on one page and currently "drift" over to the next page in a document.

9. **Insert borderlines.**

Drag   Click and drag to select all rows of the table.

                        Click to open the Borders menu.

                        Click to place lines around all cells in the table.

Click   Click anywhere to deselect the table. Your table should
                        look like Figure 4.30.

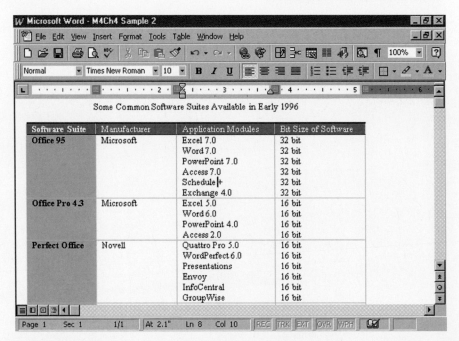

Figure 4.29
The newly formatted table.

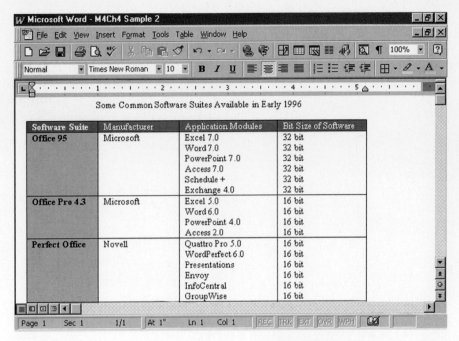

Figure 4.30
The completed table.

10. **Print the table.** Compare the results of the two print operations. Which table is more readable?

11. **Close and save the table document as M4Ch4 Sample 2.**

Reinforcing the Exercise

1. Each element in a table is called a cell. A cell can hold numbers, text, or a graphic.

2. The lines that automatically appear in a table don't print.

3. You can use the Insert Table toolbar button to create a table.

4. Once you have created a table, the Insert Table button becomes an Insert Row button.

5. You can use the Table, Table AutoFormat command sequence to control the appearance of a table.

6. You can use the Borders command to insert printable lines in a table.

TIMELY TIP

Tables can be useful for many different applications. They can, for instance, be invaluable for building a columnar-oriented résumé like the one shown in Figure 4.31. If you want to examine this résumé more closely, you can open the 4Ch4 Davis Sample Resume file, which is stored on the Web site for this book.

This résumé's light gray lines will not print. It has had the (none) AutoFormat option applied to it.

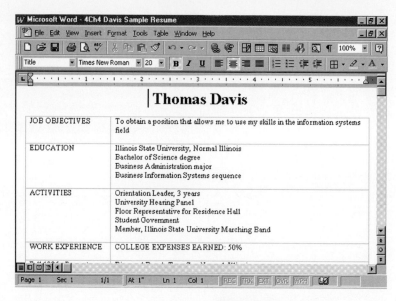

Figure 4.31
The sample résumé built using the table feature of Word, which you can access from the Web site for this text.

SORTING TEXT **T**a**ble, S**ort

To sort text, you first select the material you want to sort and then enter the command sequence Table, Sort. The Sort Text dialog box opens as shown in Figure 4.32.

You can sort by paragraphs or by field numbers. The sort types available are Text, Numeric, or Date. The sort order options are Ascending (smallest to largest, or A to Z) and Descending (largest to smallest, or Z to A). If your text doesn't contain a header row (column heading or caption), the No header row option is automatically selected in the My list has group. If your text has headings that you don't want to include in the sort, select the Header row option in the My list has group.

 **On Your Own**

Word 97 has a fun feature called Table Draw. This feature provides you with tremendous control in building tables. Some other interesting features related to tables include the following:

- The Tables and Borders button opens a toolbar of that name that provides a number of features and capabilities.
- It allows you to build a table using the freehand pencil. You can also add columns and rows using the pencil or erase a column or row using the eraser.
- Open the Clippit Office Assistant, and ask it about tables. Examine some of the Help screens. Find out about the new Table Draw feature.
- Ask Clippit about table math. Find out how to embed calculations in a table. For instance, you can generate a column sum by entering the command =sum(above) in the bottom cell of a column.
- Try generating a table that makes use of some of these features.

When the selected data (such as name, address, city, state, and zip code) are separated by something other than commas or tabs, click the Options command button in the Sort Text dialog box. The Sort Options dialog box appears as shown in Figure 4.33. Click the appropriate options under the Separate fields at group. If the data is separated by a character other than a tab or comma, select the Other option and enter the character.

Figure 4.34 shows the 4Ch4 Names List document, with names and addresses that could be sorted in various ways (for example, by last name or by zip code).

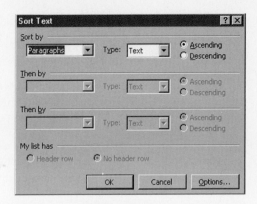

Figure 4.32
The Sort Text dialog box.

Entering and Sorting Text

How you enter text plays an important role in how Word sorts that text. Each segment of text separated by a comma or a tab is considered a separate **field.** Because Word uses this method, you must carefully plan your document and correctly enter the data. For example, if you are using columns of text without using the Table feature, enter those columns using tab stops rather than spaces. The document shown in Figure 4.34 (4Ch4 Names List) was created by pressing (TAB) to advance from one field to the next (note the tab stops in the ruler). Notice also that a field can contain several words.

If you select Paragraphs to sort by, the sort is applied to the text, number, or date that is contained in the first column. If you want to sort another column in ascending or descending order, select the particular field number (Field 2, Field 3, and so on) from the Sort by list box in the Sort Text dialog box.

A **key** is the entity (field or word) by which the text is to be sorted. For example, if you selected all the records (rows) in Figure 4.34 for sorting and you wanted to use Zip as the key field, you would choose Field 6 in the Sort by list box (Zip is the sixth field).

Figure 4.33
The Sort Options dialog box for controlling the field separators for a sort operation.

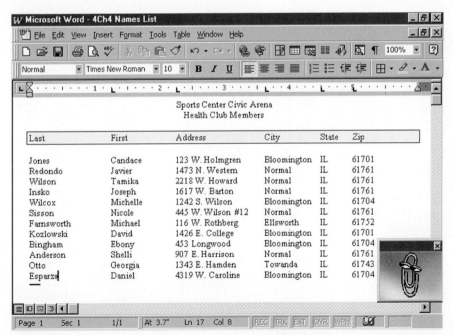

Last	First	Address	City	State	Zip
Jones	Candace	123 W. Holmgren	Bloomington	IL	61701
Redondo	Javier	1473 N. Western	Normal	IL	61761
Wilson	Tamika	2218 W. Howard	Normal	IL	61761
Insko	Joseph	1617 W. Barton	Normal	IL	61761
Wilcox	Michelle	1242 S. Wilson	Bloomington	IL	61704
Sisson	Nicole	445 W. Wilson #12	Normal	IL	61761
Farnsworth	Michael	116 W. Rothberg	Ellsworth	IL	61752
Kozlowski	David	1426 E. College	Bloomington	IL	61701
Bingham	Ebony	453 Longwood	Bloomington	IL	61704
Anderson	Shelli	907 E. Harrison	Normal	IL	61761
Otto	Georgia	1343 E. Hamden	Towanda	IL	61743
Esparza	Daniel	4319 W. Caroline	Bloomington	IL	61704

Figure 4.34
The 4Ch4 Names List document.

Hands-On Exercise: Sorting Names and Addresses

For the following exercise, clear the screen and open the file 4Ch4 Names List document. Isabel first wants to sort the name and address records of members of the sports center health club by last name. This will sort the last names in alphabetical order.

1. **Position the insertion point to the left of the first record (for Candace Jones), and click and drag to select the entire table.**

2. **Specify the sort by last name.** This will sort the last names in alphabetical order.

Ta̲ble	Click to open the Table menu.
Sort. . .	Click to to open the Sort Text dialog box (Figure 4.35). Make certain that the entries that appear in Figure 4.35 also appear on your dialog box. You should not have to make any changes.
OK	Click to perform the sort.
Click	Click anywhere to deselect the text. The records in your document should be in the alphabetical order shown in Figure 4.36. Because of the default (sorting on the first field) used by Word, you didn't have to specify any special instructions for this first sort operation.

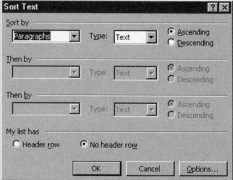

Figure 4.35
The Sort Text dialog box for the first sort operation.

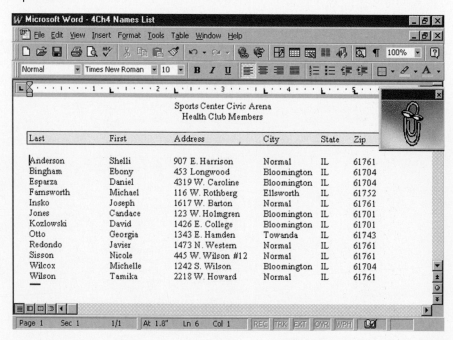

Figure 4.36
The contents of the name list sorted alphabetically by last name.

3. **Sort the City field in descending order.** Move to the left of the first record (for Shelli Anderson), and select the entire table.

Ta̲ble	Click to open the Table menu.
S̲ort. . .	Click to open the Sort Text dialog box.
▼	Click the down arrow of the Sort By list box to see the options shown in Figure 4.37.
Field 4	Click to sort by field number 4 (City).
O D̲escending	Click to sort in descending order.
OK	Click to perform the sort.
Click	Click anywhere to deselect the text. The records in your document should be in the order shown in Figure 4.38.

Figure 4.37
The options of the Sort by list box.

4. **Sort the zip codes in ascending order.** Position the insertion point to the left of the first record (for Georgia Otto), and select the entire table.

Ta̲ble	Click to open the Table menu.
S̲ort. . .	Click to open the Sort Text dialog box.
▼	Click the down arrow of the Sort by list box to open a list of fields.
Field 6	Click to sort by field number 6 (Zip).

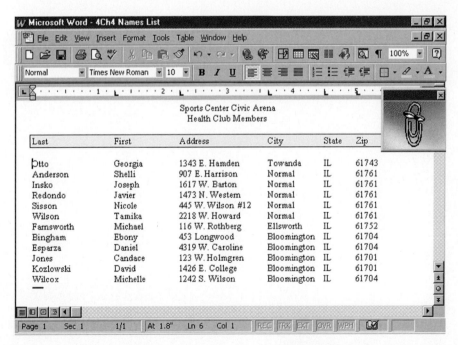

Figure 4.38
The lines sorted in alphabetically descending order by city name.

O <u>A</u>scending	Click to sort in ascending order.
[OK]	Click to perform the sort.
Click	Click anywhere to deselect the text. The records in your document should be in the order shown in Figure 4.39.

5. **Sort the lines first by city and then also by last name in ascending order.** Position the insertion point to the left of the first record (for Candace Jones), and select the entire table.

T<u>a</u>ble	Click to open the Table menu.
<u>S</u>ort. . .	Click to open the Sort Text dialog box.
▼	Click the down arrow of the Sort by list box.
Field 4	Click to select field number 4 (City) as the first field to sort by.
O <u>A</u>scending	Click to sort in ascending order.
▼	Click the down arrow of the Then by list box.
Field 1	Click to select field number 1 (Last) as the second field to sort by.
[OK]	Click to perform the sort.
Click	Click anywhere to deselect the text. The records in your document should be in the order shown in Figure 4.40.

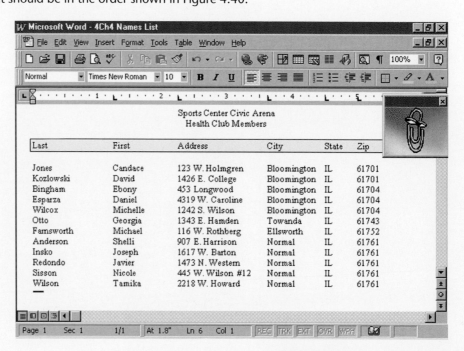

Figure 4.39
The lines sorted numerically in ascending order by zip code.

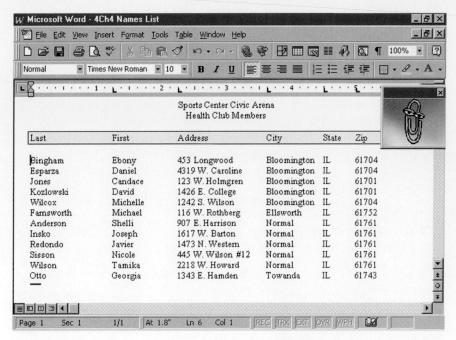

Figure 4.40
The lines sorted alphabetically by city and by last name within each city.

6.   **Print the document.**

7.   **Close the document without saving it.**

Reinforcing the Exercise

1.   You typically select text before you sort it. Otherwise, the entire document will be sorted.

2.   You open the Sort Text dialog box by issuing the Table, Sort Text command sequence.

3.   Documents are most easily sorted when the fields are separated by a tab.

4.   Sort keys are controlled via the Sort by box.

5.   You use the Sort Options dialog box to indicate when something other than tabs or commas separates fields.

 *On Your Own*

Explore sorting the contents of a table.

- Open the M4Ch4 Sample 2 table created previously.
- Select all data rows.
- Sort the table.

USING THE MACRO FEATURE

<u>T</u>ools, <u>M</u>acro, <u>R</u>ecord New Macro

Word's Macro command lets you record an often-used string of commands, called a **macro,** assign that string a name, and then replay the string of commands after by invoking the macro. By creating a macro, you perform a common task only once; therefore, you simply invoke the macro to replay the string of commands. Any set of commands that you use frequently is a candidate for placing in a macro.

Creating a Macro

You can record and execute a macro using six steps:

1. Issue the Tools, Macro, Record New Macro command sequence to begin the macro definition process.
2. Name the macro.
3. Briefly describe the macro.
4. Enter the keystrokes while the macro recording process is active.
5. End the macro definition process.
6. Execute the stored macro.

Once you have named and started recording the macro, Word records any keystrokes. Word lets you know that this recording process is in effect by displaying the REC indicator in the status bar. If you want to pause the macro momentarily, click the Pause button on the macro toolbar. To restart the macro, click the Pause button a second time.

Hands-On Exercise: Creating a Macro to Put Your Name in Boldface

In this exercise, you will create a macro that places your name in boldface type within a document. This is just the macro Isabel needs for her letterhead stationery. Start with a blank document.

1. **Create the macro name.**

<u>T</u>ools	Click to open the Tools menu.
<u>M</u>acro	Click to open the Macro menu.
<u>R</u>ecord New Macro. . .	Click to open the Record Macro dialog box (Figure 4.41).

Type the name of the macro to be saved to disk: **BOLDNAME**

2. **Specify where you want the macro stored.**

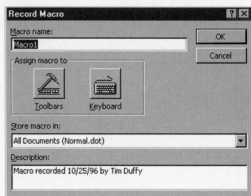

Figure 4.41
The Record Macro dialog box.

Store macro in: Check this box to make certain it displays the All Documents (Normal.dot) option. This means it will be available to any document using the Normal template.

Click   Go to the Description text box.

3. Enter a descriptive name.

Triple-click   Triple-click the description box to select the existing text.

Type a description for the macro: **Generate Boldfaced Name**

The completed Record Macro dialog box should look like Figure 4.42.

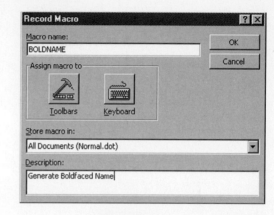

| OK | Click to close the dialog box and begin recording the macro. The macro toolbar appears, and the pointer changes to include an icon of a cassette tape (Figure 4.43). If the macro toolbar is in your way, drag it to an unused area. |

4. Enter the commands to be stored in the macro.

B   Click to issue the Bold command.

Type your name and a trailing space: ***Your Name***

B   Click to turn off boldfacing.

Figure 4.42
The completed Record Macro dialog box for the BOLDNAME macro.

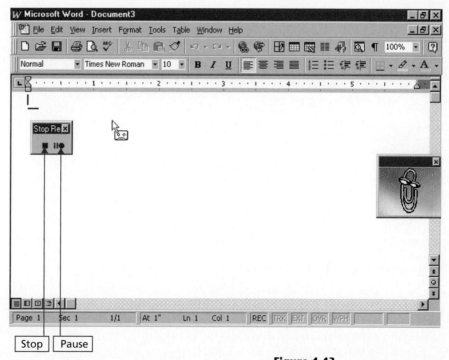

Stop   Pause

Figure 4.43
The Stop Record toolbar and the macro icon and pointer.

(ENTER)   Press to move to the next line.

5. **Turn off recording.**

      Click this button on the macro toolbar. The toolbar disap-
                   pears from the screen.

6. **Execute the macro.**

Tools   Click to open the Tools menu.

Macro   Click to open the Macro menu.

Macros. . .   Click to open the Macros dialog box (Figure 4.44). This
                   dialog box contains all of the macros that are in the Nor-
                   mal.dot template.

BOLDNAME   Double-click to run the macro. Your name should appear
                   on the screen in bold type. Each time you execute this
                   macro, your name will appear
                   on the screen.

7. **Delete the macro (you don't want it to be-
    come part of the school's common template).**

Tools   Click to open the Tools menu.

Macro   Click to open the Macro
                   menu.

Macros. . .   Click to open the Macros dia-
                   log box.

BOLDNAME   Click the macro name to se-
                   lect it.

[Delete]   Click to delete the macro. A
                   dialog box now appears re-
                   questing verification of the Delete
                   command.

[Yes]   Click to delete the macro. Its
                   name disappears from the dialog box.

[X]   Click to return to the document.

[X]   Click to Close the document without saving.

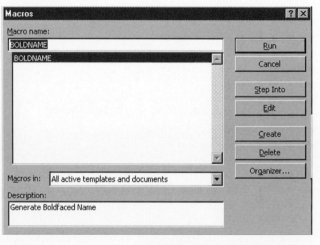

Figure 4.44
The Macros dialog box allows
you to access any macros associated with the Normal template.

Hands-On Exercise: Building a Letterhead

Isabel wants to create a letterhead that can be printed on plain stationery
and contains her work address information (Figure 4.45). In this exercise,
you create a macro called LETTERHEAD that builds this letterhead, which
uses a boldface italic font in a different style and point size than regular text
and is centered on the page.

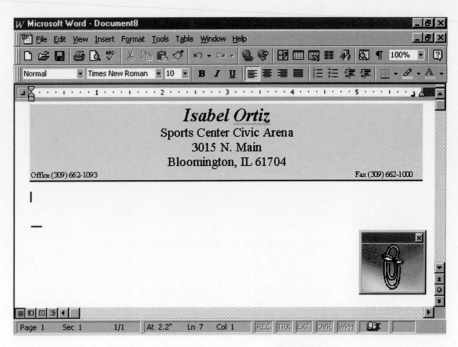

Figure 4.45
The letterhead to be generated by the macro in this exercise.

1. **Create the macro name.**

Tools   Click to open the Tools menu.

Macro   Click to open the Macro menu.

Record New   Click to open this dialog box.
   Macro. . .

Type the name of the macro to be saved to disk: **LETTERHEAD**

2. **Create the macro description.**

Click   Click the Description text box.

Triple-click   Triple-click to select all of its text.

Type a description of the macro: **Isabel's Letterhead**

Your Record Macro dialog box should look like Figure 4.46.

    Click to return to the document and start recording keystrokes.

3. **Create the first line of the letterhead.**

Click the down arrow in the Size list box in the Formatting toolbar to display the list of alternative sizes.

20   Click to select this size.

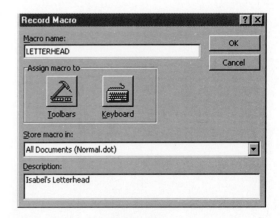

Figure 4.46
The completed Record Macro dialog box for creating the letterhead.

I   Click to issue the Italic command.

B   Click to issue the Bold command.

≡   Click to center the text.

Type Isabel's name: **Isabel Ortiz**

I   Click to turn off the Italic command.

B   Click to turn off the Bold command.

(ENTER)   Press to go to the next line. The screen should look like
                        Figure 4.47.

4. **Enter the next three lines.**

▼   Click the down arrow in the Size list box in the Format-
                        ting toolbar to display the list of alternative sizes.

14   Click to select this size.

Type the business name: **Sports Center Civic Arena**

(ENTER)   Press to go to the next line.

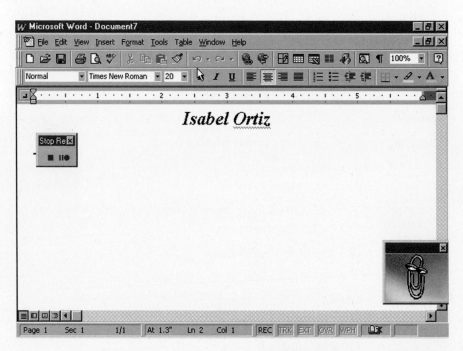

Figure 4.47
The first line of the letterhead.

Type the street address: **3015 N. Main**

(ENTER)   Press to go to the next line.

Type the city, state, and zip code: **Bloomington, IL 61704**

(ENTER)   Press to go to the next line. The screen should now look
                       like Figure 4.48.

5. **Enter the telephone and fax numbers line.**

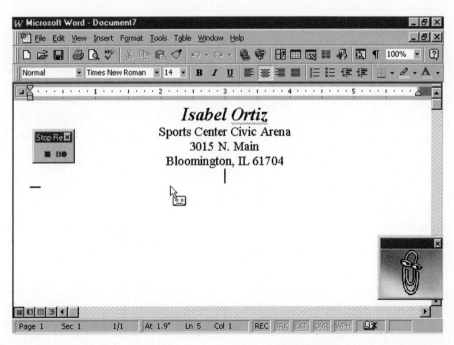

▼   Click the down arrow Size list box in the Formatting tool-
                       bar to display the list of alternative sizes.

8   Click to select this size.

                       Click to left-justify text.

┘   Click this button until the right-align indent icon appears.

5.8   Click this location on the ruler to insert a right-align
                       tab stop.

Type the telephone number: **Office (309) 662-1093**

Figure 4.48
The letterhead with the next
three lines entered.

| (TAB) | Press to move to the right-align tab stop. |

Type the fax number: **Fax (309) 662-1000**

| (ENTER) | Press to go to the next line. The letterhead should look like Figure 4.49. |

6. Change the font size and create a selection.

(ENTER)	Press to go to the next line.
	Click the Size list box in the Formatting toolbar to display the list of alternative sizes.
10	Click to select this size.
(ENTER)	Press to insert a space.
(CTRL) + (HOME)	Press to move to the beginning of the document.
(F8)	Press to enter selection mode.
(↓)	Press four times to include the first five lines in the selection.
(END)	Press to extend the selection to include the entire fifth line. Your selection should look like Figure 4.50.

7. Add shading and borders.

| **Fo**rmat | Click to open the Format menu. |
| **B**orders and Shading. . . | Click to open the Borders and Shading dialog box. |

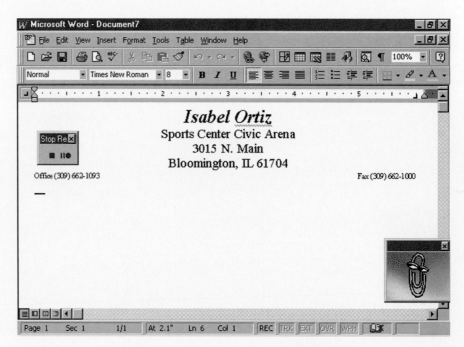

Figure 4.49
The letterhead with its five lines entered.

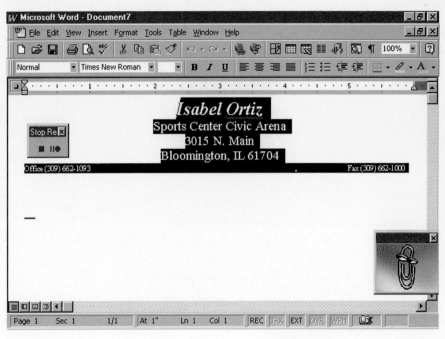

Figure 4.50
The selected text of the letterhead.

Borders	If necessary, click this tab.
Width	Click this list box to display its selections.
1½ pt——	Click this option.
Shading	Click to activate this tab of the dialog box.
Style	Click this list box to display its selections.
10%	Click to select this option. The dialog box should look like Figure 4.51.

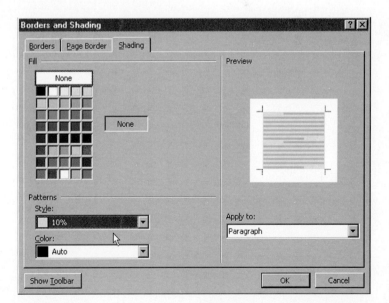

Figure 4.51
The completed Shading tab of
the Borders and Shading dialog
box.

OK	Click to return to the document.
▼	Click the down arrow of the Border button to open the Borders menu.
	Click to select this border type.
ESC, ↓, ↓	Press to turn off the selection. The letterhead should now look like Figure 4.52.

8. Turn off the macro.

■	Click this button on the macro toolbar.

9. Close the existing document without saving it.

10. Execute the macro. If necessary, open a new document in which to execute the macro.

Tools	Click to open the Tools menu.
Macro	Click to open the Macro menu.
Macros. . .	Click to open the Macros dialog box.
LETTERHEAD	Double-click to execute the macro. A completed letterhead should appear on the screen.

11. Print the letterhead.

12. After covering the next section of the chapter, erase the LETTERHEAD macro by using the same commands that you used with the BOLDFACE macro.

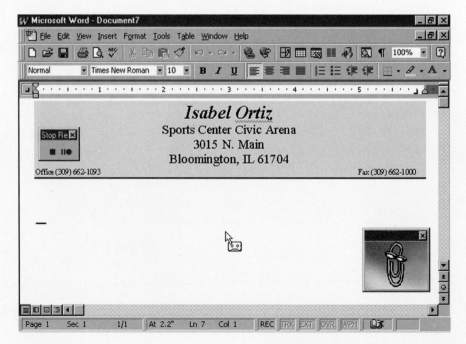

Figure 4.52
The completed letterhead for Isabel.

Reinforcing the Exercise

1. A macro is a recorded string or series of commands.

2. Begin creating a macro by issuing the Tools, Macro, Record New Macros command sequence.

3. When you are recording commands in a macro, the macro toolbar appears with the Stop and Pause buttons, and the mouse pointer looks like a cassette tape.

4. Click the Stop button of the macro toolbar when you are done recording keystrokes.

Editing a Macro

You may have a macro that you wish to change, or you may have recorded some commands by mistake. Word lets you edit the text of a macro.

You begin the editing process by following these steps:

1. Enter the Tools, Macro, Macros command sequence.

2. Select the macro you want to edit.

3. Click Edit. The Microsoft Visual Basic window shown in Figure 4.53 appears.

Figure 4.53 shows the screen for the LETTERHEAD macro. It contains the Visual Basic instructions that Word placed in the file as representations of the commands that you entered. Word records macros using **Visual Basic**—its internal language as well as the internal language of other Office products. The macro begins with the words "Sub LETTERHEAD" and ends with "End Sub." Once such a macro file is on the screen, you can edit it like any other document.

Issue the File, Print commands to print the macro instructions. Examine them at your leisure. Click the Cancel button to return to Word.

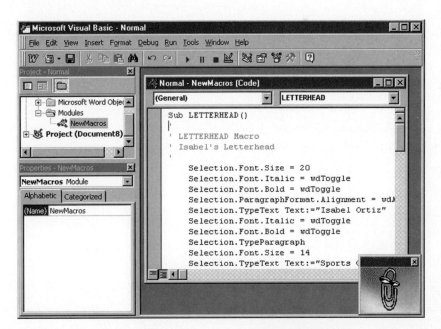

Figure 4.53
The LETTERHEAD macro instructions.

SESSION REVIEW

This session introduced some advanced document features of Word: columns, tables, sorting, and macros. For more information, consult Word's documentation.

The Columns command allows you to create such documents as newsletters with columns that snake from one column to the next and are read left to right from the top down. You can set up the entire document, or just parts of it, to contain multiple columns. If you desire, you can also place rules between the columns.

The Table command allows you to create a text entity to hold tabular data or to support parallel columns. Cells in a table can hold text, numbers, or graphics. The easiest way to define a table is by using the Insert Table button on the Standard toolbar. The Table AutoFormat command applies a number of predefined formats to a document table to give it a more finished appearance.

You can sort regular text or tabular data by issuing the Table, Sort Text command sequence. When you are entering data that you may sort later, be sure to use tabs or commas rather than spaces to separate fields from words.

The Macro feature of Word stores commands and replays them later, thus enabling you to perform complex tasks easily. Macros are an efficient way of performing repetitious operations. Macros are stored using the Visual Basic programming language.

KEY TERMS AND CONCEPTS

cell 4–160

clip art 4–153

field 4–167

key 4–167

macro 4–172

newspaper columns 4–146

parallel columns 4–146

table 4–159

Table feature 4–159

Visual Basic 4–181

SESSION QUIZ

Multiple Choice

1. Which of the following is the default separator when you are defining a sort operation?
   a. comma
   b. tab
   c. colon
   d. none of the above

2. Which of the following statements concerning sorting is/are false?
   a. You can sort on only one field at a time.
   b. The field to be sorted is called a key.
   c. The default sort order is ascending.
   d. A paragraph is a line followed by an Enter keystroke.

3. Which of the following statements concerning columns is/are false?

   a. Parallel columns can be created using the Columns command.

   b. You can choose one of five predefined columns, or you can create your own column format.

   c. Vertical lines can be inserted between existing columns from within the Columns dialog box.

   d. You can make the length of the columns on the last page equal no matter where they end originally.

4. Which of the following statements is/are true concerning Word tables?

   a. You can define a table using the Insert Table button.

   b. Once you define a table, the Insert Table button changes into an Insert Row button.

   c. The CTRL + → command is used to move easily from one column to another in a table.

   d. All of the above are true.

5. Which of the following statements about macros is/are true?

   a. A macro is really composed of Word commands that have been stored using the Visual Basic language and can be played back on demand.

   b. A macro is stored in a .WCM file.

   c. A template macro can be used only one time.

   d. A macro is opened by entering the Play, Macro command.

True/False

6. The Table command is used to create parallel columns, whereas the Columns command is used to create newspaper columns.

7. When entering data that may be sorted later, it is important to place the data in tabbed columns and use TAB to move from column to column.

8. Office has a clip art library that you can use to insert a graphic in a document.

9. A macro actually resides on disk as a separate file and is not part of any template.

10. You can use the Sort command to sort only one field at a time.

SESSION REVIEW EXERCISES

1. The command sequence _____ , _____ opens the Columns dialog box, which you use to create newspaper columns.

2. You use the _____ dialog box to create parallel columns.

3. The _____ _____ entry of the Columns dialog box is used to start columns at a specific point in the document.

4. The Columns dialog box has five _____ that can be used to define column types easily.

5. You define parallel columns by using the _____ _____ dialog box.

6. If you want to specify the comma as the separator in a text sort, you need to access the _____ dialog box from the Sort Text dialog box.

7. When you want to sort text in a document, you must first include the text in a
   _____.

8. The Sort Text dialog box opens when you issue the _____ , _____
   command sequence.

9. The _____ list box in the Sort Text dialog box specifies the first sort key.

10. The _____ list box in the Sort Text dialog box specifies the second sort key.

11. The _____ option is the default used to specify the order of the sort.

12. The _____ _____ button on the Standard toolbar is used to create
    a table composed of rows and columns.

13. Press the _____ key to move to the right through the columns of a table.

14. Issue the _____ + _____ shortcut command to move to the left
    through the columns of a table.

15. You can easily insert rows in a defined table by clicking the _____
    _____ button of the Standard toolbar.

16. A table cell can hold _____ , _____ , or _____.

17. To start recording a macro, you need to issue the _____ , _____ ,
    _____ command sequence.

18. Once a macro is recording, you can stop the recording by clicking the _____ _____
    button of the macro toolbar.

19. Executing a macro requires issuing the _____ , _____ ,
    _____ command sequence and then double-clicking the desired macro.

20. A/an _____ is really composed of commands stored in the Visual Basic lan-
    guage.

COMPUTER EXERCISES

1. Open the 4CH4 Exercise 1A document,
   which contains name and address information (Figure 4.54).
   a. Use the Save As command to save the
      document as M4Ch4 Exercise 1.
   b. Perform a sort to arrange the names in
      alphabetical order by last name. Print
      the document.
   c. Perform a sort to arrange the zip codes
      in ascending order. Print the document.
   d. Perform a sort to arrange the names in
      alphabetical order within ascending zip
      codes. Print the document.
   e. Close the document without saving any
      changes.

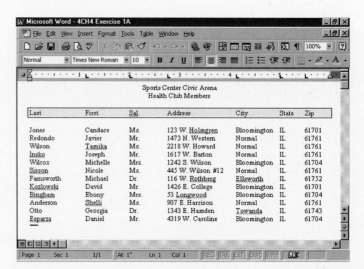

Figure 4.54
**The names in the 4CH4 Exercise
1A document.**

2. Create the following macro and save it using the name ADDRESS.
    a. Create a macro named ADDRESS that will automatically enter your name, address, and date information, left-justified, for a letter like that shown in Figure 4.55. After the date has been entered, the insertion point should move down two lines.
    b. Test your macro to make certain that it works.
    c. Save the macro.

3. Create a macro by adapting the LETTERHEAD macro you created for Isabel earlier in this session.
    a. Use your address information.
    b. Incorporate any graphics features (shadowing and borders) that you want. Check the clip art library to see if there's a clip art image you would like to add.
    c. Experiment with using two fonts: one for your name and the other for the remaining lines.
    d. Test the macro.

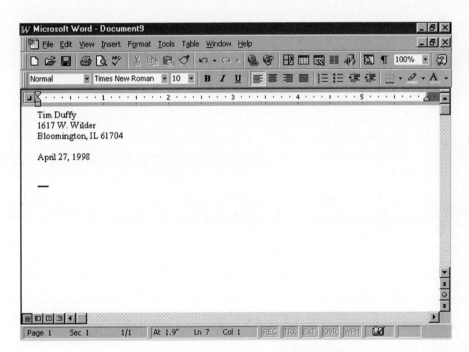

Figure 4.55
The name and date information for a letter to be entered using the ADDRESS macro.

4. Create the newsletter shown in Figure 4.56. Make certain that the font is Times Roman and the font size is 10 pt. The introductory portion of the newsletter (Figure 4.56) resides in a file called 4Ch4 Exercise 4 Introduction.

   a. Use the Insert, File command sequence to insert the first part of the newsletter. Change the city information to the name of your city. The body of the newsletter (Figure 4.57) resides in the file named 4Ch4 Newsletter Text.

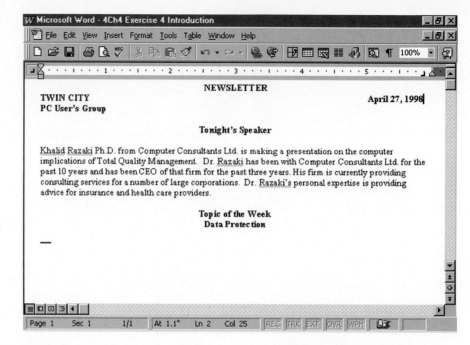

Figure 4.56
The 4Ch4 Exercise 4 Introduction file inserted at the beginning of the newsletter document.

   b. Using Figure 4.58 as a guide, prepare the introduction to receive the newsletter body. Insert any needed lines and define the columns. Your finished newsletter should look like Figure 4.58.

   c. Balance the lines at the end of the newsletter.

   d. Print the newsletter.

   e. Save the newsletter using the name M4Ch4 Exercise 4.

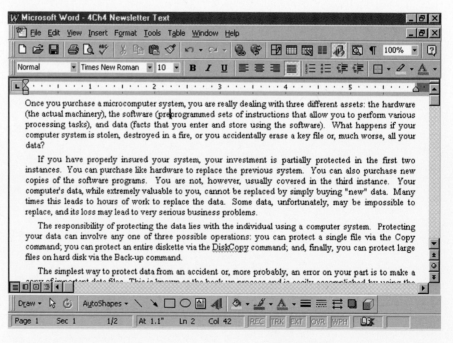

Figure 4.57
The 4Ch4 Newsletter Text document to be used for the newsletter body.

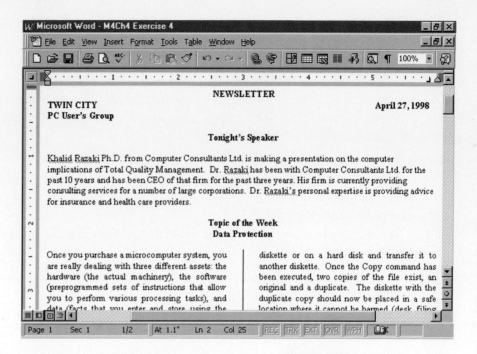

Figure 4.58
The M4Ch4 Exercise 4 newsletter with the two files inserted.

5. Add clip art to the newsletter that you created in Computer Exercise 4.

   a. From the Business category of the Microsoft Clip Gallery 3.0, insert the Information Personal Computer with Mouse and Information Diskette clip art images in the newsletter. Use Figure 4.59 as a guide for inserting the images on the first page of the newsletter.

   b. Save the new version of the newsletter using the name M4Ch4 Exercise 5.

   c. Print the newsletter.

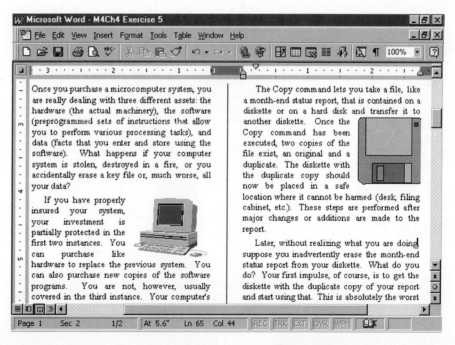

Figure 4.59
The newsletter with the inserted clip art images.

6. This exercise involves opening the document 4Ch4 Newsletter Text.
   a. Use the Save As command to save the document using the name M4Ch4 Exercise 6.
   b. Add the centered boldfaced title *Data Protection*.
   c. Incorporate the graphic file Cartridge Drive and Notebook Computer from the Technology category in the document at the designated locations shown in Figure 4.60.
   d. Enter the captions listed here. Change their font size to 8 pt. Center the text in the caption box. Get rid of the caption box lines.

Cartridge Drive figure caption:
All computers should have a hard disk backup to tape performed at regular intervals.

Notebook Computer figure caption:
The portability of some computers provides serious data security problems for organizations.

   e. On the second page of this document, place the text file called 4CH4 Exercise 6 Quotation in a text box (Figure 4.61).
   f. Use the 25% gray fill color for the text box.
   g. Print and save the document.

7. This exercise involves using the previously created M4Ch4 Exercise 4 document.
   a. Use the Save As command to save the document as M4Ch4 Exercise 7.
   b. Use the Columns command to define a three-column newsletter.
   c. Change the space between the columns to 0.25 inch.
   d. Place the page number in the lower-right corner of each page.
   e. Use the Headers and Footers command to add a borderline at the top and bottom of the document (above the page number), as shown in Figure 4.62.
   f. Print and save the document.

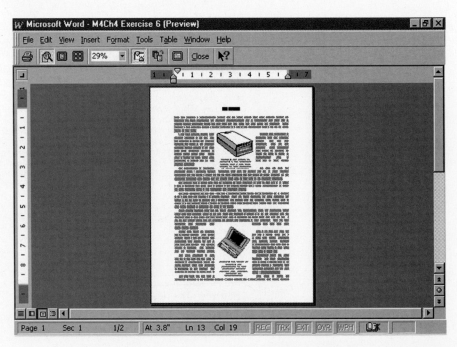

Figure 4.60
Positioning of the clip art.

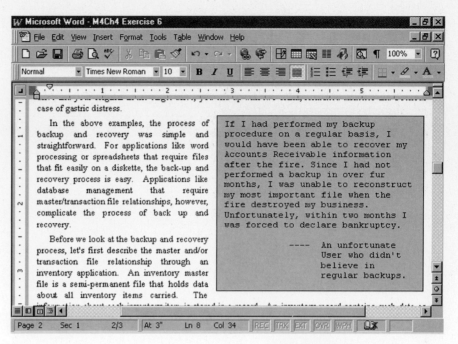

Figure 4.61
The embedded quotation.

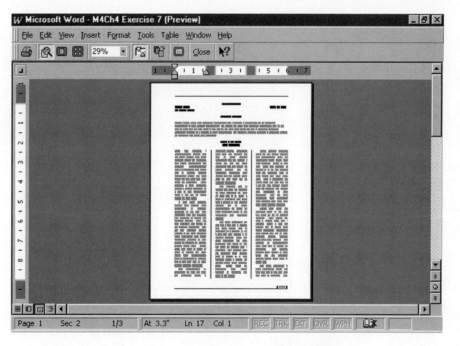

Figure 4.62
The finished M4Ch4 Exercise 7
newsletter.

8. Enter the island vacation itinerary document shown in Figure 4.63 as a table.

   a. Set up the table with three columns and five rows (the first row contains the table column heading).

   b. Using Figure 4.63 as a guide, drag the table borders to the locations indicated.

   c. Drag the right indent handle to properly center the heading over the table.

   d. Print the table.

   e. Save the table to the document named MCh4 Exercise 8.

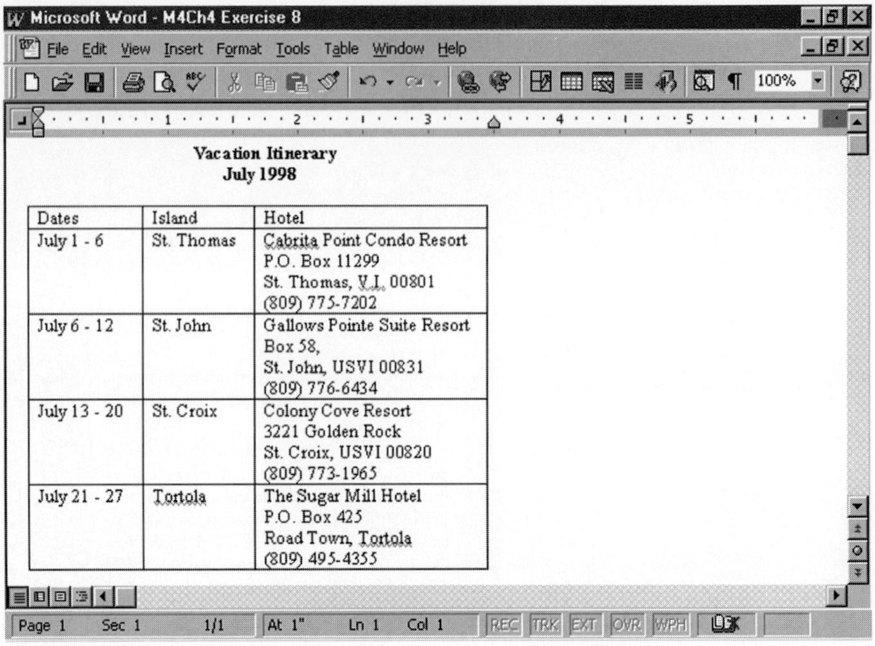

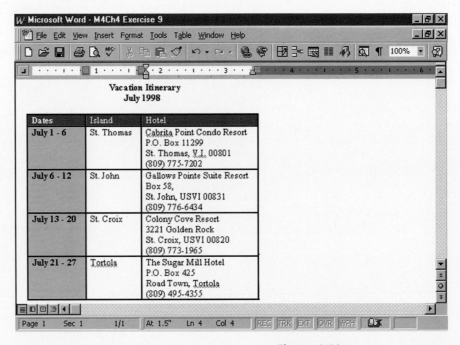

Figure 4.63
The island vacation itinerary.

9. Open the M4Ch4 Exercise 8 document.

   a. Use the Table AutoFormat command to format this table.

   b. Choose Classic 2 as the formatting option, and then place borderlines around all cells (Figure 4.64).

   c. Print the document.

   d. Save the document as M4Ch4 Exercise 9.

Figure 4.64
The vacation itinerary with the Classic 2 format applied to it and borderlines added.

10. Open the 4Ch4 Exercise 10 document shown in Figure 4.65. Perform the following operations on the table.

   a. Save the document using the name M4Ch4 Exercise 10. Sort the table in ascending order by organization name. The sorted table should look like Figure 4.66.

   b. Print the table.

   c. Save the table.

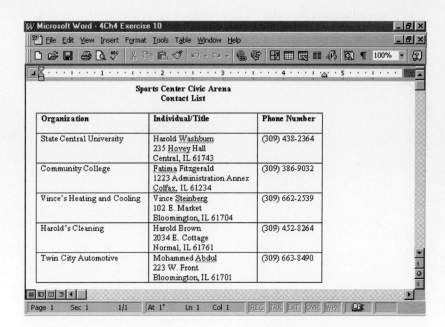

Figure 4.65
The 4Ch4 Exercise 10 document with the embedded table.

INTERNET EXERCISES

1. Build a résumé.

   a. Open and print the 4Ch4 Davis Sample Resume, 4Ch4 Tilden Sample Resume, and 4Ch4 Harper Sample Resume documents from the Web site for this text.

   b. Examine each of these résumés. Select one of these formats for building your résumé, or design your own résumé format.

   c. Save the file using the name M4Ch4 Your Name Resume.

   d. Print the résumé.

   e. Convert it to HTML format. View the résumé by loading that HTML file. How does the HTML version differ?

2. Access sample letters from the World Wide Web that you can use for a number of different typs of applications.

   a. Access the Excite Web page (http://www.excite.com) to execute a search.

   b. Enter the search text *sample letters* in the Search text box. Click the Search icon.

   c. Locate a site with sample letters.

   d. Save the desired sample letter to disk.

   e. Print a sample letter.

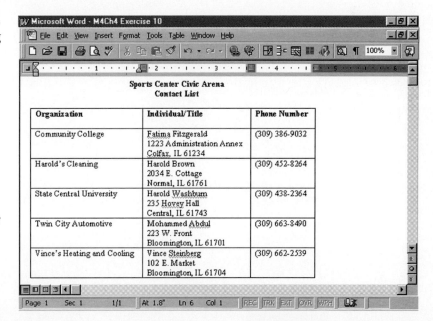

Figure 4.66
The sorted table.

SESSION 5

Word's Productivity Tools

After completing this session, you should be able to:

➤ Use the Thesaurus

➤ Perform a word count on part or all of a document

➤ Use Mail Merge to construct templates and data files

➤ Import names from an Excel workbook and use them in a merge operation

➤ Create individualized letters and labels

Isabel has received a request from the manager of the health club at the Sports Center Civic Arena for help in the preparation of a promotional mailing to health club members, informing them of an open house and offering those members a reduced rate for renewing their memberships for an additional six months. Alice, the Sports Center manager, has indicated that some of the names will have to be entered manually, while others are stored in an existing Excel workbook.

Isabel's daughter Rosa has also asked for some additional help on her term paper on ferrets.

In the course of this session, you will learn how to use some of Word's productivity tools to help Isabel respond to these requests. You will use the Thesaurus feature to find synonyms and antonyms for words. You will see how the powerful Mail Merge feature can help you create personalized form letters and other documents based on combinations of standard and individualized text. You also will learn how to perform a word count on a document.

FINDING WORDS WITH THE THESAURUS FEATURE

<u>T</u>ools, <u>L</u>anguage, <u>T</u>hesaurus

The **Thesaurus feature** of Word offers synonyms and antonyms to help you choose your words effectively when you write. A **synonym** is a word with the same meaning as another word. An **antonym** is a word that means the opposite of another word.

Starting the Thesaurus

To start the Thesaurus, place the cursor at the word you want to look up and issue the Tools, Language, Thesaurus command sequence. Alternatively, you can activate the Thesaurus and then type any word that you want to look up.

Using the Thesaurus

Figure 5.1 shows the Thesaurus dialog box that appears in response to the Thesaurus command. In this example, the word *Fools* (the first word in the 4Ch5 Thesaurus Sample document from the Student Data files) is being analyzed because the cursor is located at that word in the document window.

When you have decided on the appropriate word, select it. When you click the Replace button, Word replaces the word in the document and returns you to your document.

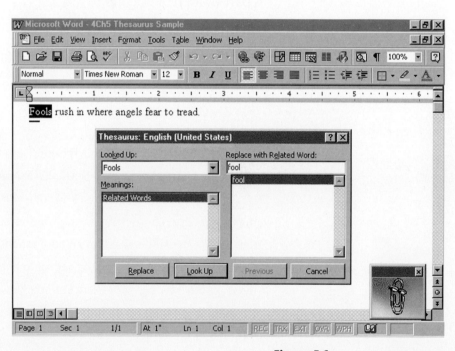

Figure 5.1
The Thesaurus dialog box.

Hands-On Exercise: Using the Thesaurus to Replace Text

Open the 4Ch5 Thesaurus Sample document that resides with your student data files. Make certain that the cursor is at the word *Fools*.

1. **Invoke the Thesaurus for the first word.**

<u>T</u>ools   Click to open the Tools menu.

<u>L</u>anguage   Click to open the Language menu.

Thesaurus . . . Click to open the Thesaurus dialog box. Your screen should look like Figure 5.1. Notice that the word *Fools* appears as selected text.

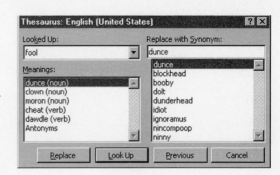

Look Up   Click this button to display alternatives for the word *fool* (Figure 5.2). Notice that several meanings of the word *fool* appear in the box on the left, and the synonyms for the selected meaning (in this case, *dunce*) appear in the box on the right.

Figure 5.2
The Thesaurus dialog box for the word *fool.*

clown (noun) Click to select this word from the Meanings box to see synonyms for this word. Your screen should now look like Figure 5.3.

buffoon Click this word. It now appears in the Replace with Synonym box.

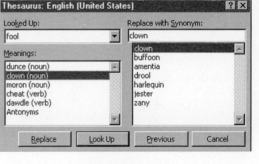

Replace   Click to replace the word *Fools.* The word *Buffoon* now appears in place of *Fools,* and the dialog box disappears.

Type: **s** to make *Buffoon* plural.

2. **Find an antonym for the word *rush.***

Click   Click on the word *rush.*

Tools Click to open the Tools menu.

Language Click to open the Language menu.

Figure 5.3
The meanings and synonyms for the word *clown.*

Thesaurus . . . Click to open the Thesaurus dialog box. Your screen should like Figure 5.4.

Look Up   Click to display alternatives for the word *haste.*

Antonyms Click the Antonyms entry in the Meanings box to generate a list of antonyms for the word *haste* (Figure 5.5).

Cancel   Click to return to the document.

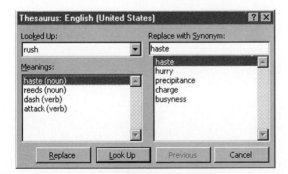

Figure 5.4
The Thesaurus dialog box for the word *rush.*

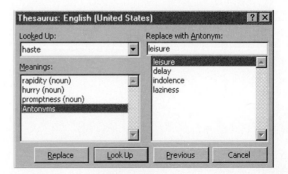

Figure 5.5
The antonyms for the word *haste.*

3.   Look up the word *tread.*

Click	Click to select the word *tread.*
Tools	Click to open the Tools menu.
Language	Click to open the Language menu.
Thesaurus . . .	Click to open the Thesaurus dialog box.
Walk	Click to select the word *walk* (not *walking*) in the Meanings list box.

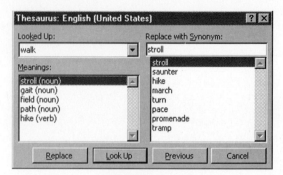

Look Up	Click the Look Up button to display additional synonyms (Figure 5.6).
Saunter	Click the word *saunter* in the Meanings box to place it in the Replace with Synonym box.
Replace	Click to put the word *saunter* in place of *tread,* and the dialog box disappears. Your sentence should now read: *Buffoons rush in where angels fear to saunter.*

Figure 5.6
Additional synonyms for the word *walk.*

4.   Close the document without saving it.

Reinforcing the Exercise

1.   You activate the Thesaurus feature by using the Tools, Language, Thesaurus command sequence.

2.   You can search for synonyms or antonyms.

3.   Use the Look Up button to find more synonyms or antonyms for the selected word.

4.   Click the Replace button to replace the selected word in the document with the word in the Replace with Synonym (or Antonym) box.

COUNTING WORDS WITH THE WORD COUNT FEATURE   **Tools, Word Count**

The Word Count command lets you count the number of pages, words, characters, paragraphs, and lines in a document. You can include footnotes and endnotes as well. The command sequence Tools, Word Count displays the Word Count dialog box that reports the count.

Hands-On Exercise: Using Word Count

Isabel's daughter Rosa has learned that her term paper on ferrets (which you worked on in Session 3 of this module) must be between 1500 and 1800 words. She wants to know if her paper meets this requirement.

1. **Open your version of the 4Ch3 Ferret Term Paper document.**

2. **Issue the Word Count command.**

Tools   Click to open the Tools menu.

Word Count   Click to open the Word Count dialog box (Figure 5.7).

3. **Include footnotes.**

Include footnotes and endnotes   Click this option in the Word Count dialog box to include footnotes in the document statistics. New numbers now appear (Figure 5.8). With or without footnotes, the ferret document fits the length requirements.

Cancel   Click to close the dialog box.

4. **Close the document without saving it.**

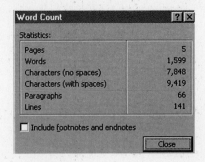

Figure 5.7
The word count for the 4Ch3 Ferret Term Paper document without including footnotes.

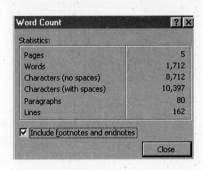

Figure 5.8
The statistics including the document footnotes.

Reinforcing the Exercise

1. You can display document statistics by using the Tools, Word Count command sequence.

2. Document statistics appear in a Word Count dialog box.

3. Word can generate document statistics either excluding or including footnotes and endnotes.

MERGING DOCUMENTS WITH THE MAIL MERGE FEATURE   Tools, Mail Merge

Despite technological advances, most communication is still conducted via the written word, and writing letters is still extremely important in business. Writing essentially the same letter to 100 different people, as often happens in business, poses some real problems. People do not like "Dear Customer" letters, so in many situations, it is important to modify each letter so that it appears to have been typed individually for the recipient.

     Of course, it is possible to create a letter, save it to disk, and type a new name and address 100 times before printing. But this is still a lot of work, and it's even worse if various references within the body of the letter also have to be changed.

Word's **Mail Merge feature** automates the task of bulk mailings. With Mail Merge and a letter-quality printer, each letter in a bulk mailing can be created efficiently and still look as though it was individually typed. Figure 5.9 shows an example of such a letter.

As its name implies, the Mail Merge command of the Tools menu is capable of combining (merging) files. Usually two files are needed. The **main document** (also called the **template file**) contains the constant data—the text to be included in all the letters—and the instructions for placing the individual data (Figure 5.10). The **data source file** (also called the secondary file) contains the variable, individualized text (Figure 5.11). The data source file provides the input to the main document template. The template is, in effect, a computer program containing instructions on what to do with the input data; the output will be an individualized letter for each recipient listed in the data source file.

Sports Center Civic Arena
Health Club
3015 N. Main
Bloomington, IL 61704

April 29, 1998

Mr. Stanley Chapman
407 W. Wood
Clinton, IL 61934

Dear Mr. Chapman;

As a token of our gratitude for your continued membership in the Sports Center Civic Arena Health Club, we would like to invite you to an Open House which will be conducted from 5:00 p.m. to 9:00 p.m. May 1st through May 4th. Healthy snacks and beverages will be served. Feel free to stop by and chat with the staff and your friends.

We would also like to extend a 10% discount to anyone who takes this opportunity to renew his or her six-month membership during the Open House.

We look forward to seeing you.

Sincerely,

Alice Plummer

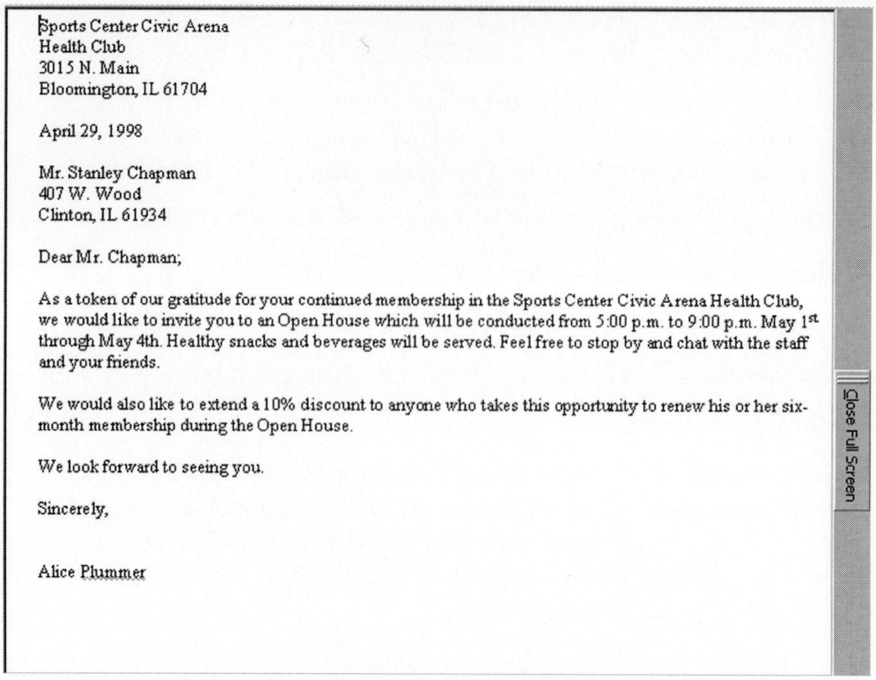

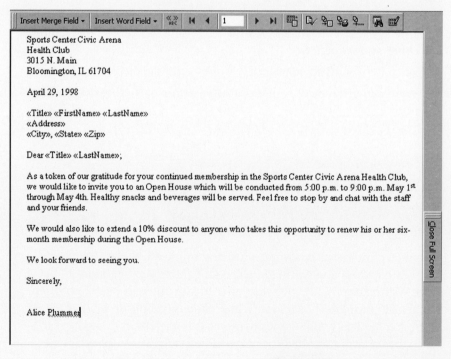

Figure 5.9
An individualized letter produced by the Mail Merge feature.

Sports Center Civic Arena
Health Club
3015 N. Main
Bloomington, IL 61704

April 29, 1998

«Title» «FirstName» «LastName»
«Address»
«City», «State» «Zip»

Dear «Title» «LastName»;

As a token of our gratitude for your continued membership in the Sports Center Civic Arena Health Club, we would like to invite you to an Open House which will be conducted from 5:00 p.m. to 9:00 p.m. May 1st through May 4th. Healthy snacks and beverages will be served. Feel free to stop by and chat with the staff and your friends.

We would also like to extend a 10% discount to anyone who takes this opportunity to renew his or her six-month membership during the Open House.

We look forward to seeing you.

Sincerely,

Alice Plummer

Figure 5.10
The M4Ch5 Letter Template document used for creating the personalized letter in Figure 5.9.

Creating the Data Source File

The data source file shown in Figure 5.11 holds the data that corresponds to the changeable parts of the individualized letters shown in Figure 5.9.

The main document accesses data from the data source file. The data for each recipient is stored in a **record** in the data source file. A **field** of the record contains a piece of data about the recipient, such as first name. Each record may have several fields.

Once you have created a data source file, you can use it with any number of main documents (templates). The names of the fields to be used in this exercise are:

- Title
- FirstName
- LastName
- Address
- City
- State
- Zip

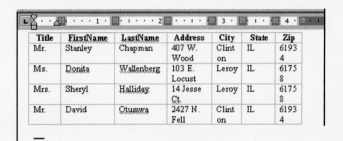

Title	FirstName	LastName	Address	City	State	Zip
Mr.	Stanley	Chapman	407 W. Wood	Clinton	IL	61934
Ms.	Donita	Wallenberg	103 E. Locust	Leroy	IL	61758
Mrs.	Sheryl	Halliday	14 Jesse Ct.	Leroy	IL	61758
Mr.	David	Otumwa	2427 N. Fell	Clinton	IL	61934

Figure 5.11
The M4Ch5 Names Source File document used in creating the personalized letter in Figure 5.9.

T I M E L Y   T I P

Your data source file will look like a table if it has 31 or fewer fields. If it has more than 31 fields, data will be separated by commas, and each record will end with a paragraph mark.

Field names must start with a letter, contain no spaces, be unique, and consist of fewer than 40 characters.

Hands-On Exercise: Creating the Data Source File

You will create a source file that contains the names of Sports Center members for Alice to use in her mailing.

1. **If necessary, open a new document that will be used as the data source file.** Make sure that you are in Normal view.

2. **Start the Mail Merge process.**

Tools   Click to open the Tools menu.

Mail Merge . . .   Click to open the Mail Merge Helper dialog box (Figure 5.12).

3. **Indicate that the main document will be a form letter, and then create the data source file.**

   Click to open the pulldown menu shown in Figure 5.13.

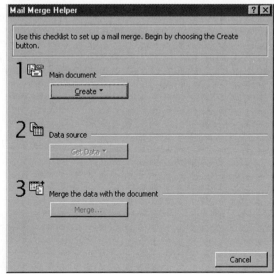

Figure 5.12
The Mail Merge Helper dialog box.

Form Letters . . .   Select this option to display the dialog box shown in Figure 5.14, which requests information about where the document should be built.

| New Main Document | Click to open a blank document and return to the Mail Merge Helper (Figure 5.15).

| Get Data ˅ | Click to open the Get Data pulldown menu (Figure 5.16).

Create Data Source . . .   Click to open the Create Data Source dialog box (Figure 5.17).

4. Remove the JobTitle field from the Field Names in header row selection box.

JobTitle   Click this entry.

| Remove Field Name | Click to remove the JobTitle entry.

5. Repeat step 4, selecting and removing the following field names that you *don't* want to add to the main document: **Company, Address1, Address2, PostalCode, Country, HomePhone,** and **WorkPhone.** The fields Title, FirstName, LastName, City, and State should be the only remaining fields. Your Create Data Source dialog box should look like Figure 5.18.

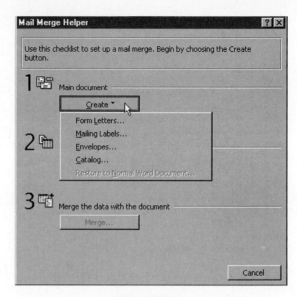

Figure 5.13
The Create pulldown menu.

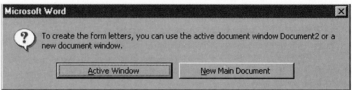

Figure 5.14
Word requests information about how the document is to be created.

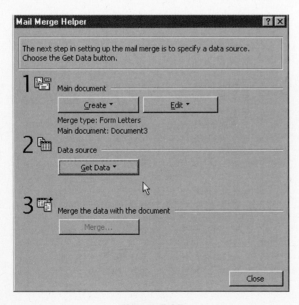

Figure 5.15
The changed Mail Merge Helper dialog box.

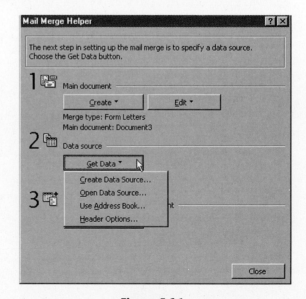

Figure 5.16
The Get Data pulldown menu prompts you about where the data will come from.

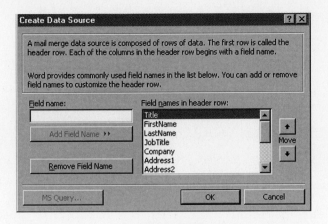

Figure 5.17
The Create Data Source dialog box used to create the field names of the source file.

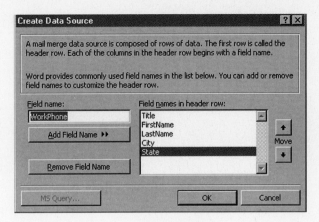

Figure 5.18
The Create Data Source dialog box with the undesired fields removed.

6. **Enter a new field name in the Field name box.**

Type: **Address** the name of a new field.

 Click to add this field to the list of fields. The Address name is now last in the field list in the Field Names in header row list box.

7. **Repeat step 6 to enter the Zip field name.**

8. **Arrange the fields in the order that they are to appear in the data source file by using the Move buttons.**

Address Click this field name.

 Click the Move Up button until the Address field appears between the LastName and City fields. Your finished dialog box should look like Figure 5.19.

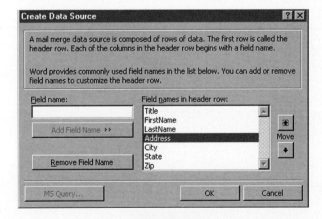

Figure 5.19
The completed field layout for the data source file.

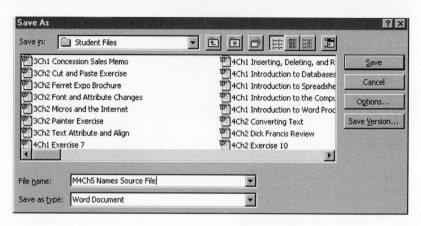

Figure 5.20
The Save As dialog box.

9. Save the field layout.

| OK | Click to open the Save As dialog box.

Type: **M4Ch5 Names Source File**

Enter the file name. The Save as dialog box should look like Figure 5.20.

(ENTER)   Press to complete the saving process. You are warned that your data source contains no data (Figure 5.21).

| Edit Data Source | Click to open the Data Form, where you can now begin adding records to your data source (See Figure 5.22).

10. Enter data for the first record.

Type: **Mr.**   in the title field.

(TAB)   Press (TAB) or (ENTER) to move to the next field.

Type: **Stanley**   in the FirstName field.

Type: **Chapman**   in the LastName field.

Type: **407 W. Wood** in the Address field.

Type: **Clinton**   in the City field; do *not* enter a comma.

Type: **IL**   in the State field.

Type: **61934**   in the Zip field. Your Data Form dialog box should look like Figure 5.23.

11. Add the record to the file.

| Add New | Click to add another record.

12. Repeat steps 10 and 11 to enter the remaining records shown in Figure 5.24.

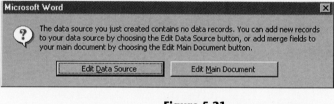

Figure 5.21
Dialog box warning that the source file is empty.

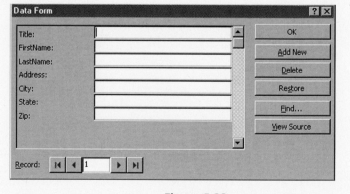

Figure 5.22
The Data Form used to add and edit records in the source file.

13. Save the data source file.

 Click to view the data source file (Figure 5.24). The first line contains the field names, and subsequent lines contain the data. Notice the Database toolbar above the table.

Click this button on the Standard toolbar to save the file.

Click the Close button for the document to close it.

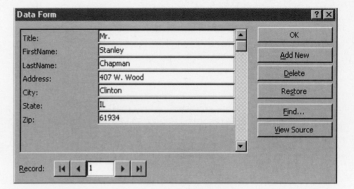

Figure 5.23
The Data Form dialog box completed for the first record.

Word created a table that lists the field names for the data source in the first row. Each row of data will be treated as a record, that is, the variable fields to be used for each form letter.

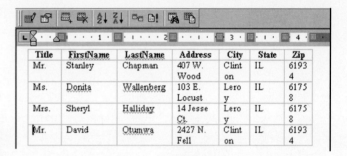

Reinforcing the Exercise

Figure 5.24
The completed data source file.

1. The Mail Merge Helper dialog box provides assistance in setting up a merge operation.

2. The Create Data Source dialog box provides you with a list of field names you can select.

3. The Data Form dialog box displays the field names and space for each field and is used to build a data source file.

4. You can display the data source file in table format.

Attaching the Data Source File to the Main Document

The main document is the form letter you want to send. It is like a normal document except that it contains **merge field codes** that indicate where merged data will appear. Figure 5.10 shows the main document for the Sports Center letter.

To complete the merge operation, you must attach the data source file to the main document. Once the data source file is attached, you use the Insert Merge Field command to insert merge field codes into the main document. Word uses these codes to extract information from the data source when the merge operation is executed. The merge fields also tell Word where to put the data. Figure 5.25 shows a blank merge document with the Mail Merge toolbar. The Mail Merge toolbar buttons are described in Table 5.1.

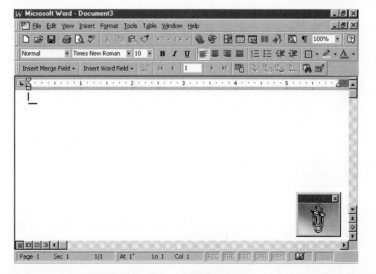

Figure 5.25
A blank merge document with the Mail Merge toolbar displayed.

Table 5.1   Mail Merge Toolbar Buttons

Button	Name	Function
Insert Merge Field ▾	Insert Merge Field	Inserts a mail merge field at the cursor location
Insert Word Field ▾	Insert Word Field	Inserts a Word field at the cursor location
« » ABC	View Merged Data	Toggles between viewing merge fields and actual data
◄	First Record	Displays the first record in the active data source file
◄	Previous Record	Displays the previous record in the data source file
1	Go to Record	Displays the specified record in the data source file
►	Next Record	Displays the next record in the data source file
►|	Last Record	Displays the last record in the data source file
	Mail Merge Helper	Prepares a main document for a merge operation
	Check for Errors	Checks for errors in a merge operation
	Merge to New Document	Collects the results of the merge in a document
	Merge to Printer	Sends the results of the merge to the printer
	Mail Merge	Invokes the Mail Merge dialog box
	Find Record	Finds a specified record in a data source file
	Edit Data Source	Opens a data source file

Hands-On Exercise: Creating the Main Document

Isabel has helped Alice enter the data for the Sports Center mailing. Now Alice needs to create the main document to be used as the form letter.

1. **Use the Mail Merge Helper to get to the main document.**

Tools   Click to open the Tools menu.

Mail Me_r_ge . . .   Click to open the Mail Merge Helper dialog box.

2. **Indicate that you want to create a form letter.**

[Create ▾]   Click to open the Create pulldown menu.

Form L_e_tters . . .   Click to open a dialog box that asks how you want to create the document (Figure 5.26).

[New Main Document]   Click to use the current document window to build the template.

[Get Data ▾]   Click to open the Get Data pulldown menu (Figure 5.27).

Open Data Source . . .   Click to open the Open Data Source dialog box (Figure 5.28).

M4Ch5 Names Source File   Double-click the filename. Word displays a dialog box that indicates that currently there are no merge fields in your document (Figure 5.29).

[Edit Main Document]   Click to open a blank document with the Mail Merge toolbar activated.

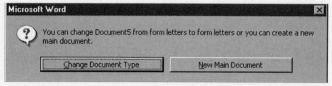

Figure 5.26
The dialog box asking how you want to create the main document.

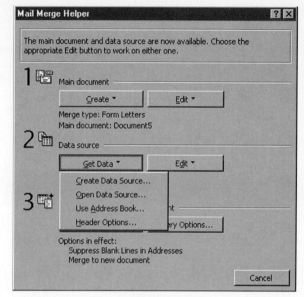

Figure 5.27
Pulldown menu for getting the data source file.

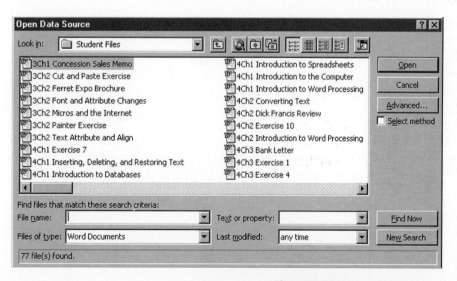

Figure 5.28
The Open Data Source dialog box.

3. Enter the first four lines of text shown in Figure 5.30, and then press (ENTER) twice.

4. Insert the date merge field code so the current date will print whenever the document is printed.

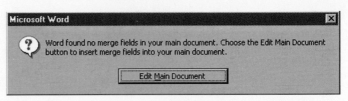

Figure 5.29
This dialog box indicates that you need to work on your main document.

Insert	Click to open the Insert menu.
Date and Time . . .	Click to open the Date and Time dialog box. Make certain that the Update Automatically option is selected.
April 27, 1998	Double-click the option that presents the date in this format.
(ENTER)	Press this key twice to insert a blank line in the letter.

Figure 5.30
The first lines of the letter template.

5. Enter the merge field codes in the letter.

Insert Merge Field ▾	Click this button on the Mail Merge toolbar to open a list of fields (Figure 5.31).
Title	Click this field name. The merge field code is now embedded in the document as <<Title>>.
(SPACE)	Press to insert a space.
Insert Merge Field ▾	Click to open the list of fields.
FirstName	Click to embed this code in the document.
(SPACE)	Press to insert a space.
Insert Merge Field ▾	Click to open the list of fields.
LastName	Click to embed this code in the document.
(ENTER)	Press to move to the next line. Your document should look like Figure 5.32.

Figure 5.31
The Insert Merge Field pulldown menu with the field names contained in the source file.

Figure 5.32
The first line of merge field codes for the salutation, first name, and last name entered in the document.

6. **Repeat step 5 to enter the next two lines of addressee information.** Use Figure 5.33 as a guide. Manually enter the comma after the City code (it wasn't entered in the data source file). When finished, press (ENTER) twice.

7. **Enter the salutation.**

Type the salutation text: **Dear.**

(SPACE)   Press to insert a space.

8. **Insert the Title and LastName fields followed by a semicolon.** Your document should look like Figure 5.33.

9. **Use Figure 5.34 as a guide for entering the body of the letter.**

10. **Save the file as M4Ch5 Letter Template.**

<u>F</u>ile   Click to open the File menu.

Save <u>A</u>s . . .   Click to open the Save As dialog box.

Type the name of the file: **M4Ch5 Letter Template**.

(ENTER)   Press to complete the save operation.

Figure 5.33
The remaining merge field codes inserted in the template letter.

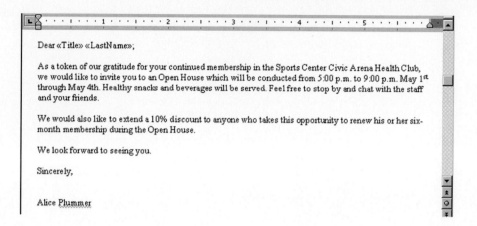

Figure 5.34
The body of the letter to be entered.

11. Test the merge operation.

Click to open the Checking and Reporting Errors dialog box (Figure 5.35).

Click to begin the checking operation. If Word finds any errors, it will report them to you. If the merge operation works correctly, the completed documents are placed in a window with the title Form Letters1 (Figure 5.36).

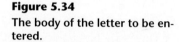

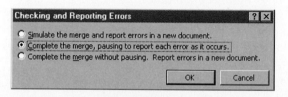

Figure 5.35
The dialog box used to check for any errors.

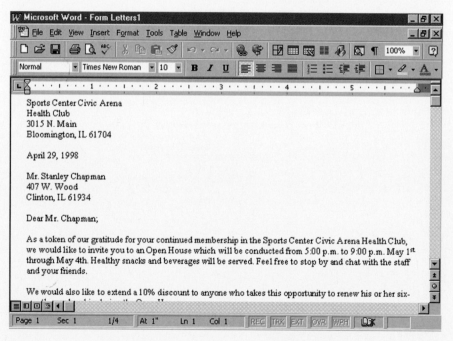

Figure 5.36
A form letter created by using merged documents.

12. Return to the main document.

Click the Close button of the document. Word asks if you want to save the form letters.

Click not to save the letters. Return to the window with the M4Ch5 Letter Template document.

13. Close the template document.

Click the Close button of the document window. Word asks if you want to save the main document file.

Click to save the file.

Reinforcing the Exercise

1. Use the Mail Merge Helper dialog box to begin building the main document.
2. Use the Insert Merge Field button of the Mail Merge toolbar to enter data fields in the document.
3. Insert the date as a field to make the main document more flexible.
4. Once you have completed a merge operation, you can test it by clicking the Check for Errors button.

Executing the Merge Operation

After creating and saving your data source and main document files, you begin a merge operation by opening your main document and clicking one of the three merge buttons on the Mail Merge toolbar:

- **Merge to New Document** Clicking this button creates the merged document and puts it in a new Word document.

- **Merge to Printer** Clicking this button creates the merged document and sends it to the printer.

- **Mail Merge** Clicking this button displays the Merge dialog box (Figure 5.37) and gives you a range of options for controlling the merge operation.

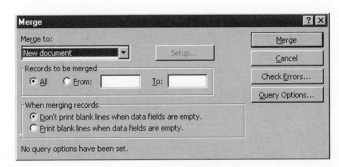

Figure 5.37
The Merge dialog box for controlling how a merge operation is executed.

TIMELY TIP

> You can preview the merged document by clicking the View Merged Data button on the Mail Merge toolbar. This allows you to view a merged record from the data source on the screen before you print it.

Hands-On Exercise: Performing the Merge Operation

Isabel is now ready to show Alice how to execute the merge operation.

1. **Open the M4Ch5 Letter Template main document.**

             Click to open the Open dialog box.

   M4Ch5 Letter   Click to select the main document.
   Template

2. **Execute the Merge command so that the letter will appear on the screen.**

             Click to send all the letters to the screen.

3. **After scrolling through the letters on the screen and noticing if the merge worked correctly, send the letters to the printer.**

             Click this button on the Standard toolbar to print the merged letters.

4. **Save and close all open files.**

Reinforcing the Exercise

1. When performing a merge operation, you must first open the main document.
2. Clicking a Mail Merge button starts the merge process.
3. You can merge directly to the printer or to a new document.

Entering Merge Data from the Keyboard

In the previous example, the main document received all its data from the data source file. But you may have an application for which you want to enter all or some data directly from the keyboard. In this situation, open the Insert Word Field menu and select the Fill-in command. You are then prompted via a dialog box for the prompt and default values to enter.

When the merge is executed, a dialog box prompts you for information. Of course, if all your variable fields are defined this way, you do not need a data source file.

When the merge operation begins, Word automatically stops at the first keyboard variable and waits for you to enter the data for this field. After you enter the data, press (ENTER) or click OK to continue the merge until it reaches the next keyboard variable.

Using an Excel Workbook as Merge Input

You may have an Excel workbook like that shown in Figure 5.38 that you want to use as your data source for a merge operation. Notice that the column headings contain the same names as you specified previously for the data source file. Any data source you use must have headings that match those specified in the main document.

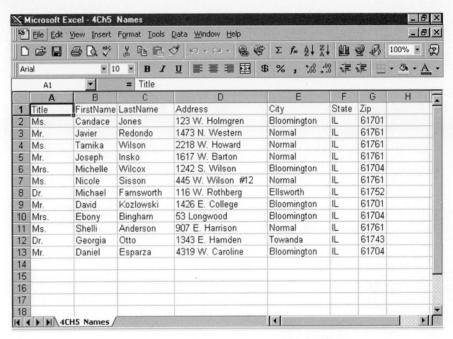

Figure 5.38
The 4Ch5 Names Excel workbook to be used as input for a merge operation.

Hands-On Exercise: Using an Excel Workbook as Input in a Merge Operation

You will finish the promotional mailing using information already stored in an Excel workbook as merger input.

1. **Open the M4Ch5 Letter Template document.**

2. **Prepare for the merge operation.**

 Click this button on the Mail Merge toolbar. The Mail Merge Helper dialog box appears (Figure 5.39).

 Click to display the pulldown menu.

 Click to open the Open Data Source dialog box (Figure 5.40).

Files of _type:_ Click to open this list box.

All Files Click this entry.

4Ch5 Names Double-click this file name. The dialog box shown in Figure 5.41 appears.

OK Click to indicate that you want to include the entire spreadsheet.

X Click to close the Mail Merge Helper dialog box.

3. **Execute the merge.**

Click this button to execute the merge operation. You should now see the letter created by the first record of the workbook (Figure 5.42). Examine other letters.

4. **Close all files without saving them.**

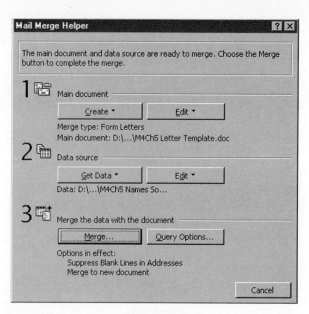

Figure 5.39
The Mail Merge Helper dialog box.

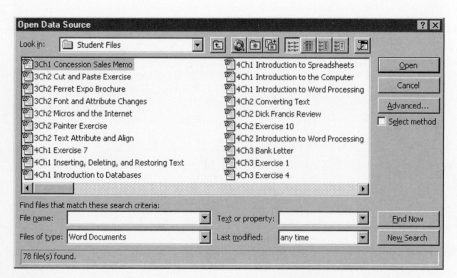

Figure 5.40
The Open Data Source dialog box.

Figure 5.41
The dialog box asking how much of the spreadsheet you want included.

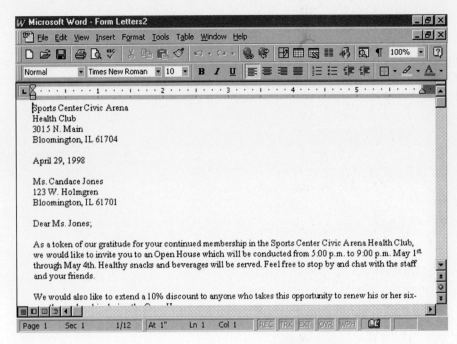

Figure 5.42
The letter created using the first workbook record.

Reinforcing the Exercise

1. You can use Excel workbook as input for a merge operation.

2. The main document defines the expected field names. The column headings in the workbook must match the field names in the main document.

3. You must specify a new data source in the Mail Merge Helper dialog box before you can use the workbook as the data source for the main document.

Generating Mailing Labels

Mailing labels are easy to create by using the Tools, Mail Merge command. The following steps let you generate standard labels that are three across on a sheet. This discussion assumes that you are using a laser or ink jet printer. Start with a blank document window.

Hands-On Exercise: Creating a Label Definition

Now it's time for Alice to mail her letters. Creating mailing labels is similar to creating form letters. This exercise uses the data source file, M4Ch5 Names Source File, created in the earlier mail merge exercise.

1. Choose the Tools, Mail Merge command.

Tools   Click open the Tools menu.

Mail Merge . . .   Click to open the Mail Merge Helper dialog box.

2. **Create mailing labels using the M4Ch5 Names Source File document.**

> **Create ▾**   Click this button in the Main document portion of the dialog box.

Mailing Labels . . .   Click to open the dialog box that asks where you want to create the template for the labels.

> **Active Window**   Click to choose this option.

> **Get Data ▾**   Click this button in the Data source portion of the dialog box.

> **Open Data Source...**   Click to open the Open Data Source dialog box.

**M4Ch5 Names   Double-click the data source
Source File**   file. Word now asks about setting up the main document.

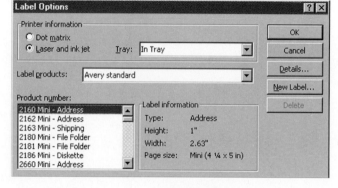

> **Set Up Main Document**   Click to open the Label Options dialog box (Figure 5.43).

Figure 5.43
The Label Options dialog box used for selecting the label type.

3. **Select the options for the label format in the Label Products text box.**

Avery standard   Click this option (the default) if necessary.

4. **Select an entry from the Product Number list box.**

5160 - Address   Click this label type.

> **Details...**   Click to see information on the label format just selected (Figure 5.44). Notice that this address label has the attributes of three columns across and a height of 1 inch.

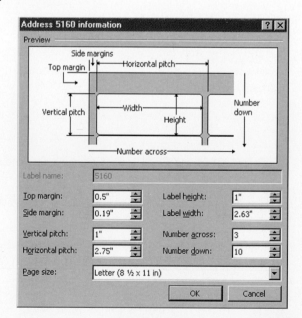

Figure 5.44
The Address 5160 information dialog box.

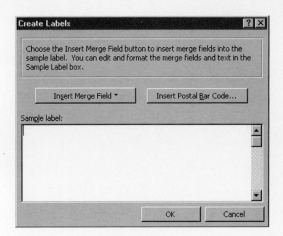

Figure 5.45
The Create Labels dialog box.

OK	Click to close the dialog box and return to the Label Options dialog box.
OK	Click to open the Create Labels dialog box (Figure 5.45).

5. Insert the fields to be merged into mailing labels.

Insert Merge Field ▼	Click this button, and then select the fields to be inserted, one at a time, into the Sample label portion of the dialog box. Use the format shown in Figure 5.46.
OK	Click to return to the Mail Merge Helper dialog box.

6. Merge the labels to the screen.

Merge	Click to display the Merge dialog box (Figure 5.47). Notice that the default Merge to setting is New Document.

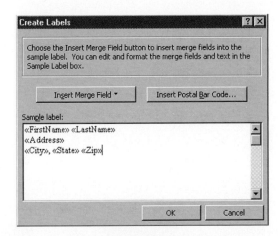

Figure 5.46
The order of the fields to be used for the label.

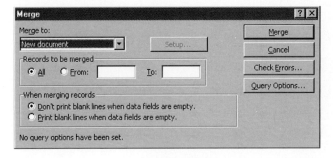

Figure 5.47
The Merge dialog box for controlling the placement of the merged document.

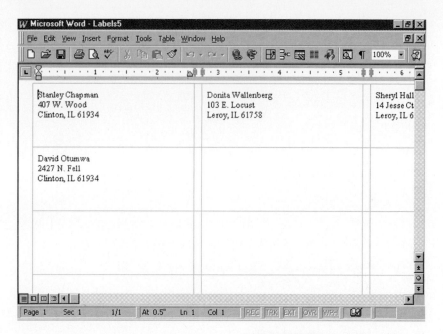

Figure 5.48
The created labels using the Merge command.

  Click this button to merge the names into the mailing labels. The screen should look like Figure 5.48.

7. **Print the label page.**

8. **Close the generated labels document.**

  Click this button on the document window to open the dialog box that asks if you want to save the labels.

  Click to indicate you do not want to save the labels. You are now returned to the label definition document (Figure 5.49).

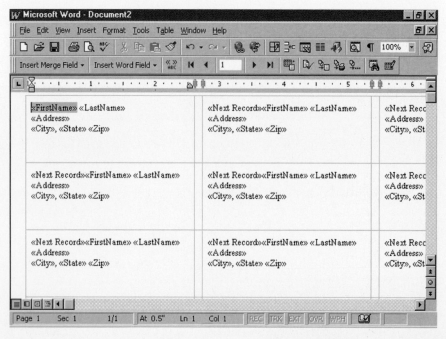

Figure 5.49
The label definition document.

9. **Save the label definition document to disk.**

File   Click to open the File menu.

Save <u>A</u>s . . .   Click to open the Save As dialog box.

Type the filename: **M4Ch5 Labels Template**.

10. **Close the file.**

Reinforcing the Exercise

1. The label definition process starts with the Mail Merge Helper dialog box.

2. You need to create a new main document to support labels.

3. Word supports a number of different label types. You select the label type from the Label Options dialog box.

4. You use the Create Labels dialog box to design the field location on the label.

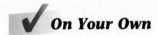 *On Your Own*

Create labels using the preceding discussion of label definition and the information in the hands-on exercise that dealt with using an Excel workbook as merge input.

- Create the labels using the M4Ch5 Labels Template. Use the 4Ch5 Names Excel workbook as the source file.

- Print the labels.

SESSION REVIEW

The Thesaurus option finds synonyms and antonyms for the word at the current cursor location. The Thesaurus looks up one word at a time. You can replace the word at the cursor location when you locate a better word.

The Word Count command prepares a number of statistics related to the document. The statistics, depending on the check box at the bottom of the dialog box, may or may not include any footnotes and endnotes.

The Mail Merge feature lets you individualize form letters by creating a main document (template file) that combines variable and constant text. The main document stays the same from one letter to the next. The individualizing (variable) text is found in a data source file that consists of records. Each record holds all data for mailing a letter to a particular recipient. The merge operation places variable data from the data source file into locations specified by merge field codes in the main document.

The data source file is composed of records of the data to be merged. This file can be used with various main document files. For instance, the same data source file used for letters can generate addresses on labels. Variable fields must remain in the same order from one record to the next within a data source file.

Word can also accept input to a merge operation from an Excel workbook.

Once the merge operation has been performed, you can tell Word to send the output to a printer.

KEY TERMS AND CONCEPTS

antonym   4–194
data source file   4–198
field   4–199
Mail Merge feature   4–198

main document   4–198
merge field codes   4–203
record   4–199

synonym   4–194
template file   4–198
Thesaurus feature   4–194

SESSION QUIZ

Multiple Choice

1. Merge lets you do which of the following?
   a. automatically place today's date in a letter
   b. send messages to the operator
   c. enter variable information from the keyboard
   d. prepare personalized form letters
   e. all of the above

2. The main document contains which of the following?
   a. constant information
   b. field numbers
   c. the data source file
   d. merge commands
   e. for a main document, all of the above

3. Which format is correct for entering a merge field in a main document?
   a. "field"
   b. 'field'
   c. <<field>>
   d. none of the above
   e. all of the above

4. Which of the following is true regarding entering data source files?
   a. The main document and the data source file must use the same field names.
   b. The order of the fields does not matter.
   c. The character used between fields is the colon (:).
   d. If a field has an embedded comma, you must enclose that field in double quotation marks (").
   e. All of the above are true.

5. When using the Thesaurus feature, which of the following options allows you to look up other words by selecting a word from the synonyms list?
   a. Replace with Antonym list box
   b. Look Up button
   c. Replace button
   d. Replace with Synonym list box
   e. None of the above can be used.

True/False

6. You can use the same data source file for a number of merge applications.

7. To execute a merge operation, you must first open the main document.

8. Main documents for merge operations can contain messages to the operator as well as accept keyboard data to fulfill a task.

9. Once you have issued the Thesaurus command, you can find information related to only one word (the one at the cursor location).

10. The Word Count feature automatically counts footnotes and endnotes.

SESSION REVIEW EXERCISES

1. Define or describe each of the following:
   a. main document
   b. data source file
   c. constant data
   d. variable data

2. The _____ feature of Word allows you to find synonyms and antonyms for a word at the cursor location.

3. A/an _____ is a word that means the same thing.

4. When you click the _____ _____ button, new entries for the highlighted word appear in the Thesaurus dialog box.

5. The _____ _____ dialog box provides a number of statistics about a document.

6. When you are using Word Count, _____ and _____ are not automatically included in the document statistics.

7. The _____ _____ feature allows you to send personalized form letters.

8. The _____ _____ file contains the individualizing data for form letters in the form of fields and records.

9. The main document for a merge operation is composed of constant and _____ data.

10. The source data file and main document for a merge operation must use the same _____ names when referencing data.

11. The _____ _____ _____ dialog box provides assistance in creating a main document or data source file.

12. The _____ _____ _____ dialog box provides a number of field names from which you can choose for creating the data source file.

13. The View Source button of the Data Form dialog box displays your data source file as a _____ .

14. When the main document appears on the screen, the _____ _____ toolbar also appears.

15. The _____ _____ _____ button is used for placing field names in the main document for a merge operation.

16. When you have a series of variable fields on a line, you usually insert a/an _____ between each field.

17. Use the _____ _____ _____ button of the Mail Merge toolbar to see if the merge operation will function properly.

18. The _____ can also be used as input for the main document in a merge operation.

19. The _____ names must be the same regardless of whether you are using a data source file or an Excel workbook as input to a main document.

20. There are a number of predetermined _____ formats from which you can select when designing a label merge operation.

COMPUTER EXERCISES

1. Enter the following names and addresses in a data source file called M4Ch5 Exercise 1 Source. Change the town names to the names of towns around your area. Enter the data so that they can be used by the Mail Merge feature.

Name and Address Data

Mr.	Eduardo	Rodriquez	#12 Haycraft Dr.	Clinton	IL	61934
Ms.	Carol	Furst	1432 W. Olive	Bloomington	IL	61701
Dr.	Sharon	Acklin	707 Vale St.	Bloomington	IL	61701
Mr.	Howard	Bennett	1207 Monroe	Normal	IL	61701
Mrs.	Denise	Adams	152 E. Grove	Bloomington	IL	61702

2. Create the following letter as the main document for a merge application in which you use the data source file that you just created. The italic items in the letter are to be read in from the data source file. Name the file M4Ch5 Exercise 1 Main Document.

Michael Dowd
1216 W. Brentwood
Danvers, IL 61763

March 21, 1997

Name
Address
City, State Zip

Dear *Sal. Lname;*

The purpose of this letter is to remind all of the friends and supporters of the Twin City Ferret Club about the Ferret Frolic being held this April 19 at the Sports Center Civic Arena from 10:00 A.M. until 4:00 P.M. Admission is $2.00 for adults and children are free. You are encouraged to bring one or all of your ferrets to participate in the various events.

There will be a reception held at 4:15 for club members and supporters in the Sunshine Room of the Civic Arena.

I look forward to seeing all of you at the Frolic.

Sincerely,

Michael Dowd

3. Use the same data source file to create a label template to generate the mailing labels for each person who will receive a letter.

INTERNET EXERCISES

1. Find more information on mail merge.
    a. Access the Microsoft Web page with your browser (http://www.microsoft.com).
    b. Click the Search button at the top of the page.
    c. On the Search page, enter the topic *mail merge* in the Search text box, click the Support and Knowledge Base option in step 3, and click the Search Now! button.
    d. Examine a few of the links displayed.
    e. Print two pages relating to mail merge operations.

OPERATIONS REFERENCE

FILE

BUTTON OR ICON	MENU OPTION	KEYS	ACTION
	Open	`ALT` + **F, O**	Opens a previously saved file.
	Exit	`ALT` + `F4`	Closes an application.
	Close	`ALT` + `F4`	Closes a document.
	Save	`SHIFT` + `F12`	Saves a document.
	Save As	`F12`	Saves an unnamed document or saves a document under a new name.
	Save As HTML	`ALT` + **F, H**	Converts a document to HTML format, which makes the document accessible from the World Wide Web.
	Print	`CTRL` + **P**	Print a document.
	Print Preview	`ALT` + **F, V**	Displays a preview of the document as it will be printed.

EDIT

BUTTON OR ICON	MENU OPTION	KEYS	ACTION
	Copy	`CTRL` + **C**	Copies selected text onto the clipboard.
	Cut	`CTRL` + **X**	Cuts selected text from a document and places it on the clipboard.
	Paste	`CTRL` + **V**	Takes text from clipboard and puts it in a document at the insertion point.

EDIT (continued)

BUTTON OR ICON	MENU OPTION	KEYS	ACTION
	Paste Special	(ALT) + **E, S**	Links documents from other Office applications to a Word document.
	Undo	(CTRL) + **Z**	Reverses the effect of the last command.
	Redo	(F4)	Re-executes the last command.
	Find	(ALT) + **E, D**	Searches for specified text.
	Replace	(ALT) + **E, P**	Replaces specified text with some other specified text.

VIEW

BUTTON OR ICON	MENU OPTION	KEYS	ACTION
	Normal	(ALT) + **V, N**	Changes the editing view to the default Normal view.
	Online Layout	(ALT) + **V, E**	Splits the screen into two panes. The left pane displays just the document's headings, and the right pane displays the complete text of the document. When you click on a heading in the left pane, that section of the document is displayed in the right pane.
	Page Layout	(ALT) + **V, P**	Displays the page as it will be printed and allows editing.
	Outline	(ALT) + **V, O**	Displays the document's outline.
	Toolbars, Drawing	(ALT) + **V, T**	Activates the Office Art feature used to draw 2-D and 3-D images.
	Header and Footer	(ALT) + **V, H**	Activates the Header and Footer toolbar used to add headers and footers to a document.

INSERT

BUTTON OR ICON	MENU OPTION	KEYS	ACTION
	Break	(ALT) + **I, B**	Creates page, section, and column breaks.
	Page Numbers	(ALT) + **I, U**	Adds page numbers to a document.
	Date and Time	(ALT) + **I, T**	Adds the date and/or time to a document.
	Picture	(ALT) + **I, P**	Inserts a graphic image for clip art in a document.
	Caption	(ALT) + **I, C**	Adds a caption to go with a graphic image.
	Footnote	(ALT) + **I, N**	Adds footnotes or endnotes to a document
	Symbol	(ALT) + **I, S**	Embeds special characters into text.
	File	(ALT) + **I, L**	Embeds a file from another Office application into a word document.

FORMAT

BUTTON OR ICON	MENU OPTION	KEYS	ACTION
B	Character	(CTRL) + **B**	Boldfaces text.
I	Character	(CTRL) + **I**	Italicizes text.
U	Character	(CTRL) + **U**	Underlines text.
	Paragraph, Indentation *or* File, Page Setup	(CTRL) + **L**	Aligns text along the left margin.
	Paragraph, Indentation *or* File, Page Setup	(CTRL) + **R**	Aligns text along the right margin.
	Paragraph, Indentation *or* File, Page Setup	(CTRL) + **E**	Centers text between the left and right margins.
	Paragraph, Indentation *or* File, Page Setup	(CTRL) + **J**	Aligns text along both the left and right margin

FORMAT (continued)

BUTTON OR ICON	MENU OPTION	KEYS	ACTION
	Tabs	ALT + **O, T**	The left edge of text aligns at the tab stop.
	Tabs	ALT + **O, T**	The right edge of text aligns at the tab stop.
	Tabs	ALT + **O, T**	The center of text aligns at the tab stop.
	Tabs	ALT + **O, T**	The decimal aligns at the tab stop.
	Borders and Shading	ALT + **O, B**	Adds borders or shading to selected text.
	Columns	ALT + **O, C**	Creates columns.
	Change Case	ALT + **O, E**	Changes text to a different case, such as lowercase, uppercase, sentence case, or title case.
	AutoFormat	ALT + **O, A**	Formats a document automatically, paragraph by paragraph, in accordance with the Normal template.
	Text Box	ALT + **O, O**	Adds a box around selected text.
	Drop Cap	ALT + **O, D**	Adds a drop cap to a document.

TOOLS

BUTTON OR ICON	MENU OPTION	KEYS	ACTION
	Bullets and Numbering		Creates a bulleted list.
	Bullets and Numbering		Creates a numbered list.
	AutoCorrect		Activates the AutoCorrect feature, which automatically checks the spelling in a document.
	Spelling	ALT + **T, S**	Opens the Spelling and Grammar dialog box used to check spelling of a document.
	Macro	ALT + **T, M**	Creates a macro.

TOOLS (continued)

BUTTON OR ICON	MENU OPTION	KEYS	ACTION
	Language, Thesaurus	ALT + **T, L, T**	Activates the Thesaurus feature used to choose synonyms and antonyms for words in a document.
	Word Count	ALT + **T, W**	Counts the number of words in a document.
	Mail Merge	ALT + **T, R**	Activates Mail Merge feature used to automate the tasks of bulk mailings and creating labels.

TABLE

BUTTON OR ICON	MENU OPTION	KEYS	ACTION
▦			Creates a table with column widths automatically set.
	Table Auto-Format	ALT + **A, F**	Formats a table.
	Sort	ALT + **A, S**	Sorts a table.

GLOSSARY

alignment character Text typed prior to this character is aligned in a particular way; text typed after this character is aligned normally.

antonym A word that means the opposite of another word.

application window Contains the title bar, application control buttons, menu bar, document control buttons, Standard and Formatting toolbars, ruler, Office Assistant, split box, status bar, scroll bars, view icons, and a blank document window.

AutoFormat feature Automatically formats a document, paragraph by paragraph, applying different formatting styles (font styles, tab settings, paragraph positioning, bullets, and so on). Any features are automatically applied from the Normal template, unless you specify some other template.

bar tab stop Places a vertical bar at the tab stop and is used to create a division between units of data.

border A box or line surrounding a block of text.

bullet A large dot at the left margin of an item in a list.

cell The intersection of a row and column.

clip art A library of graphics that you can access and place in a document. In Office, clip art is accessed through the Microsoft Clip Gallery 3.0 dialog box.

cursor Vertical line that appears in the upper-left corner of an empty screen. Also called the insertion point.

cursor movement commands Issued through the arrow keys, (PGUP), (PGDN), (HOME), (END), and any of these combined with (CTRL) to move the cursor within a document.

data source file One of the two files needed for a merge operation. The data source file contains the variable text and provides the input to the main document.

decimal alignment Typed text moves to the left until you type a period. All text in a column aligns at the decimal point.

embed To insert a document imported from another application. For example, you can embed an Excel worksheet into a Word document. You perform this task by using the Insert, File command sequence. Embedded text is static, meaning that changes made to the original document are not reflected in the embedded document.

endnote A citation of source material for a document that appears at the very end of the document.

end-of-document marker Horizontal line that appears at the end of a document.

field 1. A segment of text in a table separated from other segments by a comma or tab. 2. In a data source file, a field contains one piece of data about the recipient of a bulk mailing, such as a first or last name or an address.

footer A line of text printed just above the bottom margin of a page. Usually appears on every page of a document.

footnote A citation of source material for a document that appears at the bottom of the page.

Formatting toolbar Usually located beneath the Standard toolbar, this toolbar enables you to format characters and paragraphs. Using this toolbar, you can select formatting styles such as the font, point size, text alignment, and bold, italic, or underlined text. You can also use the Formatting toolbar to apply predefined styles to text.

handles Markers on the ruler used to define margins and indents. Using the mouse, you drag a handle to change a setting.

hanging indent The first line of a paragraph is set at a certain point and the remaining lines are indented from that point.

hard page break A page break that occurs as a result of an Insert, *Page Break* command sequence. It is marked by a dotted line with the words *Page Break* centered on it.

header A line of text printed just below the top margin of a page.

Header and Footer toolbar Appears on-screen after you issue the View, Header and Footer command sequence. You use the buttons on the Header and Footer toolbar to enter text, insert and format page numbers, insert the date and time, as well as perform other tasks.

hotspot A spot on the Word screen that, when double-clicked, displays a dialog box that allows you to perform tasks related to that spot. For example, when you double-click the ruler, the Tabs dialog box opens, and when you double-click the status bar, the Go To tab of the Find and Replace dialog box opens.

I-beam A cursor that looks like a capital *I*.

key A field or word by which a table is sorted.

line spacing The amount of space between lines of text. You can change line spacing by issuing the Format, Paragraph command sequence and selecting the Indents and Spacing tab.

link To insert an imported document by using the Edit, Paste Special command sequence. Linked documents are automatically changed when any changes are made to the original document. For example, an Excel table linked to a Word document will change automatically when you make a change to the original table in Excel.

macro An often-used string of commands recorded as one entity and given a name. To invoke that string of commands, you only need to invoke the macro.

Mail Merge feature A Word feature that automates the task of bulk mailings. With Mail Merge you can create a large number of individualized letters efficiently.

main document One of the two files needed for a merge operation. The main document contains the constant data—the text that will be included in all the output documents—and the instructions for placing the individual data. Also called the template file.

merge field code In the main document of a mail merge operation, codes that indicate where merged data will appear.

newspaper columns The type of columns you find in newspapers and newsletters, where the text goes from the top of a column down to the bottom of that column and then up to the top of the next column.

Normal view Word's default view normally used to initially build and edit a document. This view does not support the WSIWYG (what you see is what you get) feature.

Online Layout view Divides the screen into two panes: The left pane lists the elements of the document, such as section headings and table headings. The right pane displays the complete text of the document. The item selected in the left pane is the item displayed at the top of the right pane. This view is particularly good to use with long documents.

orphan The last line of a paragraph that appears alone at the top of a page.

Outline view Displays the text in outline form.

Page Layout view Shows exactly how the document will appear on the printed page.

paragraph marker (¶) A formatting code that marks the end of a paragraph.

parallel columns The type of columns you find in tables, lists, or any text or numbers you want to keep aligned. Text in parallel columns continues to flow down the same column, even if that column extends onto another page.

Picture toolbar Appears on-screen after you insert a graphic image. You use the buttons on the Picture toolbar to change the contrast and brightness of the image, crop it, wrap text around the image, format the image and control how it is displayed, as well as perform other tasks.

record In a data source file, the data for each recipient of a bulk mailing is stored in a record.

ruler Displays the tab paragraph, and margin settings for the current line.

selection bar An area along the left margin of a document. When the pointer is in the selection area, it changes to an arrow pointing up and to the right. Clicking when the pointer is in the selection bar selects an entire line of text.

shading Color or gray applied to an area surrounded by a border to give special emphasis to that area.

soft page break A page break that occurs automatically as text is entered. It is marked by a dotted line across a page that shows where one page ends and another begins.

split box Black box that appears at the end of the ruler. When you click the split box, the screen divides into two sections, allowing you to have two different views of the same document.

Standard toolbar   Located beneath the menu bar, this toolbar contains buttons that enable you to execute commands more quickly than you could using menus. Among the commands you can issue through the Standard toolbar are Open, Save, Print, Cut, Copy, Paste, and Undo.

style   A collection of formatting options applied to selected text or to the entire document. For example, a style might change the font type, size, boldfacing, and italics of a piece of selected text.

synonym   A word with the same meaning as another word.

table   A grid of rows and columns used for price lists, inventory lists, income statements, sales forecasts, budgets, or almost anything that can be constructed in a spreadsheet such as Excel.

tab leader   A dotted or solid line that fills in a blank area between tab stops.

tab stop   Set place in a document where the cursor stops when you press (TAB). By default, Word sets tab stops every 0.5 inch.

Table feature   Allows you to create columns to enter text that aligns with parallel columns across the page.

template file   *See* main document.

temporary file   Storage place in the computer's memory (RAM) for a document you open. Any changes you make to an open document do not affect the temporary file until you issue a Save command.

Thesaurus feature   Provides synonyms and antonyms of a selected word in a document.

view   A unique way of displaying a document. Word allows you to see a document in several different views so you can see the results of various features you have applied to the document. The quickest way to change views is by clicking one of the view icons displayed above the status bar.

Visual Basic   The internal language all Office applications use to record macros.

widow   The first line of a paragraph that appears alone at the bottom of a page.

word processing   The computer manipulation of text data: creating, revising, storing, retrieving, and printing text.

word wrap   A feature that automatically places a word on a new line if it does not fit at the end of a line. Because of word wrap, the only time you need to press ENTER is at the end of a paragraph.

INDEX

Address sorts, 168-171
Alignment character, 74
Antonyms
    explanation of, 194
    how to find, 195-196
Application window, 2, 3
AutoFormat command
    exercise using, 106-107
    explanation of, 100-101
AutoNumber option, 125

Backing up files, 84-85
Bar tab stop, 69
Boldface, 172-174
Borders
    exercises to insert, 111-112, 123-124
    how to create, 110-111
    on letterheads, 178-180
    in tables, 161, 164
Bullet, 101
Bulleted lists
    exercise using, 104-105, 107-108
    explanation of, 101-102

Cells, 160-161
Change Case command, 81-82
Clip art, 153-159
Columns
    how to correct, 150
    how to edit, 146
    how to resize, 160
    for newsletters, 146-152
    types of, 146
Columns dialog box, 146, 148
Cursor, 2
Cursor movement command
    explanation of, 13
    use of, 14-16

Data source file
    attached to main document, 203-204
    explanation of, 198
    how to create, 199-202
    how to save, 203
Date command, 82-83
Dates, how to enter, 83-84
Decimal alignment, 74
Deletion
    commands for, 22
    of endnote, 128
    of footnote, 128
    of page number, 99
    of text, 22-24
Document window, 4
Documents
    controlling appearance of, 25-29
    converting to HTML from Word, 33-36

deleting and restoring text in, 22-24
    moving around, 12-13
    page appearance within, 29-32
    selecting text in, 17-21
    working with page breaks in, 14-17
Double indent, 58, 65, 66

Embedding a worksheet, 129-132, 134-136
Endnotes
    explanation of, 124
    how to delete, 128
    how to insert, 125-127
    word counts to include, 197
End-of-document marker, 2
Excel workbook, 211-213

Field
    explanation of, 167
    of records, 199
Files, saving and backing up, 84-85
Find command
    explanation of, 75-76
    use of, 77-80
Footer
    exercise to insert, 121-124
    explanation of, 120
    how to create, 120
Footnotes
    explanation of, 124
    how to delete, 128
    how to insert, 125-127
    word counts to include, 197
Formatting toolbar, 5, 8

Handles, 5
Hanging indent, 58, 67
Hard page break, 14, 16
Header and Footer toolbar, 120, 121
Headers
    explanation of, 120
    how to create, 120
    how to insert, 121-124
Hotspots
    explanation of, 46
    use of, 47-48
HTML format, 33-36

I-beam, 12
Indent
    double, 58, 65, 66
    hanging, 58, 67
    how to set, 63-67
    left, 57-58, 65
Inserting text, 22-24
Internet exercises, 44, 93, 144, 191, 221

Key, 167

Layout tab, 30, 31
Left indent, 57-58, 65
Letterheads, 174-180
Line spacing, 25-29
Linking, to a worksheet, 132-136
Lists
    bulleted or numbered, 101-102, 104-108
    using tab stops to create, 74

Macro
    explanation of, 172
    how to create, 172
    how to edit, 181
    to put name in boldface, 172-174
Macros
    to build letterheads, 174-180
Mail Merge
    creating data source file for, 199-203
    creating mail document for, 203-209
    execution of, 209-211
    exercise using, 211-213
    explanation of, 198
    how to preview, 210
Mail Merge toolbar, 204
Mailing labels, 213-217
Main document
    attaching data source file to, 203, 204
    explanation of, 198
    how to create, 204-209
Margins, 57-62
Margins tab, 30
Menu bar, 5
Merge field codes, 203
Microsoft Web page, 44

Names, how to sort, 169-171
Newsletters, 146-152
Newspaper columns, 146-152
Normal template, 57
Normal views, 48
Numbered lists
    exercise using, 105-106
    explanation of, 101-102

Object linking and embedding (OLE), 129
Office Assistant, 5
Online Layout view, 55-56
Orphan, 14
Outline view
    exercise using, 54-55
    explanation of, 50

Page breaks, 14-17
Page layout, 29-32

Page Layout view
  exercise using, 52-53
  explanation of, 49-50
Page numbers
  exercise using, 97-100
  how to add, 96-97
  how to delete, 99
Page Setup dialog box, 29, 30
Paper size tab, 30
Paper source tab, 30
Paragraph codes, 12
Paragraph mark, 76
Paragraphs, indents and spacing
    within and between, 26-27
Parallel columns, 146
Picture toolbar, 109
Pictures
  exercise to insert, 111-119
  steps to insert, 108-109

Record, 199
Replace command, 77-80
Restoring text, 22-24
Ruler, 5

Saving files, 84-85
Scroll bar, 6
Selection bar, 17
Shading
  exercise using, 111-112
  how to create, 110-111
  on letterheads, 178-180
Soft page break
  explanation of, 14
  illustrations of, 15, 16

Sorts
  names and addresses, 168-171
  order options for, 166-167
  text, 167-171
Split bar, 6
Standard toolbar, 5, 7
Status bar, 6
Style
  exercise using, 102-103
  explanation of, 100
Style Gallery dialog box, 100
Symbol dialog box, 128, 129
Symbol insertions, 128-129
Synonyms, 194

Tab leader
  explanation of, 69
  how to create, 72-74
Tab stop
  bar, 69
  explanation of, 68
  used to add columnar format lists,
    74
  working with, 69-71
Table Draw, 166
Table feature
  exercise in using, 161-165
  explanation of, 160
Tables
  enhancing appearance of, 160-161
  explanation of, 159
  features related to, 166
  how to create, 160
  how to enter data in, 160
  uses for, 165

Template file, 198
Temporary file, 84
Text
  deleting and restoring, 22-24
  entering, 9-12
  how to enter and sort, 167-171
  selecting, 17-21
  sort order options for, 166-167
Thesaurus
  explanation of, 194
  how to start, 194
  used to replace text, 194-196
Title bar, 4

Undo button, 22, 23

View icon, 6, 9
Views
  exercise using, 51-56
  explanation of, 48
Visual Basic, 181

Widow, 14
Word 97, 2
Word Count, 196, 197
Word processing, 2
Word wrap, 9
Worksheets
  how to embed, 129-132, 134-136
  how to link, 132-136
World Wide Web, 33-36